INSIGHTFUL INC.

LEARNINGS FROM

Unilever

INSIGHTFUL INC.

LEARNINGS FROM Unilever

MANISH MAKHIJANI

JAICO PUBLISHING HOUSE

Ahmedabad Bangalore Chennai
Delhi Hyderabad Kolkata Mumbai

Published by Jaico Publishing House
A-2 Jash Chambers, 7-A Sir Phirozshah Mehta Road
Fort, Mumbai - 400 001
jaicopub@jaicobooks.com
www.jaicobooks.com

INSIGHTFUL INC.
ISBN 978-81-972303-3-2

First Jaico Impression: 2024

Page design and layout by Inosoft Systems, Delhi

Printed by
Thomson Press India Limited, New Delhi

Advance Praise

Insightful Inc. brings to life the insights function in a comprehensive way with many excellent examples and thoughtful perspectives drawn from Manish's extensive experience. It will be a helpful guide for people working in insights and marketing, providing great foundations for those at the start of their career and an illuminating refresher for those at later stages.

— ***Rebecca Wynberg,*** *Founder, Wy Consulting (UK)*

Insightful Inc. talks about how to integrate consumer understanding and insight into the core of an organization's values and processes. Manish uses his vast experience across categories and geographies to illustrate how market research and insight can give you an edge.
In my many years of working with Manish across the world, I have seen him not just as a highly skilled individual in crafting insights for business growth but also possessing the judgment and pragmatism to not fall into the trap of creating processes that reduce agility and speed. It's this judgment that is captured well in the book, with practical examples and learnings. I highly recommend *Insightful Inc.* as a handy reference guide for people working in the marketing and insights industry on both sides of the table, and for marketers looking to be inspired by lessons from FMCG.

— ***Samir Singh,*** *CMO, Global Personal Care, Unilever*

Manish has written a book that was a long time coming for the insights industry. He has drawn upon his years of experience with master marketer Unilever, combining it with his theoretical and practical knowledge of the craft to write a primer for the industry. Both users and practitioners of market research will find this book a valuable aid in building consumer-centricity among their clients and in their organizations. The book abounds with examples and practical tips and includes a section at the end of each chapter on implications for marketing and insights professionals.

Importantly, it also looks at how the insights business will evolve and what are the skills and capabilities that will keep insights practitioners relevant in what promises to be an exciting future. To me, the book was also a reminder of what makes our profession so unique and why it attracts so many smart people.

— ***Preethi Reddy****, former CEO and Chairperson,*
South Asia, Insights Division, Kantar

Insightful Inc. shall be on the must-read list of a variety of audiences—from students of marketing to current practitioners and the c-suite executives. This 'insights transformation guidebook' will leverage the author's immense knowledge to help leaders reap the benefits of building consumer-centric organizations.

Manish has been a friend, and a client, for several years. His quiet, and sometimes understated, demeanour hid such a vast repertoire of astute thinking and knowledge that this book brings to light. I admire the structured way in which he has synthesized his life's learning in this book. I hope this is just the first of a series of books that he will write in future.

— ***Pranesh Misra,*** *Chairman and Managing Director,*
Brandscapes Worldwide

In *Insightful Inc.*, Manish has narrated and discussed a compendium of experiential insights that have made organizations and researchers more insightful, creative, and consumer-centric. Some of the strategies that have worked for brands have come from an organizational focus that is rooted in being open to new learning, being willing to be surprised, believing in the magic of insights, and providing a fertile soil within the organization for deeper exploration, questioning, taking a holistic perspective, using numerous data sources and at the same time being strongly consumer-centric.

Manish combines the world of insights research with analytics, technology, AI and in-market experiences and learning. He underscores the value of bringing many streams of data together to be holistic and yet magically insightful. By the end of the book, one realizes that it has the potential of becoming a bible for all researchers, marketers and advertising planners who wish to create winning brands that consumers will love, respect, and desire. The book reflects the many lessons that the author has learnt while working at Unilever and from the ever-changing and complex world of the consumer.

— ***Dr. Meena Kaushik****, Chairperson,*
Quantum Consumer Solutions

To my dad, for instilling in me a love for human psychology, and my wife, Savy, for always standing by me.

Contents

Foreword

"*Nothing in life is more exciting and rewarding than the sudden flash of insight that leaves you a changed person.*" American Physicist Arthur Gordon Webster succinctly captures the importance of 'insights' in this quote. Over the years, however, in business, we have realized that although 'rewarding', insights need not always be 'sudden' or even a 'flash'. The process of capturing and evaluating insights and turning them to actionable ideas has become a veritable science in recent years.

Put simply, insights refer to a deep understanding of people, or of a situation, of cause and effect. In fact, for companies, insights have been integral to developing solutions for consumers since the very beginning. Be it the bar of Sunlight soap that was launched to address the drudgery of washing and cleaning clothes in Victorian England or Horlicks that was meant to supplement the diet of soldiers during the First World War.

As consumerism grew, the need to understand people became more distinct. From the early days of market research that involved only formal questionnaires, more qualitative practices such as focus group discussions and in-depth interviews emerged. Today, insights are the bedrock for any company that aims to deliver superior service and products to its consumers.

What traditionally used to be simple market research that supplied data to marketing teams, is now evolving into strategic insight engines across corporations, enabling them with higher levels of consumer and customer centricity. Gathering insights no longer means amassing a quantum of data but the ability to link this disparate data and extract value out of them. Consumer behaviour is evolving; and it changes often and in unexpected ways. The COVID-19 pandemic, for instance, has brought in massive and sudden shifts in consumer behaviour. In India, with people staying at home during lockdowns and tending to household chores themselves, the sale of dishwashers and dishwashing detergents saw a rise. Several other home care products that delivered on consumers' increasing need for sanitation and hygiene saw a steep rise in sales. We also saw an increasing number of consumers preferring products that deliver higher order benefits and at the same time are people and planet positive. Insights are hence no longer restricted to just the product, but relevant to the entire consumer journey.

I have always believed that insights go much beyond just product development and can support every part of the business. For example, insights into consumer shopping patterns can tell you how a product should be distributed across channels; cultural insights can tell you how to market your products. Take, for example, Hindustan Unilever's WIMI programme. 'Winning in Many Indias' (WIMI) was launched in 2014 to understand the different needs of different consumer groups across the many 'Indias'. This helped us gain local insights and act upon them with speed.

Insights can also help businesses chart their journey through rough weather. Take the last few years, for example. It has not only taught us that as leaders, we need to adapt to new situations and embrace change at all times-, but also made us realize the importance of having the ability to pull together disparate views of a situation to create a plausible understanding of the complexity around us. I call this ability, sensemaking. And to hone this ability, you need to embed a strong sense of gathering and understanding of insights. One needs to have an external orientation, build a wide network, engage with multiple stakeholders, listen with humility, see patterns in complexity and think across polarities such as efficiency versus effectiveness, or safety versus economy.

Unilever, in fact, has been one of the stalwarts in mining consumer insights not only for its brands or products but also to strengthen the entire value chain. Take the Reimagine HUL programme, for example. Witnessing the rapid growth of technology and realizing its potential in creating a meaningful difference not only to businesses but to society, HUL embarked upon the Reimagine journey. It was a vision of how we want to leverage data, harness latest technologies and emerging business models, to redefine how HUL engages with consumers, customers, and the way we operate. The objective is not only to stay abreast of the changing needs of a digitally connected ecosystem but also about creating structural capabilities that provide superior value to consumers.

Over the years, Unilever's insights mechanism has developed into one of the biggest competitive advantages for the company. Today, it is a highly connected and digitized function that drives business performance.

Manish's book navigates multiple dimensions of the consumer insights function with several examples from Unilever. It showcases the transformation of the traditional consumer insight into a highly-specialized science.

Sanjiv Mehta
Former Chairman/CEO of Hindustan Unilever

Preface

The world around is going through transformation at an accelerated pace, and the pace of change will never be this slow again. The Digital Revolution has played a significant role in this transformation journey. It has redefined rules of competition and need for speed. It has also fundamentally altered how people think and behave.

In this environment, companies need insights on people more than ever before. Providing insights faster, cheaper, and better has become a business imperative. More and more corporations are realizing that superior insights create lasting competitive advantage. However, this calls for a change in processes, mindset, and cultural transformation. However, all this is easier said than done.

This journey is never easy; it involves tremendous efforts and can sometimes be difficult and frustrating. Learning from past experiences accelerates the transformation journey. This book is a practical guide to the transformation journey of making your organization an '*Insightful Inc.*'. Drawing from true experiences within a company and blending it with robust frameworks, this book brings these insights to life with real-world case studies.

As a part of the Consumer Market Insights team at Unilever (in India and in various countries and product categories around the world), Manish has played a crucial role in driving this transformation. *Insightful Inc.*, based on his learnings from Unilever, is an invaluable guide to anyone who wants to create a sustainable competitive advantage for their business.

Create an inspiring journey, enjoy the ride, and transform the business!

Stan Sthanunathan
Former Executive Vice President – Consumer
Market Insights, Unilever

Introduction

"Wow, what an insightful presentation!" commented the American Ambassador (who was visiting Unilever office as a special guest) on a presentation I was delivering before him and his team on the Indian culture and its diversity. While the comment was obviously flattering, I wasn't sure I deserved it. Not because my presentation lacked information on Indian cultural values, rather it included more of general observations about Indian culture than actual insights. In other words, I hadn't explained why Indians behaved in certain ways or the historical and evolutionary forces that have shaped us the way we are today. Neither did I comment on the implications of the culture on business environments of the two countries or how it impacts the queues American embassy sees every day for the U.S. visa. It was an interesting presentation (even if I say so myself), but not necessarily an *insightful* one.

This got me thinking on how the definition of 'insight' is open to different interpretations and meanings depending on individuals. Having spent over 19 years in Unilever, I learnt that the organization's culture and the teams, generally speaking, are quite insightful. They religiously study consumer behaviour, dissect each data set they obtain, and try to fathom its business implications. However, does this make the entire organization insightful? Perhaps better than the most, but is that organization a true embodiment of the definition?

While reading Sudhir Sitapati's (an ex-Unilever marketer) book *The CEO Factory: Management Lessons from Hindustan Unilever*, it struck me that a lot of marketers at Unilever are inherently insightful. All examples presented in his book are rich with great insights on: how to define a problem, how the marketers go about obtaining the data and gaining a deeper understanding that could solve that problem, and so on. I think the book reflected the culture of Unilever quite well where gaining insights is not simply delegated to the consumer insights team, but is a result of a collaborative effort between different teams. Insights teams are *enablers* rather than necessarily *producers* or *owners* of insights. This, indeed, is a great place to be at because the insights team then gets to focus on newer and faster (and sometimes economical) ways of gaining insights which helps the teams to move forward.

My interest in trying to understand human behaviour perhaps dates back to my teenage years. My father had a double major (in Philosophy and Psychology) and my mother taught Hindi and History. So, naturally, our house brimmed with books on philosophy, psychology, and Hindi literature. By the time I finished school, I had already read a lot of books on psychology (which my father probably would not have allowed, had he known at that time). Although I didn't grasp much of what was written in those books then, I think my readings on psychology, with a sprinkling of philosophy and Hindi literature, made me the intuitive 'listener' that I am today.

As a curious child, I was also drawn to the world of advertising from early on. I grew up in the 1980s when Doordarshan was the only channel running on Indian television sets. The concept of TV commercials or advertisements (ads) gained popularity only in the latter half of the decade when colour TVs came in and subsequently the number of programs increased. Watching ads during these programs was always exciting (sometimes, more than the programs themselves). I would often wonder why some ads seemed better than the others because back then I was under the impression that the same Doordarshan team made the ads for all the brands that approached them for advertising. It soon dawned on me that the ads that stood out were, perhaps, a result of a better briefing that the team received as compared to others; they were clearly more entertaining and conveyed a much sharper message. Funnily enough, the importance of a good ad brief was clear to me even then as a teenager!

But all of that was quickly forgotten when my focus shifted on pursuing further education, and that's how I ended up in Veermata Jijabai Technological Institute (VJTI) to earn a mechanical engineering degree. It was only when I was quite disillusioned working as an engineer that my mind began wandering back to advertising. Heeding a valuable advice from a Human Resource personnel of a reputed ad agency back then, I joined a business school (NMIMS, Mumbai) with a clear intention of joining the world of advertising. Thankfully, before the placement season kicked in, I gave some serious thought to what I wanted to do with my career and realized that market research was a profession that uniquely combined human psychology, marketing, and statistics. I was good at research and quantitative technique courses in the B-school;

I loved marketing, and psychology came instinctively to me. So, research was an obvious choice, and I focused on pursuing research-related subjects on the campus. After learning the ropes in a few research agencies for initial few years, I found myself beginning my 19-year-long career at Unilever which I spent globetrotting in order to work on and gain consumer insights for different product categories—from Personal Care to Foods—and loved every minute of it.

What I enjoyed and gained the most from a career in consumer insights is not just the ability to understand why people behave the way they do, but to relate that understanding to product consumption and brand perceptions. And, more importantly, making the best use of this knowledge to decode the way products can be further enhanced to improve the lives of the consumers, in whatever small way.

A powerful insight is the one that reveals an aspect of a person's behaviour that's obvious in hindsight; such an insight can further be used to create an innovative product or improve an existing product or service (more on this in the next chapter). Uncovering an insight through an exploration of consumer behaviour is exciting for me, but creating a unique destination of that journey is even more exciting. A few years ago, when Unilever was encouraging everyone to find and understand their own purpose in life and therefore in the organization, I realized that my purpose is, and has always been, to *bring music into mathematics to unravel hitherto untold stories*. That is, combining the science of analytics with the art of understanding human behaviour to unearth a new aspect and create a new opportunity. This is what I enjoy doing, both in personal life (like writing this book and other articles) as well as in professional life. The idea behind this book is to present all the learnings I gained from Unilever, and I hope you, my readers, find the journey to be as exhilarating as I did.

Insights are useful not only in creating something new but also in renovating an existing brand or business. If you look around in the world of business, you will notice that all successful businesses are founded on great consumer insights. Whenever a business discovered a genuine need or a tension among consumers that needed to be resolved (and it was commercially viable, of course), they used that consumer insight to design their new product or service. Equally continuous evolution of the foundational consumer insight on which a brand or business is based, has allowed the businesses to remain relevant to consumers over decades. Below are some of the apt examples around us that show how these insights were used:

Dove: The pressure to be beautiful feeds on our tendency to focus on the negative, making beauty an unnecessary source of anxiety. (Dove offers a wide range of products that claim to moisturize and nourish your skin and provide you with 'real care'.)

Nike: The barrier to me being more of an athlete isn't the quality of my running shoes, it's the motivation it takes. (Nike's purpose that goes with the tagline—*Just do it*—is to do everything possible to expand human potential—by empowering the athlete in you.)

M&M's: The silky texture of melting chocolate looks and tastes delicious, but it also feels sticky. (M&M's candy shell prevents the chocolate from melting until it is consumed.)

Google Pay: Monetary transactions and payments seem complicated and unsafe to the uninitiated at first. At times, it makes one feel like they need deeper knowledge of the banking system or technical expertise. (Google Pay application makes such monetary transactions easier for the consumers with its simple and secure user interface, and has been helpful for everyone with minimal knowledge of conducting online payments or transactions.)

Persil/Omo/Surf: Kids always get dirty, and while it's exhausting to do their laundry every time, we do it nonetheless because we want them to continue playing as it is a healthy part of their development. (Persil believes dirt is good—it's a mark of an active and experimentative childhood; so, let them keep playing!)

Tech companies use similar insights to add a layer of latest technology to the ways existing businesses serve consumer needs. For instance, the need for easy transportation always existed and was being taken care of by different taxi companies. However, the process of hailing a cab and getting someone to chauffeur you around by a simple tap of a thumb on your smartphone needed technological simplification and accessibility. Uber—through its technology—brought in this ease of accessibility, a sense of quicker mobility and user-friendliness thereby resolving a lot of tensions in the earlier process of hailing a cab. Airbnb does the same for booking a comfortable place to stay during travel.

An insightful tech company would always make it easier and hassle free for its consumers to avail their services by deftly hiding all the complex behind-the-scene processes. A classic example here would be that of Apple vs. Android. While Apple is user-friendly and intuitive for its end users, Android is an equally powerful and innovative operating system. However, Android is said to be more of a delight for geeks than end users; this is because it gives a lot of space to flex the system in order to create a bespoke experience. A deep understanding of target audiences and what they need gives these tech companies an ability to design the right experience.

How did Unilever and other such organizations evolve to be insightful? Was it planned that way or was it just a coincidence or the passion project of a few Chief Marketing Officers (CMOs) or Chief Information Officers (CIOs)? Is it about nurturing a few insightful individuals in the team or is it about the processes laid out for people to follow? Or is it about the cutting-edge research methods? In the recent past, various companies have significantly invested into big data analytics to increase the power of organizational analytics; this has often resulted in re-engineering of the innovation process, including the State-Gate process where the decisions are driven by numbers and analytics. Does this mean that these organizations are more insightful than others? Are organizations that employ innovative practices more creative and insightful than others, or have they simply engineered their innovation processes better?

The intention of this book is to explore these questions through the lens of my nearly two decades of experience at Unilever. This book takes a closer look at the dimensions of consumer insights and what it takes for an organization to be insightful. The idea is to outline not just what insightfulness means in an organization but also how to execute an insights function. Hence, it includes both 'what' needs to be done and, equally, 'how' it can be done—by delving deeper into ways to nurture gut feelings and create processes and methods or techniques for the same; for insights is a true combination of art and science. I hope the readers find this book useful in gaining a deeper understanding of how an organization can be made insightful and consumer-centric.

CHAPTER 1

What Is an Insight?

Insight is perhaps one of the most commonly used (and abused) words in the world of marketing and research. More often than not, people use it when they make basic observations such as "the stock market crashed as soon as the budget was announced", or "the market share of the brand went up when they reduced the prices of the products". These are all observations, and not insights, because they are simply articulating the data (what they see or observe). They do not explain the phenomenon or the reasons behind these observations. The fact that these general observations are often understood as insights in itself gives us an insight: people don't tend to observe (and analyze) things around them deeply. And when they do observe closely, the results often surprise them because they spot the things they failed to notice earlier, and this makes them believe they have unearthed an insight. This tells us that the first step in being insightful is about being observant.

Insight, therefore, is an explanation and an interpretation of the observation; a deeper, astute, and more penetrating understanding of the observation. Cambridge dictionary defines insight as simply "a clear, deep, and sometimes sudden understanding of a complicated problem or situation, or the ability to have such an understanding."

Connecting the Dots

If the market share of a brand increases with price reduction, it says a lot about the brand's equity in relation to its pricing, and also about consumers' willingness to pay for the brand (or even for the category). It may also tell us something about the pricing environment in the market at that point in time. It all depends on how much one digs into the observation by collecting other observations around it. The most useful question to ask here is "why?": Why did the shares go up once the prices were reduced? Now, we need to dig deeper and pull out more information to find answers: has it happened in the past?; does it happen to other brands?; how is the brand priced against the competition?, and so on. Finding these answers and connecting them with the "why?" gives us an insight. 'Connecting the dots' is, therefore, the next step for gaining an insight once we gather enough observations.

In the above example, after connecting the dots, let's say we conclude that the brand equity wasn't strong enough to command higher pricing, and hence the reduction in price led to increase in sales and market share. Now, is this an insight about the brand or about the people buying the brand? It is a bit of both, but it is an important distinction to think about nevertheless. If you are looking for insights on the brand to understand it better in order to manage it well, the observations (and connecting-the-dots exercise) have to be around brand's performance in different situations. But if you are looking for consumer insight so that you can manage consumer expectations from the category (that your brand belongs to) well, then the observations have to be about consumer behaviour around different brands in different situations. If it's the latter, you will need to look for observations across brands in the category (that your brand belongs to) on what people buy at different prices, the benefits they seek, what they think of the other brands, what they remember of the brand from its advertising, and so on. As a result, you gain an in-depth understanding of how to make the brand more appealing to consumers.

This leads to the notion that the *objective* of gathering insights has to be very clear upfront. Otherwise, it could be like running aimlessly in different directions with several observations without yielding anything worthwhile and useful. Sometimes, it's better to start with a hypothesis rather than an objective. Some marketers think that the bolder the hypothesis, the more interesting the insight, especially when it's being developed for communication design. The importance of being clear about the objective upfront cannot be overemphasized, given how often the analysis tends to start without a clear objective (or under the guise of 'exploration') which results in teams running in circles quite aimlessly.

Moving on, let's assume that you have a clear objective, which is stemming from a key observation that needs to be understood and you start gathering observations by seeking answers to "why" questions. How do you know when to stop asking "why", to stop digging deeper, and how would you know that you have a deep enough insight? Let's look at this with an example.

Insight for a Fashion Brand

Objective: You work for a women's fashion brand and want to gain an insight on how women buy clothes for themselves. It can be a difficult one to start with because understanding how women shop for clothes is like trying to navigate a labyrinth where one can easily get lost given the way women look for and make choices in their clothes. Let's try with one simple observation a woman respondent made (hypothetically) in your research.

Initial observation: *"I want to buy clothes that I can wear to the office but with brighter colours."*

WHY SPECIFIC CLOTHES FOR OFFICE	WHY BRIGHTER COLOURS
Why 1: Because you can only wear certain type of clothes to office, and I need those.	**Why 1:** Because colour palette for office clothes is usually pretty subtle, muted, and dull.
Why 2: Because you are expected to dress in a certain professional way at workplace.	**Why 2:** Because wearing subtle colour clothes would be quite boring and won't make me stand out.

WHY SPECIFIC CLOTHES FOR OFFICE	WHY BRIGHTER COLOURS
Why 3: Because I don't want to break the mould and be conspicuous.	**Why 3:** I like bright colours and I think they make me glow.
Why 4: Because that will make me fit into the office group and belong.	**Why 4:** I want to be able to have my distinct identity and not disappear in the crowd.
Why 5: Because that will give me the peace of mind to focus on my work instead of worrying about people's opinions about me.	**Why 5:** Because that will make me feel confident and good about myself, which would help me work better.
Why 6: Because that will make me more successful.	**Why 6:** Because that will make me more successful.
Why 7: Because I will be happy and have peace of mind when I am successful.	**Why 7:** Because I will be happy and have peace of mind when I am successful.

There are a few interesting things to observe here:

1. You could go on and on, all the digging eventually will lead to reasons like 'peace of my mind' or 'world peace' or some such big lofty purpose which might be quite useless for a brand to tap into.

2. The trick is to stop at a level that is interesting; in other words, a level that provides a different perspective into

the consumer mind and a unique angle for the brand to use.

3. In this case, if you stop at level 2 on both the tracks, then the insight would be: *I want to dress in a way that makes me look professional but also enables me to stand out.*

If you are a fashion brand wanting to target working women, this could be an interesting angle to explore. This would not only allow you to design the communication around this insight, but also design your products and pricing accordingly. This is the power of a good insight. It can be like a stepping stone (or a guiding reference) for all the thoughts and the fountainhead of all the decisions you make for your product or brand.

If an insight has to be a fountainhead to shape your brand around it, then it needs to be articulated in a way that's concise, sharp, but also inspiring. As Sudhir Sitapati (author of *THE CEO FACTORY: Management Lessons from Hindustan Unilever,* as referenced earlier) puts it, "an insight needs to be expressed pithily." And that requires significant amount of work, too. You need a clear understanding of the consumer tension and the ability to eloquently articulate that thought (tension) so that it is easy to understand and inspires several thoughts. This then converts it from what the late Jeremy Bullmore (former member of the WPP Advisory Board and famously known as the most admired man in the advertising industry) called 'low-potency' insight into a 'high-potency' insight. Low-potency insight often covers the observation quite well but is not inspiring enough, whereas high-potency insight is something that immediately provokes thoughts.

Consider this example from Jeremy's insight on insights:

Product satisfaction arises less from inherent construction and performance than consumers' internalized perception of personal utility—this is a low-potency insight. Because it's clunky and conveys the message, it takes a few times of reading before you can internalize it. You spend a lot more time understanding it than getting inspired and thinking of ideas from it. Now, consider a high-potency articulation of the same: *People don't want quarter-inch drills, they want quarter-inch holes.* This immediately elicits an exultant response, "Yes, of course! That's exactly how it is!".

Let's go back to our previous example of women buying clothes for work and turn it into a high-potency insight: *I want to dress in a way that makes me look professional but also enables me to stand out from the rest.* The tension here is the balance that she wants to achieve while buying clothes for workplace: she wants to fit into her workplace by looking professional *like everyone else,* but also wants to stand out or express her own personality through the way she dresses. How can we express it more cleverly? It does require some revisiting of the key thought you have zeroed in on and coming up with the right words. It can be an intensely creative act as it often requires—to quote Jeremy Bullmore—"a massive injection of imagination". Working with people who have a way with words by using just the right metaphors and quotes that are evocative and inspiring, and also with the ones who are economic with words while stringing sentences together often helps at this stage.

Let's try different expressions for our example by working on different angles:

1. *Same same, but different*: This sums it up but doesn't express the tension of the context very well.
2. *Professional dress that expresses who I am:* Doesn't bring out the consumer tension that well.
3. *Dress that makes me feel that I belong, but also stand out*: Doesn't bring out the professional context that well (this insight could be for any situation.)
4. *Women wear similar clothes at work, but I want something that sets me apart*: Doesn't articulate the tension between 'the wanting to belong to the workplace' and 'still retain your individuality' that well.
5. *I do want to belong to my workplace by dressing up professionally but that doesn't have to mean looking same as everyone else! I want my own personality to be reflected in the way I dress*: Quite long and not as pithy but does convey the tension.
6. *I want to dress professionally at work but with a dress that also expresses my unique identity*: Conveys the context and the tension, and also implies that professional dressing often means merging into the crowd, which is not desirable by some.
7. *I want a dress that doesn't hide who I am, even at workplace*: Now, this, suddenly sounds more interesting. Clothes are, in reality, meant to cover your body, and sometimes, hide your insecurities, but this articulation presents a contrast and thereby a tension—about wanting to remain one's true self in the dress. And 'even in the workplace' provides the reference to context.

You can go on till you reach an expression that you are happy with. In terms of process, this is usually done in a small group where you bounce off different thoughts and expressions (know more about the process later in the book). Sometimes, pictures and manifestations of the insight can help in the articulation. For the above example you can use the following picture:

The woman in the picture is Hollywood actor Reese Witherspoon from the movie *Legally Blonde* where she decides to wear the formal lawyer coat but a pink one instead.[1] A popular culture reference or a prop like this can sometimes help articulate a thought better and bring an idea to life.

[1] Today, pink is thankfully no longer considered a gender-specific colour. Legally Blonde was released back in 2001 when pink was popularly associated with femininity. So, the lead character, who wanted to make her mark differently in the male-dominated legal profession (where lawyers mostly wore black suits), chose to wear a pink lawyer's suit.

To continue with the previous example of you working with a fashion brand, you might take this insight (as discussed above) and make your brand to be 'unapologetically feminine'. Here, you are taking the insight—the tension between wanting to belong to a workplace, yet be distinctly yourself—and converting it into a brand idea. 'Unapologetically feminine' is not an insight in itself but a brand idea that is based on the insight, and you have added the dimension of femininity in it (because you are a woman's fashion brand) to express what the brand brings to the table and the reasons behind it in two words. And if that is your brand's central thought, then you can see how all your product design ideas, advertising ideas, pricing, where and how you sell it, etc., can be derived from this central thought. Driving consistency through all aspects of the brand then becomes easier as well. And all of this came out from a compelling insight based on a simple statement that a woman made at the beginning of this hypothetical journey!

To get there, you do need to have a good understanding of what the brand needs to do and an expertise of consumer understanding to decide the level at which you want to stop. This is one of the key capabilities of an insightful organization that sets them apart—they know how to mine for an insight!

Different Definitions of Insight

While the concept of insight is the same, its articulation by different people and organizations does vary with accent on different nuances in their definitions. Let's take a look at some of the definitions I have come across:

1. A resounding truth that throws new light on what we know or reveals the unknown to unlock fresh thinking. (Unilever.)
2. A good insight is like a refrigerator; the moment you look into it, a light comes on! (Jeremy Bullmore, one of the most influential thinkers on advertising and brands.)
3. Insights are unspoken human truths, truths the subconscious recognizes when it sees them. (Mark Pollard, Big Spaceship, New York.)
4. Insight is the advice of an expert fisherman: instead of trolling to the bottom of the river and dredging up garbage, insight tells you which bait to use to hook the right fish directly to your line. (Jason Theodore, Creative Director, Publicis Canada.)
5. Insight is a deep, penetrating observation or interpretation thereof, that unlocks growth and provides inputs into strategy and a launch pad for ideas. A good insight is fresh, deep, focussed, and directional. (Faris Yakob, Principal, Genis Steals New York.)
6. I think of insight as the truth that hasn't really been told before. Mr. ABC is good at stripping away the bullshit and telling that truth, and I guess that makes him "insightful". (Dave Burg, Head of Planning, Roundhouse Portland.)
7. A fresh observation that unlocks creativity. (Bud Caddell, Partner, Undercurrent LA.)

8. To me insight is any piece of information or knowledge that reshapes how I see a situation. (Adrian Ho, Partner, Zeus Jones, Minneapolis.)
9. A revelation. Something that makes you go "f*#k me I never thought of it that way"! That's interesting. (Lucy Goode, VP Planning, Publicis Montreal.)
10. An insight is like a cocoon; lots of butterflies can come out of it. (Caitlin Ryan, Executive Creative Director, Kamarama London.)
11. Insight is something that's retrospectively self-evident. (Stan Sthanunathan, Ex-Global CMI head, Unilever.)
12. The 'why' of what that inspires a breakthrough. (Stan Sthanunathan, Ex-Global CMI head, Unilever.)

Implications of Insight on Marketing and Insights Professionals

There is no one fixed definition of insight, and all different definitions centre around the same central idea. Marketers and insights professionals in an organization should define what an insight means for them and instill the practice of converting observations into insight. That would not just lead to development of a lot more consumer-centric product concepts and advertising ideas, but start a culture where people would examine every aspect of business and see how it would benefit the consumer. This simple idea can revolutionize the way of thinking in an effective manner.

To summarize what an 'insight' is:

- It has to explain one or a few key observations about the question you are trying to address.
- It has to be deep enough to be meaningful, but not so deep that you can't do anything with it (remember you are seeking an insight for your brand, and not working as a therapist).
- It has to have tension between two opposite things; something that's obvious in the hindsight when you express it.
- It has to have an 'aha' moment—a surprising revelation that's obvious in the hindsight when you read it.
- It has to be expressed pithily; an articulation that proves to be a springboard for ideas.
- It should be useful for the purpose it is being created (for the business in this case) and not just an interesting poetic thought.
- It should have flashes of inspiration, or in other words, a stepping stone for all the ideas of your business.

CHAPTER 2

What Makes a Person Insightful?

Have you ever noticed that there are some people around you who seem to be more 'insightful' than others? These are the ones who usually have a knack of explaining something in a simple manner that seems very obvious when you hear it, but not something that might have occurred to you on your own. You will find these kinds of people among poets, stand-up comedians, creative directors, and so on, who do this quite often, though insightfulness by no means is restricted to such creative professionals. Consider the famous lines given to us by the Urdu poet Mirza Ghalib:

Hazāroñ ḳhvāhisheñ aisī ki har ḳhvāhish pe dam nikle
bahut nikle mire armān lekin phir bhī kam nikle

I have a thousand yearnings, each one afflicts me so
Many were fulfilled for sure, not enough although[2]

Ghalib not only understands but also succinctly expresses the vagaries of human desire in these lines, which might otherwise take an essay to articulate. Or, consider this paragraph written by Shrayana Bhattacharya—in her book *Desperately Seeking Shak Rukh: India's Lonely Young Women and the Search for Intimacy and Independence*—where she describes the life of elite Indian men (and women) through her relationship with a man she calls as 'The One'. It speaks volumes about the shallowness of the so-called elite. This articulation by Bhattacharya not only reveals her insight about that segment of Indian society but also highlights her abilities to express it well:

"The social texture of this wealth ladder revealed itself to me during my days and evenings spent in love with The One. Despite being neighbours on the economic spectrum, an invisible partition divided this man's world and mine. This partition was discriminating; it allowed sex and flirtation but prohibited authenticity and camaraderie. He hated talking about work, considering it low form of culture. From his mother to his family friends, glamorous, unemployed women for whom marriage was an insurance policy were the norm in his social circle. The men, meanwhile, were a gallery of competitive anxieties, hanging by the skin of their teeth to their family legacies..."

So, we come back to: How some people get to be more insightful than others. It's quite well-known that a powerful insight comes from exploring the 'why' behind an observation

[2] Couplet and translation source: Rekhta org.

but equally knowing when to stop asking that 'why' (being aware that you have dug deep enough). Clearly, some are naturally attuned to doing that than others; such people can observe or probe in a very non-intrusive way and gain an understanding behind what they see and hear. Additionally, not only do they have a knack of knowing when to stop probing but also have a trove of observations in their minds that they can relate to and add things up in their minds as they go along. Is this ability natural or can it be fine-tuned? In other words, can people be trained to be insightful?

During my conversations with Rebecca Wynberg, one of the world's leading qualitative researchers, she said that insightful people have a few following common traits:

1. **They are observant:** They have a keen eye that notices little things about people that most others may not. They notice the bedside manners, so to speak, and that is not just about the behaviour but even the way people react to different situations and how they express themselves. They tend to be a lot more observant in the areas or subjects of their interest (than everything in general). For instance, a photographer is likely to be observant about things around them from a point of view of what would make a great shot or a great subject of a photo, but those interested in human behaviour would be a lot more observant of the people around them.

2. **They are curious:** Insightful people don't have to make a lot of effort to observe others, it comes naturally to them because they are genuinely curious. They are curious about how people behave, how people think, and

what makes them tick—they don't have to be experts in human psychology (although that helps), but they have an intuitive sense. My friend Poonam Kumar, who is the leading global expert in the NeedScope model of Kantar TNS, often used to share with me that we researchers are in the field of insights because we have 'vulgar curiosity' about people. This term 'vulgar curiosity' stayed with me because it aptly described almost uncontrollable urge to observe, understand, and analyze people that becomes a habit and sometimes a compulsion.

3. **They can connect the dots:** When you are curious about something and observing things about that phenomenon, you are constantly connecting dots and trying to understand that phenomenon. You are then automatically generating hypotheses and testing them at the back of your mind till you arrive at a hypothesis that tests positive with good amount of evidence you have observed. It is a bit like what your mind is going through when you are watching a gripping murder mystery—you keenly watch all characters and try to guess who the real murderer is at the back of your mind. No one trains you for guessing a murderer, but if you are interested, you get drawn and start self-learning as you watch more such movies. "Good insights people are 'reflective', they are able to reflect on what they have learnt no matter what the source of information is," shared Chitkala Nishandar, head of Insights for the Asia-Pacific region at 3M, when I was interviewing her about insights and the way they approach it at 3M.

4. **They can cut to the chase or express pithily:** If you have really understood a phenomenon and have given it considerable thought, you would be able to articulate it clearly and succinctly. Key ingredients for this are: clear understanding, considerable amount of thinking or poking, and prodding from different angles to get full clarity on the best way of expressing it. This does not happen spontaneously, unless you are gifted with words or are a writer, but requires a good amount of effort.
5. **They can articulate the implications clearly:** This last part is particularly important for insights professionals and business problem-solvers (and would not apply to insightful people like poets and comedians). It is the ability to go beyond the articulation of the insight and define the actions that need to be taken. After understanding "what" the problem is, the "so what" and "now what" have to follow for the insight to be actionable. Otherwise, the insight can remain in the realm of 'nice, interesting thing to know' without any purpose.

To answer the question posed earlier: can people be trained in being insightful? Is it an art or science? I think it's a combination of both. Not only you need to be curious about people and their behaviour but you also need some training on understanding the behaviour, connecting the dots, creating and testing hypotheses. Expressing it in a concise manner also takes practice, but can be done with the help of people who are more articulate and fluent. Poets are good at this because they have a knack of expressing an emotion quite succinctly (though they also need good amount of training and practice to get there).

And this skill is not only useful for understanding consumers but also for solving any problem. Sherlock Holmes used this skill for solving crimes; he not only generated hypotheses but also eliminated them as he connected different dots. Supply chain experts use this skill to observe the system and get insights on the bottlenecks and come up with solutions that could improve the system. This is a versatile skill that indeed goes well beyond consumer insights and comes in handy to solve any kind of problem, for this is the very foundation of critical thinking.

CHAPTER 3

How Do You Make an Organization Insightful?

If being curious, observant, possessing the ability to connect the dots and cut to the chase make people insightful, can the same be said for corporate organizations? How are some of the world's most consumer-centric organizations able to bring this ability to everyone in the organization? And how can one make corporates, which are not particularly consumer-centric, more insightful and focused around their consumers? In other words, can the model of what makes a person insightful be applied to organizations as well?

In my experience, you may have to counter several challenges while accomplishing this. One of the biggest challenges is to make the organizations evolve from a 'knowing' culture to a 'learning' one. In other words, evolving from a culture that largely depends on the heuristics to make the decisions to a culture that is much more objective and consumer-data driven. The challenge in that is not so much the cost, but sometimes ignorance about not being consumer-centric, sometimes inertia, and sometimes sheer lack of imagination on how to change it.

Recently, during a conversation with the officials of a large bank on consumer centricity, they mentioned to me that they knew exactly how many counters a branch should have. They had a person assigned specifically to help customers walking into the bank and guide them to the right counter. Additionally, they had also deployed a coupon system to ensure that people got their requisite services in the right order, and so on. But their customer experience scores still weren't improving. This was due to sheer lack of customer centricity; a simple walk-in and observing the process in a few branches over a couple of days clearly showed them that some branches were far more crowded than the others. Besides, the person helping customers didn't understand much about peoples' banking needs to be able to guide them to the right counters, and the coupon machine would break down frequently. The bank thought they 'knew' what was needed, but wasn't willing to see the experience through customers' eyes to learn better ways of serving them. Eventually, a little bit of mystery shopping exercise was enough for them to start making changes to their branches and dramatically improve customer service.

There are several such examples today where, as a customer, it is obvious to you which particular product or service needs improvement, but the company seems quite oblivious to it, and worse, never listen to your feedback. Think of fuel stations where you refuel your car and how they are often designed for efficient running of the gas station rather than ease of customers; think of several generic emails you get from your bank despite them knowing everything about you and your financial situation and very rarely getting one email or an offer that actually gives you a relevant suggestion. On the other hand, think of a large supermarket (like TESCO or Walmart) where despite having millions of products and them not knowing you personally, you can find your way to what you are looking for quite easily; or think of a smartphone which is quite intuitive for anyone to use without too much of training or complex manuals. It isn't a coincidence that some companies manage to make it quite simple for consumers whereas some have their customers struggling to optimally use their products or services. The difference between the two is consumer centricity—it is how well attuned the organization is to listen to its customers or consumers.

Consumer centricity needs to be embedded into the corporate culture, into the systems and processes, into the ways of working and into the decision-making for the company's offering to be really simple and easy for its customers. It isn't a 'job' to be delegated to the marketing or consumer insights division, but a responsibility that everyone in the organization, from CEO to trainee, from salesman to the factory worker, needs to carry. But how do you start that journey and move the organization along? Let's try and translate the traits of insightful people into the organizational traits. And that gives us some interesting clues.

TRAIT	WHAT IT MEANS FOR PEOPLE	WHAT IT MEANS FOR ORGANIZATIONS
Curious	Innate curiosity to understand people	Inculcated 'consumer curiosity' to understand how people shop and use the category and brands
Observant	Naturally observing things they are curious about	Right tools and systems to observe and understand people + easy access to information
Connecting the dots	Generating and testing hypotheses intuitively	Critical-thinking mindset
Express pithily the insights and its implications	Cut to the chase and articulate simply	Clear articulation of the insight, its implications, and resulting actions

This chapter explores each of these aspects in detail.

Making an Organization Curious: Inculcating Consumer[3] Curiosity

Curiosity is about being genuinely interested in a subject and, therefore, having your antenna naturally alert all the time. Notice how young boys (it's usually boys, though obviously not restricted to them) tend to notice the cars and know the brand or model by just one look! In a corporate environment, it is imperative to make the marketing and other customer-facing functions (and, in fact, everyone across functions) genuinely interested in the category and, more importantly, in the consumer behaviour within the category. The business teams may not be naturally 'curious' about it, either because they think the consumer behaviour in the category is quite obvious, particularly if they have also been regular users themselves of the products they make, or because they think there is not much to know about it. For instance, in the banking example in previous section, the bank managers thought they knew a lot about the banking needs of their customers because they served them every day and engaged with them regularly. But customers don't have 'banking needs' per se; rather they require financial services to take care of their money and other monetary obligations. This is crucial to know if you want to understand

---

[3] In Unilever terminology, the 'consumer' is differentiated from that of 'customer'. In FMCG or CPG organizations, the two can be different. The retailer is typically the real 'customer' for the company and 'consumer' is the person who buys from the retailer and consumes the product. But in other industries, the consumer and customer might be the same person in which case they can be used interchangeably.

why people choose or avoid banking with your organization, or how the banking services can be improved.

Ironically, despite everyone being regular users of soaps, shampoos, and detergents, FMCG companies tend to be among the biggest spenders on consumer research—P&G is said to be the biggest spender on market research globally with Unilever running a close second. So, if marketers are consumers of FMCG products themselves, why do they then need to spend money on research? Because they understand that products used are just solutions and, therefore, you must have an in-depth understanding of the problem they are trying to solve.

Let's take an example of a brand like Lux—a soap brand positioned in most markets globally as a glamorous soap used by film stars. The brand has been selling for over 80 years on that positioning, and some of the largest markets (e.g., India) still use film stars to endorse the brand. While the world has changed dramatically in the last eight decades, the brand continues to sell on this positioning. In today's world, particularly where celebrities and film stars are a lot more 'accessible' (via Instagram, X, etc.), and arguably a lot less iconic, why do women (core users of the brand) use it? Do its users really believe that they would start looking like the film stars endorsing the brand? If not, then is it only the functional benefits (fragrance, lather, etc.) that drive them to it, or sheer availability, or a convenient price point? If you are part of the team Lux—doing any role for the brand in marketing or outside of it, you must intuitively understand what draws consumers to the brand. Because if you don't, you might take the wrong decision about the usage of celebrities which could damage the brand equity.

Although there would be several market research reports available for you to read as a Lux manager, it's spending time with the consumers, understanding their context, seeing their life through their eyes, and the role a soap like Lux plays in their context, can you really begin to understand and internalize the insight on how Lux makes the glamour *accessible* to women and makes them feel special even if it is for a few moments. That is when we say you have begun developing a 'gut feeling'—about the brand and the category—which is crucial to ensure right advertising and product development of the brand. It is this insight and its effective implementation at every consumer touch point by everyone in the team that makes Lux the leading soap brand in India for decades.

Source: Archives of Brand Lux

Malcom Gladwell, in his bestseller *Outliers: The Story of Success,* argues that one can become an expert in a subject after spending 10,000 hours on it. Similar argument can be applied while developing a 'gut feeling' about a product category and its consumers. The business teams need to spend time with the consumers, see them interact with the category, understand their life context, talk to them about the brand, know what they think of the advertising, and so on, before they begin to really 'internalize' the insights and make them intuitive. Unilever has a robust practice in this space; their program 'Consumer Connect' enables anyone in the organization to book a 'connect' with the consumers anywhere in the country through an app–and the consumer visit is organized with the help of back-end field agencies. In fact, some of the categories mandate newly recruited employees to spend at least 100 hours with the consumers in the first three months of their joining before they are even allowed to express any opinion in the meetings.

This practice is followed in addition to the formal research that Unilever commissions through their research agency partners. In some of the largest Unilever markets like India, there are as many as 20,000 yearly consumer connects by employees working not just in their marketing department but across functions. Such a practice brings in consumer centricity like nothing else and ensures that all the conversations (and decisions) are rooted in consumer reality and not driven by internal corporate complexity.

Most large-scale organizations have a lot of internal process complexity—to create the products and services, logistics of go-to-market strategy, marketing processes, sales systems, accounting practices, and so on. Employees of an organization live and breathe that complexity every day because they have created it for themselves and for smoother functioning of their organization. But often enveloped in that complexity, people sometimes forget that the ultimate aim of all that complexity is for them to serve their consumers. If the consumer is at the heart of all the decisions or 'brought to the boardroom' so to speak, then the decisions can often be quite simple. Consumer centricity is about taking each and every business decision by asking what would benefit the consumer and in what ways can that be maximized without compromising organization's bottom line. If the decision benefits the consumer, it will benefit the business; there is no way around that and no way to cut corners.

Consumer centricity is, therefore, not about commissioning market research through an agency; that would be, what I call, a 'second-hand' consumer centricity. Of course, formal research has its role to play and quite a critical one at that. Research studies conducted on a large scale give you a good perspective on the consumer landscape and existing consumer behaviour, which would be infeasible to achieve through personal connects. Furthermore, there is a great value in the findings obtained by an independent research unit or an outside professional who looks at the category with a fresh, yet experienced eye. Market research and consumer connects should thus complement each other to bring in or enhance consumer centricity in an organization.

Making an Organization Observant

Once the curiosity about consumer behaviour in people working in an organization has been heightened, they begin to notice minute details and develop an appetite to devour copious amounts of information. There was a time when information used to be heavily guarded and made accessible to a select few within an organization. With increasing number of people sharing their thoughts and ideas fearlessly on the internet, the mindset of guarding information has changed significantly in the corporate world. Today, the power is not merely about access to data and information, it's about what you do with it. Of course, confidential information of an organization—corporate performance, for example—still remains protected and shared sensibly in line with market regulations, but most of the other information can be truly empowering for people.

Employees, once they become curious, say about a category, they need to have ways and means to 'observe'—to access information about their categories and consumers. Initiatives like Unilever's Consumer Connect Program, formal or informal market research, and other collected consumer data are the observations available for employees to access. However, mere availability of information does not mean they will access it and necessarily have a look at it. There are a few rules, in my view, which need to be followed for employees to use the available information to make decisions (instead of following the heuristics):

1. **Information should be easily accessible:** Lengthy research reports running into hundreds of pages or cumbersome library systems are major deterrents in

ease of access to information. When employees can access information through simple Google search today, you can't expect them to be any less demanding at their workplace in this aspect. Stan Sthanunathan, former Consumer and Market Insights (CMI) Head at Unilever, once said, "The Googlization of the insight world has happened completely... the CMI teams should tell businesses that they have all the answers—now what is your question?" This turns the notion of writing briefs for conducting research on its head completely and suggests that the insights team should be prepared well in advance and have all the answers ready, without anyone asking them the questions.

2. **Information should be available in bite-size digestible form:** Social media has considerably reduced the attention span at large. If you are unable to effectively explain your point in a few minutes, in an engaging manner, you will certainly lose them. Therefore, research presentations that go on for hours and involve poring over tables and graphs are a passé today. However, smaller nuggets like videos, infographics, or stories articulating the insight and ideas springing from it are used a lot more. And that not only requires thorough understanding of the insight to know what's really important and what isn't, but also the art of storytelling—a new muscle that the research professionals have had to build. When an organization starts using small videos, podcasts, and catchy newsletters to disseminate information about their consumers, it begins to notice the change in the

conversations among their employees from internal complexity of businesses to what consumers really want.

The journey to make information easily available usually leads to creation of two types of systems:

1. **Information dashboards:** These store information on sales data, market shares, ad spends, etc., and are regularly updated. Dashboards, today, play an increasingly crucial role in the organizations. Interestingly, the better looking they are, the more they get used. Gone are the days when people used to gatekeep information. Now, organizations design multiple dashboards for different sets of information (which can also create a problem because you need a dashboard to navigate the dashboards).

Unilever used to have different dashboards for sales, financials, and marketing data (like market share, ad spends, brand penetration, equity score, etc.), but a significant effort was spent on creating a system called 'Livewire' that integrates all the data so that people can look at the full picture in one go. Subsequently, with the introduction of AI, there is an intelligent system that sits on top of that which can pull out information based on questions people ask, instead of them having to look through the entire dashboard. Creating a system like that takes substantial amount of time and investment and requires working with a suitable tech solution. Hence, an upfront commitment from the leadership team is a must. One must note that it makes the information democratic and gives the power in the hands of the people (employees), rather than relying solely on the insights or analytics team to access

For example, the dashboard above shows vital information of key competitive brands in two sub categories (household care and fabric cleaning) of Home Care in five different markets. It shows market shares, growth rate, brand penetration, and change in the penetration over a year. Only in one glimpse, you will be able to summarize the threat posed by the competition. There are further tabs in the dashboard (not shown here) that can be clicked for a more detailed analysis.

the information. Furthermore, this also enables insights team to focus on developing insights and ideas from the already gathered information, rather than spending time on collecting and extracting data from different sources for the business. This, therefore, plays a massive role in moving the organization up on the insights' evolution curve.

2. **Catalogued library of research documents, images, videos, etc.:** A catalogued library or a knowledge management system that enables people to easily search for information. This is typically for research documents collected as a part of formal or informal research. Organizations tend to have a lot of those but if not stored properly, it leads to huge inefficiency and non-usage (like conducting similar research again every few years that answers same questions that are already answered). To avoid this, Unilever has created a system called the 'People World' that enables all the insights team to commission research through it, and archives the reports and insights for everyone to access and use. It also has a sophisticated in-built AI that searches and summarizes the information archived in it, making it easier for the team to pull out nuggets of information rather than voluminous reports. For instance, one could ask a question like "What are the preferred fragrances in a soap for people in North Mexico?", and the system responds with a short one-or two-page summary based on all the research done on the subject. Consulting companies like McKinsey and Boston Consulting Group usually excel in this area in order to retain and grow their in-house expertise in different areas.

The good news is that organizations don't have to build their bespoke systems like these anymore because there are 'off-the-shelf' knowledge management systems available now. For instance, a company called 'Big Sofa' catalogues and builds search capabilities on all the videos that an organization might have in order to make them a lot more user-friendly.

Making an Organization Connect the Dots

When you have abundance of information, accurately arriving at the insights and conclusions requires connecting the dots. This is done by asking the question "why" as earlier chapter illustrates and following the 'critical thinking' mindset. It then becomes a bit like the popular fictional detective Sherlock Holmes' style—critical and deductive thinking—where you generate several possible hypotheses, examine everything in minute detail, and eliminate the ones that don't fit. People who are insightful do it out of habit, but in the context of businesses, it can require some training and guidance for people to start thinking in that mode. And with some practice, people can always tune into their 'investigative' mode.

There has been a lot of thinking and development on defining and refining the critical thinking in the academic circles for the past 50 years; but the origins of critical thinking can be traced to the teachings of Socrates (as recorded by Plato). Critical thinking is generally defined as the intellectually disciplined process of actively and skillfully conceptualizing, applying, analyzing, synthesizing and evaluating the information gathered from or generated by observation, experience, reflection, reasoning, or communication, as a guide to belief or action.

Generally speaking, there are a few steps in the critical thinking followed in every work stream:

1. **Define the problem:** Having a clear problem statement is half the battle won. For example, is declining product sale the problem or declining market share? If the sales are declining, it could be an issue with the product or the sales system, but market share is a relative measure and needs comparative analysis of the problem. At times, it may not even be a problem that needs to be solved, but looked upon as an opportunity to explore. For instance, the business wanting to identify the next $100 million opportunity.

2. **Generate hypotheses:** This entails listing potential reasons for the problem and areas to be explored.

3. **Gather information, data, opinions, etc.:** For each of the hypotheses, it is crucial to identify and gather sufficient information, data, and opinions needed and the analysis that would test the hypothesis. For instance, is the product not good enough to sell could be a hypothesis for declining absolute sales and that would need information on product test to see if it delivers on expectations.

4. **Analyze the data:** Having clarity on the question that needs answering leads to the right path of analysis. Depending on the complexity of the data and the question explored, the analysis could be based on a simple or complex analytical modelling. In case of complex analytics, one can seek help from data analysts

or scientists who understand the right method and technique of analysis.

5. **Establish significance:** Is the analysis conclusive enough? Is it valid (reflecting reality) and reliable (would result in the same conclusion, if repeated) enough for the business to use while making crucial decisions? Moreover, how to sift through the huge amount of information that can be used in the decision-making? Again, here, having clarity on the objective of the analysis is paramount.
6. **Conclude:** Identifying various attainable conclusions and arriving at the one that's supported by evidence. Make a decision on the action that the business needs to take with the conclusion.
7. **Present or communicate:** Presenting the conclusion and recommended action to relevant stakeholders with the right justifications. The art of storytelling becomes crucial at this stage so that stakeholders don't get lost in the labyrinth of analysis and techniques used for analysis but focus on what the findings mean to the business and what potential actions they could take.

Before diving into some examples, let's take a look at few rules—borrowed from the literature on inculcating thinking like Sherlock Holmes—in order to get into the 'critical thinking' mindset:

1. **Listen to or observe the details:** This is all a part of the gathering observations (see previous section) with emphasis on paying attention to details and scanning all

the information available to you before the 'hypotheses' are formed.

2. **Be aware of your own biases:** You might have preferences for and biases towards certain things, or might value opinions of some people over others; this can impact the analysis. Here is where independent teams of insights can add a lot of value because they can be objective about the analysis without being emotionally attached to the business or product or project.
3. **Be objective or examine everything with healthy skepticism:** Watch your own thoughts, be aware of what is influencing them, and try to be a bit 'distant' from the problem.
4. **Be more engaged:** Lean in more to counteract the 'auto-pilot' like initial judgment.
5. **Keep learning:** Continuously educate yourself on the subject.

Critical Mindset: An Inside Look at Unilever's Approach

Let us go back to the financial year 2009-2010 when Unilever (then called Hindustan Lever Ltd.) had five shampoo brands in the market with the total value market share of about 45% by the end of 2009. One of its brands, 'Clear', had value market share of 11% in 2007, which declined to 6.1% by June 2010[4]. Ajay Verma (fictitious name), brand manager of Clear

[4] Source of market share data is NielsenIQ Retail Measurement Services (RMS)

shampoo, scratched his head trying to understand why the brand had been losing its value market share. Ajay decided to don his detective hat and investigate this dip in the share. Like Sherlock Holmes, he was determined to figure out a solution by thinking critically, observing acutely, creating and testing hypotheses to eliminate possibilities and zero down on the real cause. He called his Insights team partner Vidya Swaminathan (fictitious name of a CMI manager), and both of them decided to embark on this investigative journey together. Now, how would they identify the cause of the dip and its solution? Let's accompany them in their journey by donning our 'critical thinking' hats and thinking like Sherlock Holmes.

Problem definition: 'Clear' is losing market share. Therefore, they need to identify the cause so that actions can be taken to arrest the decline and increase the share. You can clearly see the yearly and quarterly decrease in value shares of the brand given below:

VALUE SHARES	2007	2008	2009	Q2 09	Q3 09	Q4 09	Q1 10	Q2 10
Clear Shampoo	11.0	9.4	7.3	7.2	7.1	6.6	6.6	6.1

(Source: NielsenIQ RMS)

First question or hypothesis: Is 'Clear' losing share because it is losing out on product sales, or, even with steady sales, the products are not selling as fast as others, resulting in the share loss? Because if it is losing sales, then the problem is far more grave than just relative competitiveness. The sales data showed the following trend:

The first hypothesis turned out to be true; the declining sales were indeed shrinking Clear's value market share. The obvious questions followed: Why were the sales declining? Moreover, are the sales dipping only for the Clear brand or is the entire shampoo category witnessing this decline?

Next hypothesis: The sales of the entire shampoo category is declining (negative growth) which is affecting the sales of 'Clear' as well.

Data was extracted from NielsenIQ RMS once again to look at the category volume and value growth:

GROWTH YA %	2008	2009	Q2 09	Q3 09	Q4 09	Q1 10	Q2 10	APR 10	MAY 10	JUN 10
Value	18.4	10.7	11.1	12.8	5.6	5.9	11.8	11.2	12.1	12.0
Volume	12.4	7.8	8.7	10.3	2.0	2.2	8.6	7.9	8.7	9.0

The value of the category is growing in double digits, backed by healthy volume growth as well. So, the hypothesis that the entire category is declining turned out to be false.

Next hypothesis: Shares of all Unilever brands are declining—indicating a systemic issue—which is also affecting Clear Shampoo. Market share data of all the brands from the same source answers that question.

VALUE SHARES	2007	2008	2009	Q2 09	Q3 09	Q4 09	Q1 10	Q2 10
Unilever	47.5	46.0	45.1	45.3	45.5	45.0	45.6	46.9
Sunsilk	11.3	11.3	11.0	11.1	11.2	10.7	10.5	10.7
Dove	0.9	3.2	5.5	5.3	6.0	6.1	6.9	7.4
Clear	11.0	9.4	7.3	7.2	7.1	6.6	6.6	6.1
Clinic Plus	22.0	20.2	19.7	19.9	19.4	19.9	20.0	21.1
Lux	1.9	1.8	1.7	1.7	1.7	1.6	1.6	1.6

This hypothesis, too, turned out to be false. While Unilever lost share in 2009 (45.1), it started gaining steadily by the end of 2009 (45.5). Sunsilk and Clinic Plus were also the ones with declining share, however, they had sprung back in the last quarter of 2009. Dove saw a steady rise, while Lux was stable throughout 2009. 'Clear' shampoo was clearly the problem child.

Ajay and Vidya then zeroed in on identifying the problem for 'Clear'. The focus of the analysis then turned fully to the brand, but before looking into the reasons causing the loss, it is important to understand the extent of the problem. Was the brand losing sales because not enough consumers were buying it or, was it because consumers were buying less and less quantity of it over a period of time? In other words, was it losing market penetration or share of requirement[5]? The results were quite telling....

PENETRATION	2008	2009	Q2 09	Q3 09	Q4 09	Q1 10	Q2 10
Sunsilk	19.9	19.7	9.7	9.9	9.1	9.2	9.6
Clinic Plus	69.6	69.7	45.4	45.7	45.2	46	47.1
Clear	13.5	11.5	5.1	4.1	4.1	4.1	3.8
Dove	3.4	6	2.4	2.5	2.6	2.9	3.1
Lux	13.5	12.6	7.2	7.1	7.5	6.8	6.7

[5] SOR—Share of Requirement is defined as percentage of the category volume consumed by a household that is contributed by the brand. For example, if a household consumes 500 ml of shampoo in a year and 100ml of that is from the brand Clear, then Clear has 20% SOR. This is measured by Kantar World Panel, which has few thousand households across the country; that is used to measure purchase of FMCG products in households.

SOR VALUE	2008	2009	Q2 09	Q3 09	Q4 09	Q1 10	Q2 10
Sunsilk	27.9	28.9	49.5	50.8	52	49.8	47.9
Clinic Plus	48	47.8	64.1	63.7	62.4	62.9	63.4
Clear	15.1	15	31.9	32.6	34.3	36.2	36
Dove	16.7	18.5	39.2	42.5	42.7	43.5	44
LUX	38.2	32.5	51.6	54.5	52.4	54	53.6

The brand was not losing SOR but was losing penetration. This meant that it was not able to gain new users, but at the same time, existing users were consuming it more. In other words, the brand wasn't appealing enough to its non-users to bring them into the fold but its existing users were happy with it.

This piece of information was crucial as the entire focus of diagnostics would now shift to study the non-users. Ajay and Vidya then carried out a diagnostic analysis using a tool called '6P' analysis. This analysis involved looking into the details of all the Ps of marketing—proposition, promotion, product, price, pack, and place—to narrow down the issue to one or more Ps that can be corrected.

Proposition

Clear was positioned as an anti-dandruff shampoo competing with Head & Shoulders (H&S) from Procter & Gamble. The hypothesis now was that the brand has NOT weakened on its proposition and is still as compelling. Here is what the data suggested on how well the brands were defined in consumers' minds on the key positioning attribute:

Share of endorsement (SOE)[6] on the attribute "effective against dandruff" for Clear and H&S.

SHARE OF ENDORSEMENT	Q1 09	Q1 10	Q2 10
Clear	21	20	16
H&S	14	26	22

Clear had stronger endorsement than H&S in early 2009, but H&S had secured more endorsements since then and had become a stronger brand. Obviously then the new users looking for anti-dandruff shampoo were more likely to choose H&S.

While, the overall 'equity' of the brand (measured through the same Kantar Millward Brown track) remained stable for Clear, it soared for H&S.

[6] SOE is measured via brand track—done by Kantar Millward Brown for Unilever. Brand tracks measure awareness and equity of brands in the category. For SOE, respondents are shown a set of brands and asked to associate a fixed set of pre-defined attributes with those brands. The share of those associations is SOE.

BRAND EQUITY INDEX[7]	Q1 09	Q1 10
Clear	19.1	19
H&S	13.8	26.9

Promotion

This P is about effectiveness of advertising—both in terms of quality (of ads) and quantity (spends). Hypothesis being brand is doing good quality advertising and is spending enough money on media, for the brand to grow.

Clear had launched a new ad with Indian film actors John Abraham and Bipasha Basu in the early months of 2009. John

[7] Brand Equity Index is a proprietary score of Unilever, calculated by looking at some equity attributes included in the Brand Health Track done by Kantar Millward Brown.

and Bipasha were two leading stars of the Indian film industry who were also seeing each other at that time. Therefore, pairing them in the same ad was a major coup in generating curiosity and a lot of 'talk' around the ad. The pre-testing of the ad was done using 'Preview' or 'Link Test' by Kantar Millward Brown (elaborated later in the book). A 'preview' looks at the engagement of consumers with the ad, the memorability, the persuasion ability, and the key message takeaway—all this was done by showing the ad to respondents in a 'controlled environment'. The preview results usually predict the on-air performance quite well and hence are used for understanding how the ad is working (or not) and is used extensively to decide if the ad is worth airing. The preview for Clear's ad had shown that it would *not* perform well in the northern states of India and was *risky* (not likely to perform well) in the southern states as well. The Clear ad was aired despite these preview results and that resulted in SOR declining compared to H&S.

Furthermore, the quantity of advertising—media spends—were in line with the recommendations by the media team. In other words, the brand did not under or overspend on media. This meant that the hypothesis of not spending enough on the advertising was rejected.

Place

Place is about where the brand sells, i.e., retail shops, both general and modern trade (and increasingly e-commerce). Hypothesis being that Clear was increasing the number of shops it was selling in, and it was available in the 'key' shops (the ones that sell a lot of shampoo). This is assessed by numerical distribution, which is the percentage of all the shops in India (that sell the category) the brand is available in. The larger the numeric distribution, the better is the actual reach of the brand. Weighted distribution is the measure of 'effective reach'; if a brand is available in the shops that sell a lot of the category, then it is present in the right shops. For instance, if Tim's Family Mart sells a lot of shampoo in a suburb and if the brand is not present in Tim's Mart, then it is missing out on the consumers who buy lot of shampoo from that store. This calculated nationally is reflected in the form of 'weighted distribution' (distribution weighted by category sales). Available usually from Retail Measurement Service (RMS, offered by NielsenIQ in several countries around the world).

The distribution data for Clear looked as follows:

	Q1 09	Q2 10
Numerical Distribution	78.9%	73%
Weighted Value	53%	43%
Average SKUs per store	2.7	2.5

The data clearly indicated that distribution for the brand was an issue as well. It was selling in fewer and critically less 'important' shops. Penetration change for a brand is often correlated strongly with the distribution change and this needed correction.

Price

Clear of Unilever and Head & Shoulders of P&G were both positioned as dandruff removal shampoos and were priced at premium as compared to the average shampoos in the market. A simple measure of price premium is Average Price Index (API) which is the brand price vs. the category average price. Reported by NielsenIQ in the Retail Measurement Services, this is an effective way of not only deciding how expensive the brand is against the market average but also helps in keeping track of all the price changes of competition brands and promotions offered alongside. The category average price is indexed at 100 and the average price of all the brands is indexed against that 100. For instance, a brand with API of 110 means it is 10% more expensive than the 'average' shampoo in the market, and API of 90 means it is 10% cheaper than the 'average' shampoo, and so on.

API for Clear was 154 while H&S was 161, so strategically, the brand was priced right because its 'eyeball' competitor H&S was priced around the similar range. Given the loss in endorsement on the key attribute of 'anti-dandruff efficacy', the price modelling suggested that the brand had become more price elastic. In other words, since it was not seen to be as effective on anti-dandruff, any increase in price (particularly compared to H&S) was likely to reduce the volume sales of the brand.

Therefore, it was concluded that the brand was priced right per se but should not be changed, certainly not on the higher side, when compared to H&S.

Product

Hypothesis here was that the product delivered on the anti-dandruff attribute and was better than the products offered by its competition. Product-testing results (blind test) showed that Clear did deliver on the anti-dandruff attribute and its score on that attribute was as good as competition (called 'parity', in research parlance), but not superior to competition.

This meant that if competition were to increase their salience and availability, parity product would impact the sales of the brand negatively; and this was exactly what was happening! Clear shampoo, therefore, needed product improvement for the brand performance to go up.

Companies like Unilever follow extensive product-testing protocols—deployed during the product development stage—that enable the teams to test the product in isolation. It further assesses if the product is capable of competing with other brands and delivering on key attributes and expectations the consumers have from the category. For instance, in this case, Clear was expected to be a good shampoo for anyone to use (usually referred to as "overall opinion"), but was also expected to deliver particularly well on treating dandruff. So, the testing is done to establish its performance as a shampoo but also on its abilities to reduce dandruff as an independent product, as well as in comparison with a large anti-dandruff competing shampoo brand (like Head & Shoulders). It is important for any organization to have such protocols in place to ensure that it is geared to deliver on its expectations.

CBP	BRAND	VARIANT NAME	FORMAT	EXTERNAL BENCH-MARK BRAND	EXTERNAL BENCH-MARK VARIANT	OVERALL OPINION	OVERALL OPINION FRAGRANCE	VARIANT KEY ATTRIBUTES	CATEGORY KEY ATTRIBUTES
Scalp (Male)	Clear	Active care	Sh	H&S	Silky & smooth	*2009			
Scalp (Female)	Clear	Active care	Sh	H&S	Silky & smooth	2009			

Pack

Hypothesis for the pack was that it stood out on the shelf from the other shampoos and the packaging was found to be attractive enough to draw attention of the consumers.

No shelf test was done in the past (since the product was largely available in general trade, where products are often not very visible on the shelf to the consumers). But the pack had scored well on its attractive packaging during a pack test and the scores were steady over a period of time. (No data available to show here.) Packaging, therefore, was concluded to be not an issue.

Articulating the Problems and Recommendations Pithily

In the above example, Ajay and Vidya were able to use the critical analysis to gather that the brand was losing its differentiation on the anti-dandruff proposition in both absolute and relative terms. The advertising developed for it wasn't delivering on the intended message and needed to be changed. The product was as good as the competition (and was priced equally) but wasn't delivering the results better than the competition. Additionally, it wasn't as widely available as before. This had resulted in a decline in equity and consumer pull, while the competition brand H&S continued to march ahead.

These 6Ps are usually summarized in the form of traffic signal code by the brand and CMI team (Ajay and Vidya, in this case), which is a good example of expressing the insights pithily. Also, it gives clear guidance to teams on the improvements needed for the brand sales to turn around.

Consider the following traffic signal colour codes for the 6Ps in the table below:

Proposition: RED
Promotion: AMBER
Place: RED
Price: GREEN
Product: AMBER
Pack: GREEN

CLEAR SHAMPOO	Q2 2010
Proposition	
Promotion	
Place	
Price	
Product	
Pack	

But the job doesn't end here. It is equally critical to articulate well on the actions to be taken from the outcome of the analyses: What needs to be done when a 'P' is green to sustain it, what can be done to reverse a 'P' that's in red to green. These recommendations should be clearly articulated and agreed with the team. The insights team then follows up on the actions to be taken and reviews them regularly to track the consequences of the actions.

Implications for Marketing and Insights Professionals

This Sherlock Holmes' style of critical thinking in the form of '6P analysis' was developed about two decades ago, and is now the standard practice across the Unilever world. It's carried out every quarter with the data made available with the help of dashboards so that marketers can understand the underlying issues by themselves without any other external help. This is a good example of data democratization (which is not just about having access to data but also ensuring everyone looks at the same set of data in the same way), and also of institutionalizing the ability to connect the dots and get to the bottom of the problem.

All things said and done, it takes a lot to make an entire organization think critically. It takes passion, time, and commitment to setup this kind of a process. It involves designing the right process, implementing it, getting the buy-in from the senior stakeholders to use this for all decision-making, persistently demonstrating the impact of the system to the teams, and so on. The needs of every organization are different so they would need to setup a different system accordingly. Different sections of this book focus on the way to bring in right culture, and some of the systems and processes an organization would need to bring in. But it all starts from the commitment to bring in consumer centricity and things start flowing from there.

The CMOs should look at how they can instill this insightful thinking in their organizations. There is a simple checklist that can be used for it:

Trait	***What it means for organizations***	***Actions to kick start the trait***
Curious	Inculcate consumer curiosity.	• For every business decision, ask what consumers would want the decision to be. • Lead by example. Leaders should demonstrate their consumer curiosity and understanding.
Observant	Right tools to understand people and easy access to information.	• Setup a discipline of meeting certain number of consumers every month—through formal research or consumer connects. • Make it mandatory for everyone in the organization. • Create a system for people to talk to consumers easily and make information democratic.

Connecting the dots	Instill critical-thinking mindset	• Encourage people to think of consumer hypotheses around a problem and obtain data to test those hypotheses. • Lead by example—no assumptions to be made but gather data to test the hypotheses. • Discuss and debate the data to arrive at conclusions.
Express pithily	Clear articulation of insights	• Articulate the insight clearly. • Codify it in the system (through easily accessible documents and reports) so that the organization learns and doesn't have to keep discovering the same things time and again.

Actions	Articulate the implications and actions coming out of them	• No insights should be without an action. Work out actions to be taken. • Create a tracker of actions to be taken and follow up regularly to assess the impact.

CHAPTER 4

Evolution of an Organization Towards Consumer Centricity

Making the organization consumer-centric goes far beyond making people in the organization insightful, though making them insightful is the essential foundation. Making people insightful is about embedding the culture of critical thinking, but making the organization consumer-centric is about having the systems and infrastructure that enable the entire organization to put the consumer first in all its decision-making.

Consumer centricity is different from having a market research function within the organization. Often that function is run with old market research techniques with a mindset where market researchers 'take orders' to get research done rather than act as strategic partners generating insights in collaboration

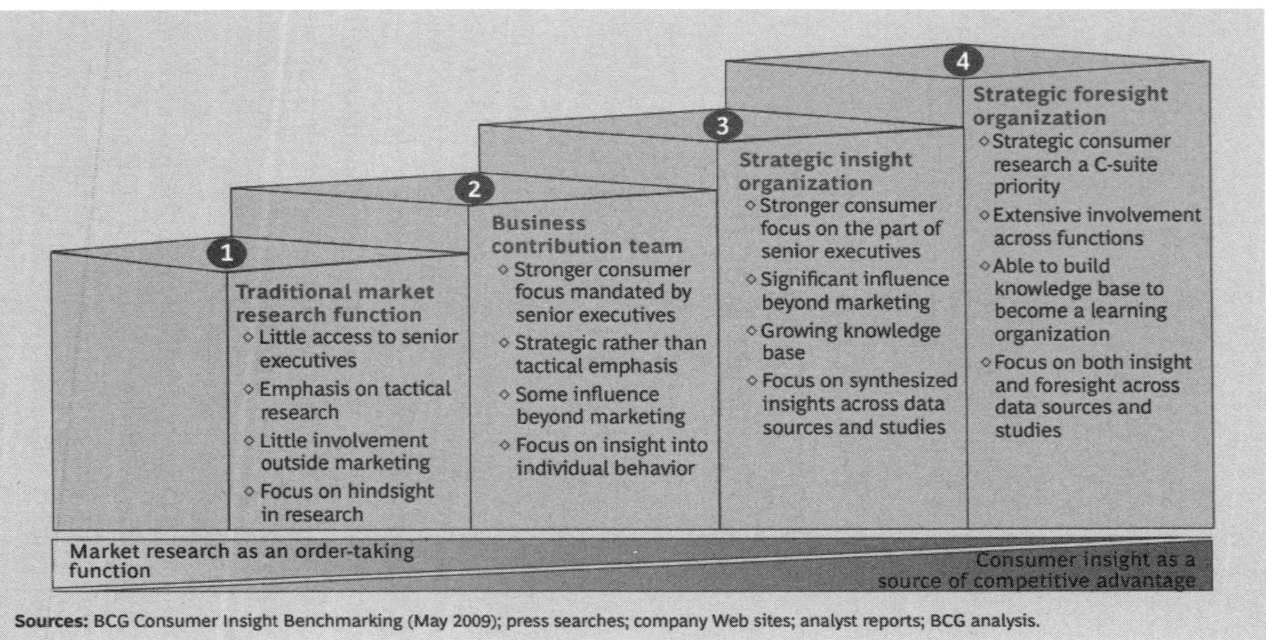

Sources: BCG Consumer Insight Benchmarking (May 2009); press searches; company Web sites; analyst reports; BCG analysis.

with research agencies and partners. As per research done by Boston Consulting Group (BCG) on this subject,[8] there are CEOs that express frustration about the fact that they spend a lot of money to get research done, yet they don't get any 'insights'. BCG, in the same paper, also identifies a framework of four stages of consumer insights on a continuum.

We will use that framework to explore how Unilever moved along the journey towards being more consumer-centric and what other organizations can gain from that experience.

Stage 1: Traditional Market Research Function

In companies at this stage of consumer centricity, consumer insights team has limited access to the senior executives who make crucial decisions. Usually, only marketing staff members tend to engage with the consumer insights team, while other functions such as product development or sales do not. As a result, the market research teams tend to focus on tactical work such as organizing focus group discussions or conducting advertising pre-test. The insights team, therefore, primarily acts more as an 'order-taking' function, interacting in a project-driven fashion to produce data and respond to data requests. They only take leadership in identifying the appropriate methodology and the research agencies to conduct the research.

---

[8] Paper from BCG called *The Consumer's Voice—Can Your Company Hear It?* published in November 2009. This chapter is based on the ideas presented in the paper but expands on them using Unilever's experience.

Till a couple of decades ago, Unilever used to have a department called the 'Market Research Department' which acted as a bridge between marketing and the research agencies. The only difference was that the department existed for several decades and pioneered some of the best practices in the industry. For instance, in India, the oldest research report that exists in the system is a brand equity report on the brand 'Dalda'—one of the first brands launched by Hindustan Lever in India in the 1930s. However, it was sold off to Bunge Limited in 2003. This report was released by the department to marketing teams on August 23, 1947. This is of particular significance because India got independence from the British rule on August 15, 1947, which means that while the country was gaining its independence, some people in the market research department were busy writing this report.

There are other interesting anecdotes from Unilever's history of market research department, too:

1. Research Bureau Limited (RBL): It was a research agency founded in the United Kingdom in 1962 by merging Unilever's market research department with the then Unilever's in-house advertising department, Lintas— which later went on to become an independent advertising agency. The purpose of RBL was to offer Unilever's long-standing marketing research expertise as a service to other companies. Eileen Cole, who had been a group leader with the Unilever's Market Research Department since 1948, became RBL's Managing Director and grew its business. RBL later became Research International (RI) and expanded its operations in multiple global markets and was eventually acquired by Kantar.

VANASPATI OPINION TEST

23rd August 1947.

OBJECT

Production of Vanaspati was suspended for a few months as a result of Government action. The Government of India also published a statement implying that consumption of Vanaspati may cause blindness. The Vanaspati manufacturers denied the truth of the statement, both arguments being featured in the Press.

The object of this test is to discover the public's attitude towards Vanaspati now the controversy is over, and the production of Vanaspati has been resumed.

METHOD & EXTENT

A test of this nature should be carried out on a national scale and in each strata of the population. It was impossible, however, to contemplate such a wide enquiry as the answer to the problem was required within a relatively short time and at a time when the Market Research Department was in the process of formation. The only possible way of dealing with the problem was to include it in the programme for training of investigators and such a procedure must inevitably reflect on the quality of the test. The method and extent described below, are, therefore, in the nature of compromise objectives.

Vanaspati is bought by men and women, depending on the buying habits of the household and the arguments about Vanaspati may have been read by either men or women; both groups have therefore been interviewed. Furthermore, the discussion is likely to have influenced people to a different extent depending on their level of literacy and on their intellectual attainments. It is broadly true that these differences are fairly clearly represented by the differences in the social classes and by the occupations followed. The test was, therefore, carried out among 315 women of the social classes representing the main market for Vanaspati, i.e. Upper Middle, Lower Middle and Working Classes, and also amongst 300 men, contacted in offices and factories, divided on an occupational basis, i.e. office, workers and coolies.

Because of convenience in training, the test was restricted to Bombay, a fact which limits further the value of the findings:

QUESTIONNAIRE

The questionnaire will be found at the beginning of the Statistical Appendix.

DATE

The fieldwork was carried out between 25th July and 7th August 1947.

--------o0o--------

2. Unilever in India (Hindustan Unilever Ltd.): Their market research department established and managed its own household panel consisting of thousands of households across the country. This allowed them to closely monitor purchase behaviour and gain a significant competitive edge for several years. It was eventually acquired by Indian Market Research Bureau (run by Kantar—a global expert in the panel management) in the early 2000s when Unilever's market research department evolved into a strategic business contributor rather than just carrying out research tasks (as shown in the second stage in the BCG model).

There are several organizations around the globe that are at this stage of the evolution of the insights function. Though it's not right to generalize, companies that are product- and R&D-driven tend to be at this stage because marketing is not the core driver of their businesses. However, the growing realization that their customers are at the core of the business is bringing in more customer understanding in these organizations. I may be generalizing once again, however, in my experience, banks around the world probably have the poorest customer centricity, which is quite ironic because unlike a lot of other businesses, banks know almost everything about their customers. But we as customers still find navigating our transactions with the banks quite an ordeal.

Companies like 3M, on the other hand, that are traditionally driven by innovation (which is primarily the responsibility of their R&D teams) have invested significantly in expanding their customer centricity. According to Chitkala Nishandar, who has been leading the insights function for APAC region at 3M, the teams at 3M now do a lot more exploratory work upfront when conceptualizing an idea. A lot of research is carried out at this stage to truly understand the problems customers face, solutions they deploy to address those problems, and a potential role a new product can play in resolving those issues. This tends to be quite beneficial (and sometimes eye opening) for the development teams, as they are no longer working on an 'interesting idea' that someone had but are focused on solving real customer problems.

Stage 2: Business Contribution Team

At this stage, the organization focuses more on its consumers (or customers) and the insights team gains better access to senior leaders. The studies become more strategic in nature and the output is not just data but the recommendations for the business to act upon. However, the focus still remains on individual research studies, often developed and analyzed in isolation. The research team then develops standardized protocols for different types of studies. For instance, concept and product tests are done in a specific manner or identifying key drivers of brand performance is done consistently, making comparisons across geographies and brands possible. The identification and alignment with different research agencies for different protocols tends to happen a lot more at this stage. However, each agency and protocol still operate quite on their own, limiting their impact and potential. The nature of interaction between the research team and decision makers can still be quite transactional, focused on specific studies.

Unilever teams went through this transition a couple of decades ago. Historically, Unilever has operated in every market almost as an independent entity making its own decisions on brands and businesses. A lot has changed on that front since then, but in that earlier environment, the 'Market Research Department' began consolidating the way studies were conducted and began developing protocols that could be followed everywhere across markets and brands. It was the first semblance of a research team to work and think independently, and the time was right for it to be re-christened as the Consumer and Market Insights (CMI) team.

Robust protocols were created for conducting all the research for developing innovations as well as for tracking the business performance on the ground. Those protocols continue to be in practice today (though have been evolving over a period of time) and form the very foundation of the insights team at Unilever. The latter part of the book details some of those protocols and processes. Meanwhile, the marketing function was evolving as well and came up with a funnel approach that filtered projects from ideas to new launches through a rigorous process that involved market research at different stages of the filtering process. This led to the embedding of the CMI teams into the very fabric of marketing like never before.

Arguably, this is what makes an organization 'process-driven' (and, therefore, less agile) where teams feel that they have to jump through several hoops before anything hits the market. That's a fair argument, and it does make an organization less agile, particularly when compared to the newer world of start-ups. However, these very systems and processes ensure that the products developed are meaningful and useful to their consumers while they are being developed, rather than discovering the real value these products bring in only after they hit the marketplace (like in the case of several start-ups). The challenge is to maintain a healthy balance between the two: have robust processes in place to check consumer responses but also ensure that those processes become increasingly agile with

Typical innovation funnel: projects go through different 'gates' and different research is done to support the decision at each gate

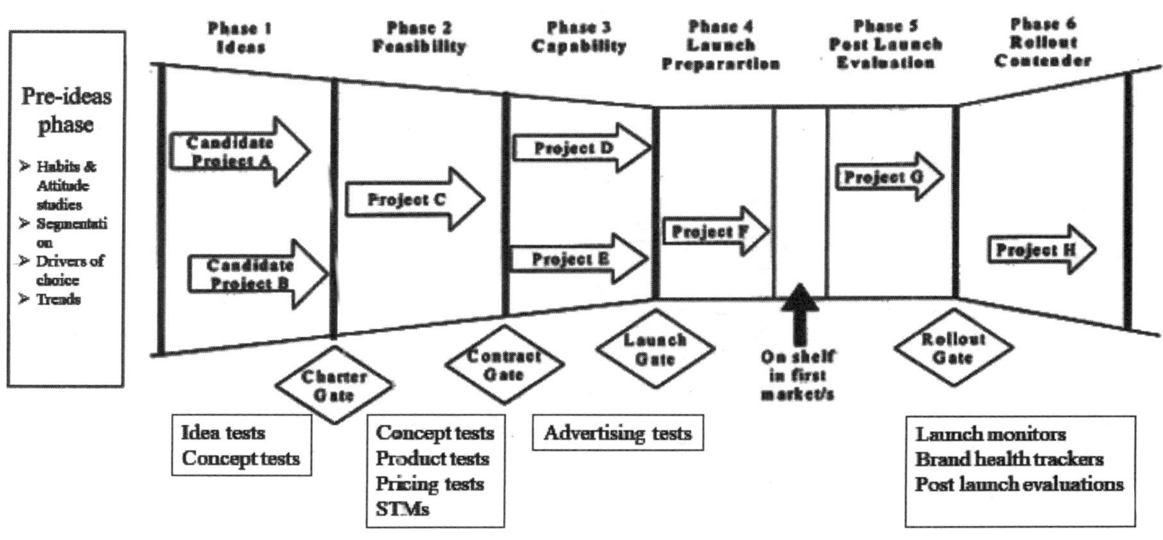

the passing time. And that is exactly one of the key focus areas of CMI teams in organizations like Unilever.

Stage 3: Strategic Insights Organization

At this stage, senior executives believe that all major decisions should be guided by consumer insights. These organizations begin to ensure that the engagement in consumer insights starts to cross functional lines and is, therefore, not just restricted to marketing department but is further expanded and reflected in the decision-making processes of other functions such as sales, research and development, supply chain, technology, etc. The data and information available across the organization get synthesized together rather than being used in silos. The data then is not restricted to market research data alone but multiple sources of data are leveraged from within and outside the organization.

The insights' function tends to enjoy greater autonomy, budget authority, and influence over its research agenda. Plus, organizations have very different approach to professional development of the insight function. Individuals from diverse career backgrounds are especially hired, trained, and rotated into a high-performance consumer insights team. Their managers value critical thinking and business judgment as much (if not more) than they value their research skills. They are integrated into day-to-day fabric of the line management meetings rather than limited to episodic and study-focused interactions. The leadership teams, including the CEO, makes research a strategic priority and that is reflected in the budgets, engagement levels, and the democratization of the data across the organization. The insights team is no longer seen to be just 'research experts' or only being 'responsible for the consumer voice', but its role expands to translating detailed knowledge about the consumers into business implications. This, therefore, allows the organization as a whole to come closer to the hearts and minds of their target consumers.

Unilever evolved to this stage in mid 2000s when Consumer and Market Insights (CMI) became an independent global function. Though still part of the 'marketing department', CMI teams stopped reporting to the marketing or business heads, but began reporting vertically to their global function (CMI) heads while 'partnering' the businesses. This was a crucial step in giving CMI an independent, objective, and unified global voice in the system. While the business head's feedback remained an important input in the performance evaluation of the CMI team and the function, CMI got the freedom to take decisions on how it wanted the insights system to develop for the growth of the business. Correspondingly, it also got the liberty to take a call on the career progression and movement of the insights talent within the organization and partnerships with the research providers outside the organization. This independence in voice was a key step in the evolution of the CMI and reflected not just the organization's emphasis on consumer centricity but also on the leadership capabilities of the insight talent.

At this stage, the structure starts to look something like this (see chart below). If the organization has a network of 'categories' and 'markets' (e.g., home care, foods, etc., are categories led globally by business heads across markets, while countries like

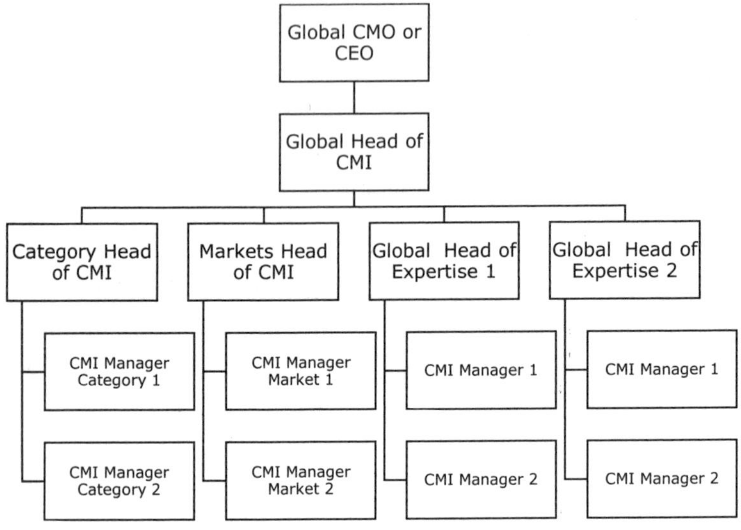

the U.S., India, European countries, etc., are markets which are led by business heads across categories), then there are CMI leads appointed for each category and market with their teams. They work closely with their respective businesses but report to one functional lead who drives the best practices, relationship with research and analytics agencies, etc. The insight team is well 'balanced' - looking 'externally' into the businesses and partnering with them and looking 'internally' within the insights team to borrow best practices and expertise. Often Centres of Expertise (COEs) get created at this stage with experts focusing only on developing an expertise internally (like shopper insights or social listening) which is used by the CMI teams of categories and businesses to solve the business questions.

Having clear established systems and processes to carry out research is an important precursor to this stage without which it would be extremely difficult for the insights function to become independent. Once the CMI teams discontinue reporting into businesses because of them being independent, it is important they move into a 'partnership' role with these businesses instead. This means that they often get a seat at the decision-making table; and, now, they must not only understand the business challenges and strategies to meet those challenges, but also bring in an objective, independent voice of the consumer to the table that enables businesses to take decisions that are right for the consumers.

Is it important for CMI to not report to the business teams they are partnering with but be an independent function? Ultimately, CMI is a part of the business, so, is this just a minor technicality that CMI teams working in business teams don't report to those business heads but vertically into a function? I think it's a significant change because this way insights teams can have the autonomy on the methods and processes, make the best usage of the insights budget, and so on. However, they still will be accountable to deliver the insights that the business needs. Finance managers, in a similar fashion, work with the businesses but tend to report vertically into the finance function to maintain their objectivity and expertise.

In my experience, this role of insight manager is the hardest one and quite challenging. Imagine sitting in meetings with the business heads and functional leads of supply chain, finance, etc., who are experts and experienced in running the business, and trying to argue about what consumers want. And if the insight manager's argument is going against what the business wants, then the onus invariably lies on that poor insight manager to muster the courage and produce the evidence to back their argument. Having the right culture where business teams appreciate this challenge that the insights teams face is important, however, empowering the insights team to raise the consumer voice, giving them right tools and methods to know what consumers want are the key ingredients as well for this to work. Having been in such 'difficult' situations hundreds of times during my career at Unilever, I often used to think that it's unfair for only insights managers to have to walk the tight rope trying to balance between what the business and consumers want. Because it does put tremendous pressure on insights managers. But in the end, the company's products and services turning far more consumer-centric and thereby resulting in the success of the company is what makes all this worth it.

Stage 4: Strategic Foresight Organization

Still an aspirational stage for most organizations, this stage requires going a lot further than the previous stages. The Stage 3 approach is applied not just within each business unit but across the corporate portfolio. The consumer insights team has a corporate-wide mandate that extends across business units and influences cross-company decisions such as acquisitions, prioritization of brands and markets, and resource allocation. A synthesis of insights is used not just for near-term decisions but also for foresight and prediction, to anticipate new trends and opportunities well ahead of its competitors.

At this stage, an insights manager is virtually indistinguishable from a marketing or a business manager because both understand insights and the business functions *almost* equally well and both are accountable for the business growth. The head of insights function within different units tend to be a part of the leadership or executive teams of that unit, driving the agenda using insights. There is a clear ownership of the end-to-end research agenda including budgets and other resources. And the output of the insights team is not about the number of studies conducted, but the ideas and actionable recommendations provided that promote business growth.

That proverbial 'seat at the table' for the insights professionals in the Unilever world is quite hard-earned. The CMI teams of Unilever are hired not only for their conceptual skills in research but also for their business, communication, and leadership skills. It is not unusual for the insights person to get into general management position within the business for this very reason. The insights team often takes up the challenge of providing avenues for additional growth purely based on consumer insights—by analyzing consumer trends (which, in itself, is an elaborate activity carried out by a team of internal experts), identifying opportunities for growth of existing brands via mergers and acquisitions.

A look at Unilever's strategy clearly reflects the role played by consumer insights and doesn't need any further elaboration (sourced from Unilever websites and other press releases):

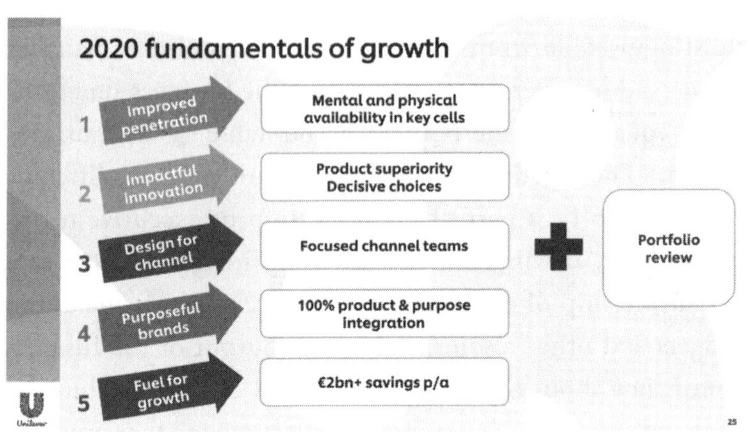
2020 fundamentals of growth
1 Improved penetration
Mental and physical availability in key cells
2 Impactful innovation
Product superiority Decisive choices
3 Design for channel
Focused channel teams
4 Purposeful brands
100% product & purpose integration
5 Fuel for growth
€2bn+ savings p/a
Portfolio review
25

What we depend on...
Relationships
Purposeful people
Trusted suppliers
Committed partners
Resources
Input materials
For example: agricultural raw materials, packaging materials and chemicals
Financial resources
For example: capital from our financial stakeholders
Intangible assets
For example: our culture, brands and intellectual property
Tangible assets
For example: factories, offices, R&D labs and logistics warehouses
What we do...
1. Consumer insights
2. Innovation
3. Sourcing
4. Manufacturing
5. Logistics
6. Marketing
7. Sales
8. Consumer use
Dove
The value we create for...
Consumers
Our people
Society
Planet
Customers
Shareholders

Implications for Marketing and Insights Professionals

The BCG model quite well explains the evolution that insights teams at Unilever have gone through. Different organizations are at different stages of this model and each stage presents its own challenges that need to be countered in order to move ahead. The key enablers are:

- Commitment from senior management for bringing in consumer centricity.
- Strong leadership of the insights function that can have the vision of what's right for the organization.
- Expertise to create right systems and processes.
- Training of insights managers on developing critical thinking skills.
- Empowerment of insights teams to maintain a tight balance between business needs and customer needs.

CHAPTER 5

Future of Insights Function within Organizations

Once the insights' function and capabilities are embedded into the very fabric of business thinking and decision-making, how does it evolve further? One of the recent developments that offers some clues is: the increasing role of technology in the space of marketing and consumer understanding. Traditional question and answer-based research is giving way to behavioural monitoring, while the advancements in data engineering, data collation, and integration have greatly expanded analytics capabilities. These developments have allowed insights organizations to holistically integrate with the 'MarTech' (market technology) stack and potentially broaden their role beyond marketing.

Analytics, as a function, has been a part of businesses for over a century, but it was not integrated into market research until recently. As far back as early 1900s, Henry Ford—impressed by Fredrick Taylor's scientific management system—is said to have hired him to measure the performance of the assembly line of his famous Ford Model T. In the 1950s, IBM introduced hard disks that allowed users to store vast amounts of data collected for the analysis of the business performance. Since then, analytics has evolved significantly and has become the backbone of decision-making process in organizations.

According to the Gartner Ascendancy Model, developed by Gartner in 2012, the maturity of usage of analytics has four stages, a fifth one has been recently added by some experts in this space. An organization could be mature in all the analytics they undertake, or, could be at different stages for analytics of different areas, depending on their needs.

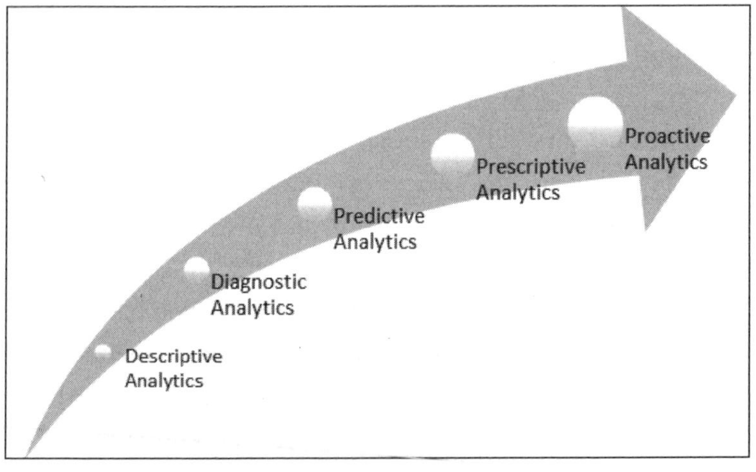

Gartner Ascendancy Model

1. **Descriptive analytics:** It simply answers: "What happened?". This stage is mainly about data collection and simple (sometimes, manual) analysis of the data to describe an activity or a phenomenon. For example, the web traffic a particular website receives, number of trucks used to deliver shipment from factory to warehouse, etc. At this stage, dashboards are increasingly used to visualize the data.
2. **Diagnostic analytics:** This stage helps us find answers to: "Why did it happen?". For instance, the reasons for the traffic on the website being of certain levels and the causes for it to increase or decrease over time. This allows the teams to take clear actions for the business.
3. **Predictive analytics:** This stage goes beyond explaining the phenomenon, and tries to answer: "What will happen?". To do this, it uses historical data to predict future events. For instance, at this stage, a marketer might ask: what would happen if you were to increase advertising spends on the brand? How much would the brand volumes grow if the brand were to reduce the price by 10%? This thinking enables the businesses not only to gain insight on the business performance but also to estimate future potential by using the driving levers of the performance. This stage is a lot more sophisticated; use of machine learning, for instance, goes up significantly at this stage. And hence, it requires not only advanced statistical techniques but also complex algorithms and systems to manage large volumes of

data. Hence, an organization might head to this stage only in certain spaces while restricting other analytics to diagnostic stage.

4. **Prescriptive analytics:** This is the stage where data analytics drive business actions. Machine learning, artificial intelligence, and other analytical tools working at their optimum level are capable of recommending a clear set of actions by analyzing the past historical patterns and objectives set for the future. For example, market mix modelling in the earlier 'Predictive' stage can inform about the elasticity that the brand has with advertising, pricing, distribution, etc., and allows the brand to simulate the results with changes in these variables. At the prescriptive stage, the model takes in the sales objectives of the next month and spells out the levels at which the brand needs to operate for advertising, distribution, and pricing. A month later, it would take in the actual sales, analyze them against the predicted, and auto-correct the model. This is a continuous loop. This way these tools help the CMI teams to obtain and strengthen the recommendations.

5. **Proactive analytics:** Some marketing experts in this space suggest another level in addition to the above four levels suggested by Gartner, which is Proactive analytics. Here, the machines work on their own with minimal manual intervention to achieve maximum returns for a pre-determined purpose. Some real examples of proactive analysis include programmatic

buying in the world of digital media, stock trading in the stock market, etc. We are likely to see a lot more of these in the future, such as driverless cars, robots programmed to do household chores, and so on. These are advanced cases of proactive analytics where machines not only understand "What happened?" and "Why it happened?" but also proactively work towards the targets and use that learning to carry out the tasks to meet those targets.

In several organizations, analytics and market research have traditionally operated as two separate functions. This may be because analytics is not just restricted to marketing alone, or, because the systems and the capabilities required differ significantly (or, it could be both!). Analytics teams consists of people skilled in data science and data engineering, while research team comprises people skilled in research methodologies. However, both provide insights about consumers that businesses use for growth. As a result, these two functions are bound to come together once they reach a certain maturity, and organizations like Unilever have witnessed that in the last few years.

I believe this trend of integrating the insights and analytics will only accelerate in the future, leading to the creation of what I call the 'Augmented Insights Engine' (A.I.E). The A.I.E would have three pillars integrated seamlessly with each other, which today work in silos within the organizations:

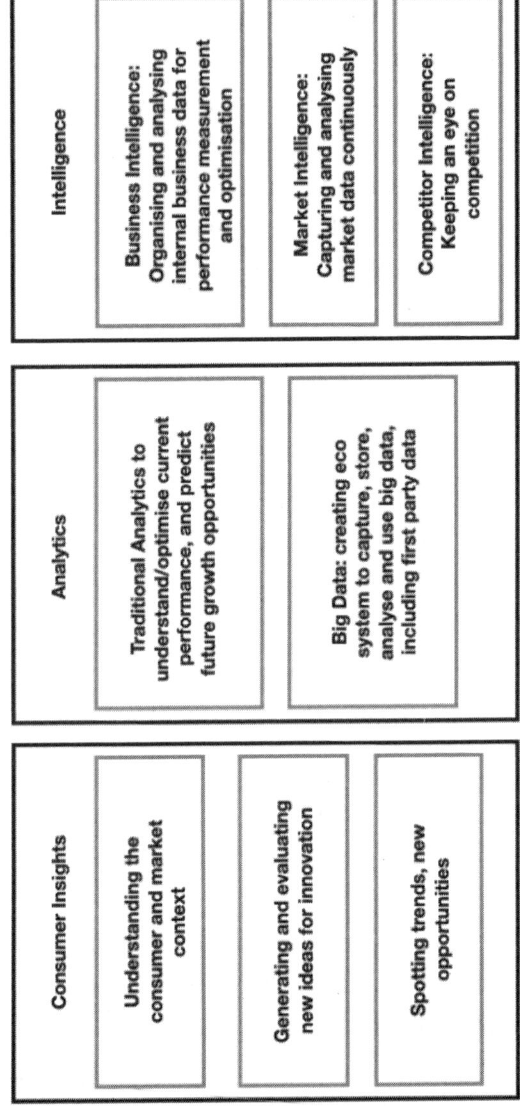
Augmented Insights Engine
Consumer Insights
Understanding the consumer and market context
Generating and evaluating new ideas for innovation
Spotting trends, new opportunities
Analytics
Traditional Analytics to understand/optimise current performance, and predict future growth opportunities
Big Data: creating eco system to capture, store, analyse and use big data, including first party data
Intelligence
Business Intelligence: Organising and analysing internal business data for performance measurement and optimisation
Market Intelligence: Capturing and analysing market data continuously
Competitor Intelligence: Keeping an eye on competition

1. **Consumer Insights:** This is the pillar of market research that brings the outside in and focuses on understanding lives, preferences, and consumption patterns of consumers, as well as identifying the trends. It also plays a significant role in developing and generating new ideas for future innovations through the innovation development process, which is becoming increasingly agile and tech-driven over time. Spotting and building on trends is another key part of consumer insights which enables the organization to identify new growth opportunities and stay relevant with the brands and services.
2. **Analytics:** This pillar would include both predictive and prescriptive analytics that use internal business numbers, market data, consumer data (including big data) to understand the ways of optimizing and growing the business. Some examples include: market mix modelling, modelling to identify levers of category upgradation, measuring and optimizing the performance of digital creatives in different cohorts, and so on. It would get integrated with the organization's capability of collecting and managing big data, including first-party data of its consumers or customers, to create a cutting-edge analytics capability supported with data science and technology.

Technology already enables capturing of consumer behaviour on the digital ecosystems created by the businesses, including its digital ads, apps, websites, etc. This data is captured not only to monitor behaviour, but also to segment people into different 'audiences' and target them for different products and campaigns. The performance of those is also captured and continuously analyzed for further optimization. The ecosystem needed for this kind of big data analytics not only requires understanding of data architecture and engineering but also good consumer insight to create meaningful audiences for the business. The integration of traditional analytics with big data and 'Martech' would make this pillar a powerhouse for generating growth for the business.

3. **Intelligence:** This pillar is about reporting and giving access to information in a meaningful and bite-size manner, which makes people more observant—a key requirement for being insightful. There is a huge volume of business and market information flowing in continuously within a system and different parts are needed for different decisions to be made. Typically, three types of intelligence systems exist within an organization—business, market, and competition intelligence. Creating and managing an ecosystem that not only presents this data meaningfully but also combines them intelligently can make things easier for the decision-makers. Technology again comes to the rescue to manage and organize this data efficiently.

Thus, A.I.E. can potentially become a strategic advisor to the CEO and the leadership team, and can also partner with all the functions of the business.

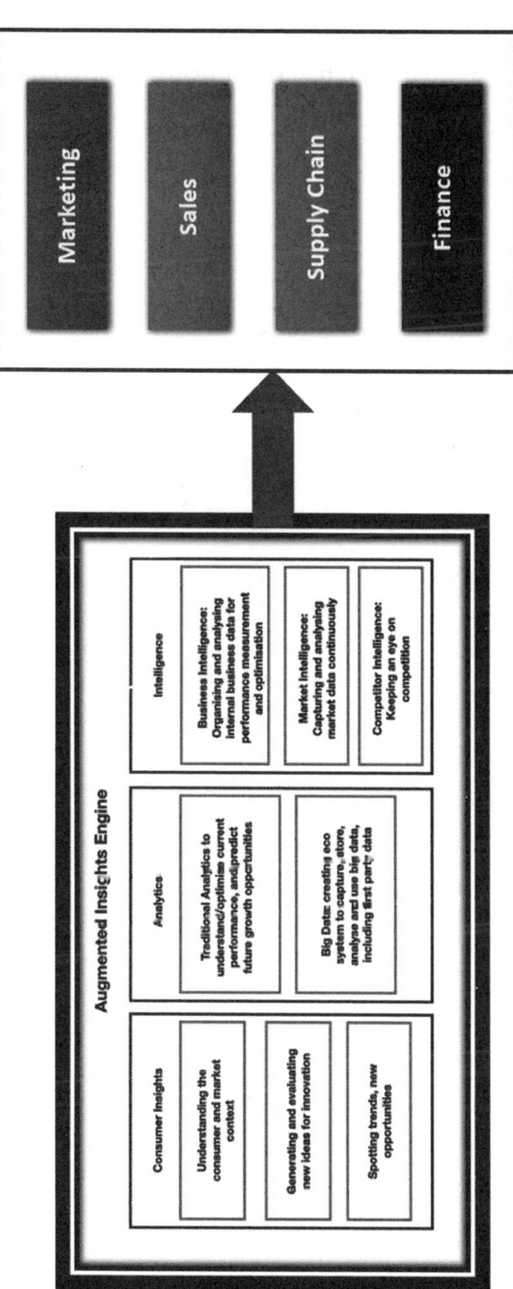
Marketing
Sales
Supply Chain
Finance
Augmented Insights Engine
Consumer Insights
Understanding the consumer and market context
Generating and evaluating new ideas for innovation
Spotting trends, new opportunities
Analytics
Traditional Analytics to understand/optimise current performance, and predict future growth opportunities
Big Data: creating eco system to capture, store, analyse and use big data, including first party data
Intelligence
Business Intelligence: Organising and analysing internal business data for performance measurement and optimisation
Market Intelligence: Capturing and analysing market data continuously
Competitor Intelligence: Keeping an eye on competition

This evolution articulated above is still about "what" the insights teams can do for the business. Arguably, a lot of progress would happen on "how" things are done.

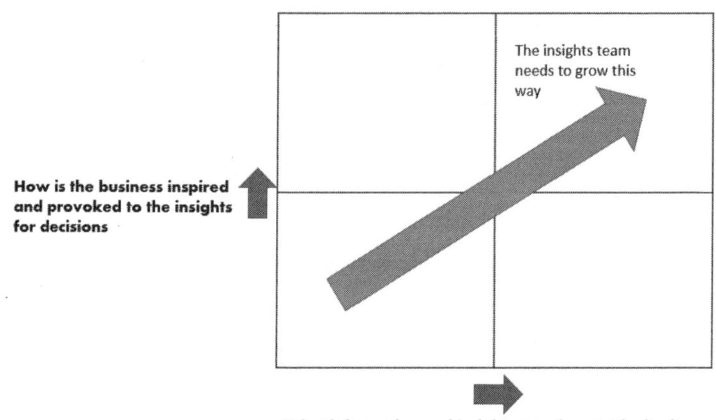

Traditionally, most people in the research and insights industry have been good at 'logic' because insights team have, for a long time, focused primarily on the numbers and data. But it's the infusion of 'magic' with the 'logic' that creates the real impact. According to Nitesh Priyadarshi, former CMI Head of Unilever South Asia, the "how" is about insights teams showing empathy towards their customers (marketers or decision makers), and this comes from:

- Understanding the ambition of the business and business managers, and the language or the corporate jargon they use to express that ambition.

- The ability to 'frame' the solution in the same language (jargon) so that they are able to understand the issue and promptly take action. Because, ultimately, driving an action should be the main focus of insights.

Unilever CMI leaders focus on training their managers on "how" the insights teams function as much as on "what" they do, if not more. The "what" is about the work they do and the insights they bring to the table which comes from their functional skills, but "how" is about the softer skills, including the emotional quotient (EQ), which enables the insight managers to truly understand the business partners and find ways to frame and land the insights in the business in an effective manner (in other words, action is taken on the insights). Some of the dimensions of these "how" skills in Unilever include:

1. **Growth mindset:** This is a competitive way of thinking (mindset) that focusses on finding different ways of expanding the business. Individuals with a high growth mindset proactively seek out growth opportunities and ensure that every insight brief and solution is geared towards achieving success in the marketplace.
2. **Consumer or customer-focused:** It's about external orientation. It's crucial to have a real passion to make a difference in the lives of the consumers and be their objective voice in all decision making.
3. **Bias for action:** Researchers are often criticized of being too nerdy and data-oriented or even occasionally indulging in exaltation of having found a great insight. Bias for action refers to the ability to identify the

actionable steps that businesses can take based on an insight and bring those steps to life in debriefs and presentations.

4. **Accountability and responsibility:** This is about being responsible for knowing the best practices and skills needed to answer the question; laying out clearly what can be expected from the research or analysis, but equally holding the business teams accountable for the action to be taken from the insights. This is, perhaps, the most daunting aspect of being an insights manager, and hence, mentoring and guiding them on this is crucial for them to be able to do real justice to their jobs.

5. **Building talent and teams:** Insights team not only works extensively with the teams of internal insights or analytics or data scientists but also with the external agencies and providers. The ability to inspire them with the right briefs, right actions, and challenging them to deliver their best by investing in their capabilities and bringing out the best in them are a part of this competency. It's not unusual to see someone from the agency team moving to the client's insight team and starting to act difficult with the agencies because they think they have the power now, having moved to the other side of the table. Therefore, getting them to be collaborative with the external teams, instead of being 'bossy', needs to be an integral part of the grooming of the new managers.

Coming back to the concept of A.I.E, Nitesh has a slightly different take on the AIE approach; he calls it the 'Enterprise Approach'. This approach is not only a combination of "what" the insights team does and "how" they do it but is also about the notion that the insights team can be open to collaborations in order to solve the problems of *any* function within the entire organization through their strategic approach.

The genesis of this 'Enterprise Approach' stems from recently arising notion in the organizations that it is not up to just one function to take the lead to generate innovative ideas for businesses to work on (used to be sales in some companies, marketing in some, and R&D in some). Ideas can come from anywhere and may not necessarily be about solving a consumer problem. For instance, an idea that solves a supply chain problem can become a new service idea for consumers. With the rise of online shopping, what used to be called the 'last mile' in the business (when consumers put the products in their basket), is now the 'first mile' for many categories. This is because consumers today spend a lot more time browsing about products online than they typically spend in physical shops. And this way consumers would end up buying more or completely different products than they would have offline. Hence, the insights teams need to break out of their 'silos' of being purely consumer problem-driven and collaborate with other functions to innovate and seek new business solutions for the entire 'enterprise'.

Preeti Reddy, CEO of Kantar's, South Asia division, affirms that the role of market research is to give 'insights that spark the corporate imagination'.

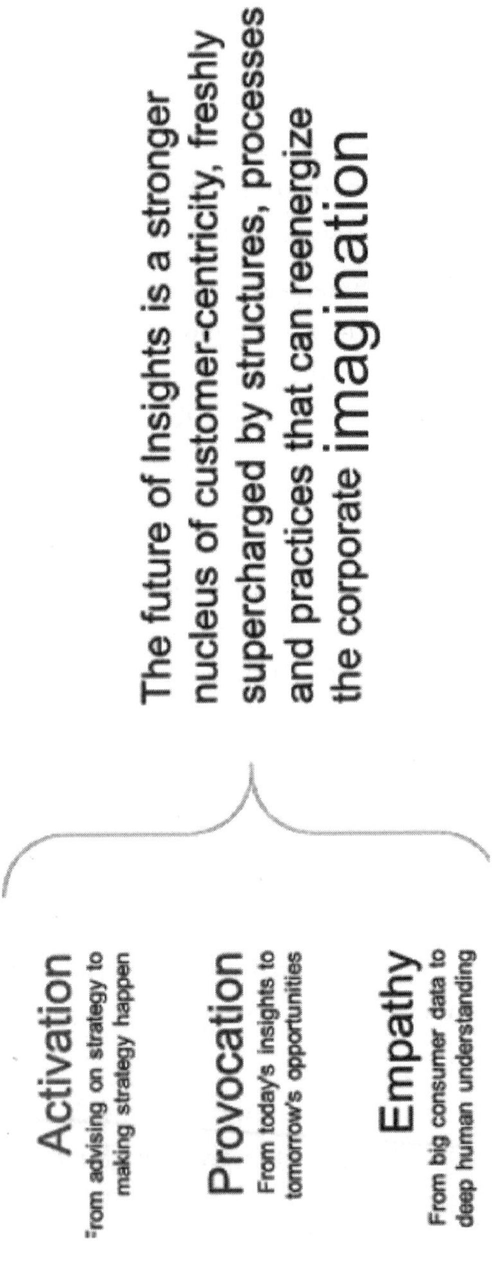

Activation
From advising on strategy to making strategy happen

Provocation
From today's insights to tomorrow's opportunities

Empathy
From big consumer data to deep human understanding

The future of Insights is a stronger nucleus of customer-centricity, freshly supercharged by structures, processes and practices that can reenergize the corporate **imagination**

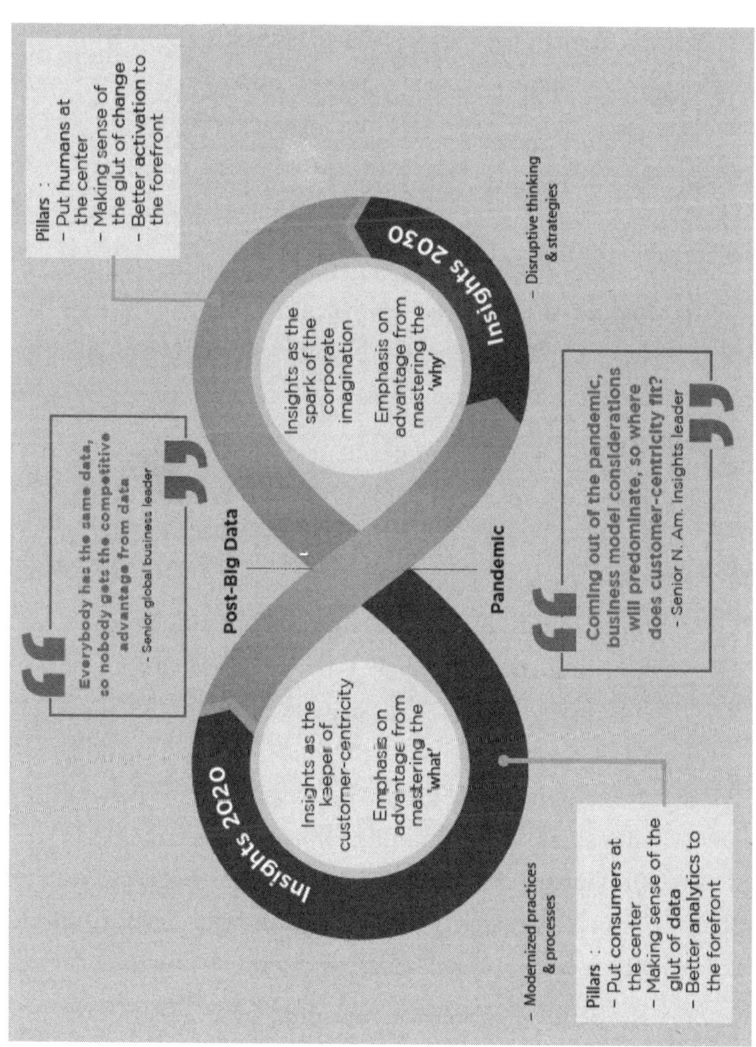
Pillars :
- Put consumers at the center
- Making sense of the glut of data
- Better analytics to the forefront
- Modernized practices & processes
Insights 2020
Insights as the keeper of customer-centricity
Emphasis on advantage from mastering the 'what'
Everybody has the same data, so nobody gets the competitive advantage from data
- Senior global business leader
Post-Big Data
Pandemic
Coming out of the pandemic, business model considerations will predominate, so where does customer-centricity fit?
- Senior N. Am. Insights leader
Insights as the spark of the corporate imagination
Emphasis on advantage from mastering the 'why'
Insights 2030
- Disruptive thinking & strategies
Pillars :
- Put humans at the center
- Making sense of the glut of change
- Better activation to the forefront

Implications for Marketing and Insights Professionals

I don't believe the debate on this is about these predictions being an accurate reflection of the future but it's about how can we encourage the organizations to move towards consumer centricity by using insights, analytics, and technological capabilities. Key actions that leaders in an organization can undertake to nurture the insights teams and their capabilities are:

- Just like a marketing manager's job is not to 'make advertisements' but to create a realistic yet inspiring marketing plan for the growth of the business (which the ad agencies can eventually use to create ads), an insight manager's job is to create an 'insights plan' that would help the business and find the right agency partners to bring those insights to the table and work with the business to implement those insights. Leadership skills are as critical in the insights staff as the general managers. Their training should focus equally on the skills and competencies. Just like all managers, "how" an insights team functions is as critical, if not more so, than "what" it does.
- Evaluate the role of insights and analytics in business decision-making process and explore opportunities to bring them together.

- Identify potential growth paths for the insights and analytics professionals within the organization. Without a clear growth path, their abilities would be restricted only to being research coordinators.

CHAPTER 6

When Research Impedes Judgment

Research is meant to aid judgment and help decision-making, but can it impede good judgment? Are there times when you are better off not doing any research? Referring to the evolution of the research function within an organization, do organizations consistently evolve or can they decline after the second or third stage of the BCG framework discussed in the previous chapter?

There is certainly a relationship between the amount of good quality research done and the right decisions it enables. But if that relationship is not nurtured, there is a good chance of it being more like an inverted U-shaped curve (see below image). The more you understand the consumer through your research, the better consumer-facing decisions you make.

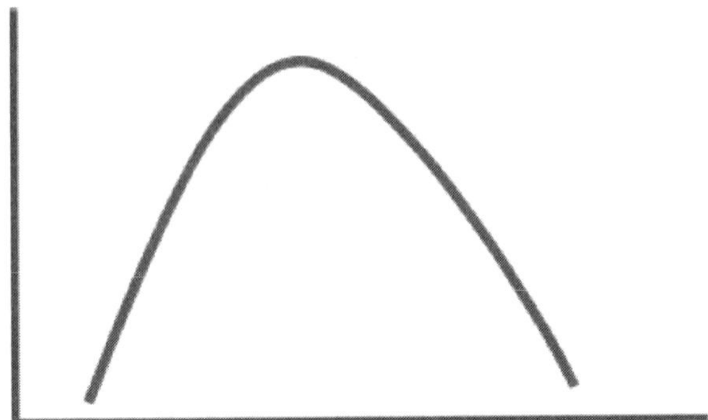

However, excessive research could also hinder this decision-making process if certain pitfalls are not avoided.

Let me explain why. An organization that is at the top of the inverted U-shaped curve typically finds itself in the second stage of the insights evolution journey, as explained in the previous chapter, where research is quite well-entrenched within the organizational framework. All decisions are made by scrutinizing consumer data with research terms being a part of the conversation: "What was the repeat rate?"; "Do you have green Link™ test?"; "Is the purchase intention of the concept stable or growing against the previous one?", etc. People think in terms of consumer metrics and base all their decisions on the available information as they understand, or at least they think they do, the way the information is obtained and analyzed.

However, beyond that, comes a time when marketers stop thinking like a marketer and start using research as a crutch. They think that consumer research would give them new ideas, evaluate those ideas, estimate potential, tell them what right advertising is, and so on. Marketing then starts running on autopilot of sorts, not unlike the 'proactive analytics' stage referred to in the previous chapter. Conversations happen around what research needs to be done rather than what innovation could be ahead of the curve. Entire thinking process revolves around getting the right research output that can convince stakeholders ("the right narrative") rather than strategy and innovations that would meet consumer needs. When the conversations begin to focus more on the research that needs to be done to meet the launch deadlines, or how the idea needs to be expressed in the form of stimuli for research, or worse, the narratives that would convince the stakeholders rather than how end consumers would finally see and experience your products that meets their needs, you are pretty close to the downward slide from the top of that curve. And to make matters worse, researchers or insight professionals in the team may also be criticized of having taken over all the innovation processes in the company since everyone is just obsessed with getting research stimuli and meeting the research deadlines.

I sometimes think of research as instruments on a plane. The sharper and clearer they are, the better directions they provide to the pilot. But you would still need a pilot to operate those instruments, even if the plane is on *autopilot*. Improving the quality of those existing instruments or installing high-end instruments doesn't mean that these instruments want to take total control of the plane; they are meaningless until someone actually uses them. A little insight into the insights team: most instruments (read insights people) actually are not interested in running the plane, they simply thrive on the act of measurements and providing directions.

Some companies, like Apple, go to the other extreme and claim that they don't conduct any market research. This, of course, isn't true. They certainly carry out a lot of research, especially after launching a product to measure customer satisfaction. Even in the innovation phase, while they may not carry out research in the way FMCG companies do, they do explore and seek to understand consumers' current behaviour around the problem or the need area. In such companies, the innovators are usually heavy users of the products themselves and completely understand what product delight means. Thus, they design the products for themselves more than for anyone else. But, they also speak to other like-minded people during the innovation process—their friends or relatives who are equally passionate about technology products—and seek their opinions on prototypes. That, in essence, is market research.

This may not be how it is done in FMCG or CPG businesses because they have millions of consumers using the product category and many of them are loyal to specific brands. In this context, market research is the process of talking to customers and understanding them. But the moment we stop applying our own judgment about products and consumer experiences and substitute it with just research data, it becomes a problem. That's because we lose sight of our own judgments and opinions. Something like that would probably never happen in the way Apple deals with innovation.

Evidently, all this doesn't mean we should stop conducting research. But there are ways in which the curve can continue progressing upwards instead of sliding down. I think that happens when we, as marketers and researchers, start using consumer understanding to sharpen our intuitions that can be used to design products and brands, rather than merely validate ideas. All of us, fortunately, are regular consumers of FMCGs; so, it isn't difficult to understand what consumers are saying and internalize it. The best marketers are those who strike a perfect balance between the two. The best creative people are those who are insightful, and who understand consumers as people with all their concerns and aspirations. They create their best advertising ideas when they combine an understanding of people with insights garnered from research about products or brands. The job of researchers should be to aid marketers and creative professionals in their judgment about people and products rather than replace it.

If that is what good consumer understanding is about, then marketing trainings in the initial few years should involve acquiring a deeper understanding of how to tell good products from the bad ones (and, indeed, good branding strategies from the bad ones). Tea marketers, for instance, should learn what good tea smells and tastes like. Soap marketers should learn what good soap smells and feels like, so that when they look at consumer data about product usage, they would understand exactly what problems consumers are highlighting, and what solutions should be offered. How many companies really do that? There is a lot of training about marketing theories and research methodologies, which is great, but the emphasis has to be on what it really means and how one can apply the learnings to develop brands and grow businesses. That is exactly like how learning about equipment used on a plane alone doesn't make you a pilot or train you on the direction in which you want to fly. To learn how to be a pilot, one needs holistic training on commanding a plane.

So, what are the traps that researchers need to avoid to ensure that the curve continues to go upward instead of down? Here are some thought starters:

1. An elementary but often-ignored point is that research objectives and decision-making criteria should be absolutely clear. Different people have different opinions about what the decision-making criteria should be or what the research is seeking to find out. For instance, should you launch with parity product results or not? Here, parity means when your product performance is on par with the competition but not superior. Why should there ever be a debate on it? If you are a heavy or regular user of the product yourself, you would know that a delightful product goes a long way towards establishing loyalty well after the advertising has been consumed and forgotten. So, if you tap into your gut feeling, you would want a superior product and you would know what elements of a product make it superior (without having to wait for a key driver analysis of the product).

2. The decision-making criteria should not be too complicated. Most consumer products are simple to use and are used day in and day out. Consumers don't think too much about them (except for some high-involvement categories), but that doesn't mean we, as marketers or insight professionals, shouldn't either.

If we maintain a balanced perspective, we can surely simplify decision-making criteria.

3. Complicated or confusing research designs should be avoided. People spend a lot of time debating and discussing the research design (sometimes at the debrief, annoyingly enough)—too many control cells, a large amount of variables, interim period forecasts, etc. This does not help the research process. The topic of design should be left to expert researchers. Equally, researchers or insight professionals need to earn that trust.
4. One should also avoid complex techniques that are more accurate but are incomprehensible to most people. I would cite discrete choice modelling for pricing research as an example, at the risk of offending my friends who are passionate about it. It is a brilliant technique which works really well to understand the trade-offs that consumers make at various price points, and it is very simple in terms of the kind of answers respondents have to provide. But analyzing and understanding results in this method is highly complex. It needs not just an expertise in analysis but also a comprehensive understanding of consumer behaviour in the category. Sometimes simpler methods are easier to deploy even if they are less accurate.
5. The conclusions and recommendations should be crystal clear.
    a) If the decision to be taken and the decision-making criteria are simple, then the recommendations should be clear too.

b) Splitting data into meaningless segments to get better scores in some segment, dissecting it in many directions, or using complicated multivariate make the recommendations unclear. The analysis needed should, of course, stem from the objectives and action standards.

6. One should not abuse the research by using it for a purpose that it is not meant for. Some examples being:

   a) Quick and dirty shortcuts instead of rigour. Carrying out qualitative research as a substitute for a quantitative study, for instance. Taking decisions on the basis of toplines without waiting for the details is another way of abusing research.

   b) Considering the testing of the execution as validation for the overall strategy. Consumers don't write strategy, but strategy can be developed with some good fundamental consumer understanding. Consumers can evaluate the manifestation of a strategy in the form of advertising or concepts or product ideas. But, for this, research has to be designed with a specific brief of either writing a strategy or checking the efficacy of a strategy through an execution. For instance, pre-testing ads before airing them is just copy testing; it is not the testing of advertising strategy or the communication idea. A communication idea can be developed with good insights about the way consumers think and feel about a product or a brand. But pre-testing only evaluates the execution of the idea.

7. Researchers or insight teams need to take a stand. The job of the insights professionals is not only to put the data on the table but also to take a stand on the recommendations. Marketers may choose to agree or disagree, and a discussion may be necessary. And often, the insights professionals would need to tap into their experiences and intuition (which is developed with experience gained by working on the category) to make recommendations, as long as they are supported with ample information from consumer studies.

8. Finally, marketers need to develop an intuition and gut feeling about the product categories and the way consumers use those products. No amount of research can be a substitute for that. It is not ironic that a book on insights is recommending that marketers should develop a gut feeling because intuitive feeling is essential for making good consumer-oriented decisions. If marketers have never washed clothes in their lives, how can they really understand what consumers look for in a detergent? If they have never stood in a queue to open a bank account or to access other banking services, they would never know different types of services banks offer. Consumer immersion, which entails understanding product usage, brand choice drivers, shopping experience, etc., is crucial to develop this gut feeling.

Implications for Marketing and Insights Professionals

More consumer research is not always a good thing; it could mean that research is being used as a crutch for decision-making. Business teams need to be 'insightful' about the consumers and the choices they make rather than 'researchful' (resourceful to do a lot of research). And the ball is not only in the court of marketers, but the responsibility also lies with research teams. They need to be mindful of the role of research in the organization but also need to be empowered to push back and say "no" when they think research is being abused.

It takes significant effort from the organization, marketers, and researchers to reach the top of the curve. It would be unfortunate if there were only a decline after that. All the research teams in organizations must go through that journey to reach the peak, but after that, they need to have the right perspective and stakeholder management within the organization to continue growing along the curve.

CHAPTER 7

Qualitative Research and Its Evolving Nature in Problem-Solving

Qualitative research (qual research) has been the backbone of insights for decades. This chapter outlines the evolution of qual research and some thoughts on where it could potentially be heading, especially if we consider the emergence of technology in the space of consumer listening and analysis. My thoughts are based on my conversations with practitioners and users of qual research across the world, integrated with my own.

Qual research has a long history and has existed for as long as the field of sociology has been established. Sociology itself has roots in the work of some Western philosophers like Aristotle and Plato, as well as some Eastern philosophers like Confucius. Although the contributions of psychologists like

Sigmund Freud and Carl Jung have also influenced qualitative research, some consider Paul Felix Lazarsfeld as the 'father' of qualitative research. By the beginning of the twentieth century, psychoanalysis had begun to enter the commercial world. By mid-twentieth century, Lazarsfeld had demonstrated how psychology could provide a framework to interpret human behaviour. He introduced the world to unstructured interviewing and group discussions and stressed the importance of answering the crucial 'why?' question.

Interestingly, the so called 'pro-quantitative' orthodoxy was at its peak during the 1930s and 40s and it swept aside any 'non-scientific' explanations of behaviour—anything that didn't have hard numerical data generated through empirical research and subjected to a battery of statistical analyses. Lazarsfeld, with qualifications in mathematics and psychology, was truly thinking 'out of the box' at the time. When 'questionnaire' was the only term available for a research instrument, he was hinting at using a topic guide to understand the 'why' questions. He began working commercially by late 1930s to research questions like "How do women decide where to buy their clothes?". Qualitative research was just beginning to be established as an alternative to empirical methods for identifying and documenting behavioural patterns of individuals and groups.

During the twentieth century, qual research saw significant strides—projective techniques were introduced by Ernst Dichter (a student of Lazarsfeld); the effective dismissal of long-running qual vs quant argument within market research; and rapid expansion and proliferation of agencies specializing in it. If you look at the latest ESOMAR report, the size of the qualitative research industry today is close to US $9 billion—clearly suggesting that it has been hugely successful in the last 100 years.

At the heart of it, qual research has always been about understanding human behaviour, understanding people in all its richness and messiness. Human mind is quite intricate and muddy in the way it thinks and navigates emotions; qual research is about mapping this complex labyrinth of human psyche. It is about developing an 'intuition' about how people think and what leads to different behaviour. That core has not changed and would probably remain unchanged. But there have been changes in the context and the way it is run in this twenty-first century.

Let's take a look at the changes in the qualitative research in this century through four lenses:

1. The client role
2. The business problems
3. The methods
4. The role of technology

1. The Client Role

Let's start by looking at how the clients have changed, in terms of how they issue briefs and what they expect.

At the beginning of the twentieth century, clients demanded more methodological thinking and expected researchers to infuse different techniques in the research based on their requirements; this was partly driven by a bit of an anxiety of not knowing what would finally yield that interesting nugget. The more exotic the methods—be it ethnography, or semiotics—the better was the proposal. During fieldwork, one would more likely see individuals from the research department or insight function sitting behind a one-way mirror and often nervously passing slips to the moderator to ensure that all the questions that their clients needed were asked.

The presentations or the outputs of the qual too consequently followed a similar philosophy. The clients expected to see 'evidence' that indeed all the proposed exotic methodologies were used, that the fieldwork was carried out in all locations and in languages that it was proposed to be in. So, the presentations had a collage of output from different methodologies and locations (like country reports) and, in the end, an attempt to combine all of this into one global summary or broader insights that the client could use. It did have an advantage because a lot of details and nuances captured during fieldwork were part of the report and people preserved those reports so that they could go back to them and pull out interesting nuggets like quotes or pictures of audio clips when needed.

A lot has changed on that front now. In marketing-savvy and consumer-centric organizations, insights' function has developed an identity and importance of its own. They are no longer 'carrier of insights' between agencies and marketing but tend to have a seat at the decision-making table to identify the way insights would be used by the business. As a result, you are more likely to see marketers in the fieldwork as well, and not just nervous people from insights team. The presentations are not a re-collage of various modules but documents outlining key insights and implications for the business. With reducing attention spans, the appetite to sit through long presentations has vanished and people expect shorter, snappier presentations preferably in video formats—you almost have to create short TikTok videos for marketing teams, else they won't even pay attention. But equally, there is a lot more pragmatism in the way the insights are discussed—these are not intellectual, academic discussions but a means to an end, which is business growth. So, you don't need to build the whole story and aura around how you got to the insight. Rather, the emphasis is on being pragmatic about what the insight truly means to the business. Give me the information I need to make a decision and let's move on (save the nuances for later).

Having said that, it doesn't mean that all clients have become savvier. There are enough who are not interested in exploring the subject broadly or use methods that provide different perspectives. They are merely interested in that one nugget which they can take to the decision-making table and hence, the briefs can be very 'transactional' in nature. Needless to say, a qual project shouldn't be going wide just for the sake of it, but its very nature allows for explorations along the way and restrictive or transactional briefs can limit those significantly.

2. The Business Problems

Business problems that qual research or any other stream of research deals with have undergone extensive changes as well.

There were days when the qual briefs were about 'triggers and barriers', 'usage and attitudes', or 'semiotics on packaging' wherein the expectation was to examine just a sliver of the consumer life. As a result, the researchers were more like ostriches with their heads buried in the sand of the triggers and barriers or usage and attitudes, and didn't examine the broader context in as much detail.

The brands and businesses today are living in a complex world. The briefs shared by the clients no longer care whether your expertise is in qual or quant research, they expect you to be an expert in solving a business problem. As a result, the briefs have evolved, too, and are a lot more holistic than they used to be. Think of questions like: "Where my next business growth is going to come from?", or "How do we support African American Lesbian women in the biases they face in this world?", etc. For broad strategic questions like this, the researcher often doesn't know from where to begin the exploration and what internal prejudices and biases to challenge first. Or, think of issues like understanding vaccine hesitancy—the complexity driven by the role that gender, literacy, political orientation, cast, geography, etc., plays in it.

This coupled with the change in the role of the client has led to the realization that the real value of work being done by research lies in the usability of the work, the outcomes it is creating, and the tangibility of the business results. Qualitative research that has always had a huge overlap with academic research now has begun to greatly overlap with the business results too.

3. The Methods

Qual and Quant methods used to be defined in 'contrast' to each other, in terms of what the other sciences were unable to do. Qualitative research has always been consumer-centric, but in the last few years, with increasing complexity of briefs coupled with changing role of clients and availability of tech solutions, it has become a lot more human-centric. There has been a realization that nuances like memory structures, culture, human biases, etc., have a massive role to play in consumer behaviour. New perspectives on human brain and behavioural economics have become mainstream. The briefs becoming more complex and holistic, therefore, has gone hand-in-hand with the methodology becoming holistic.

Qualitative research has always been about integrating several data points that are totally unstructured and coming from different sources. But the data points have now multiplied, and the sources can be quite unstructured and limited only by your imagination. Social conversations, search analytics, digital ethnography, self-data captured by respondents, analytical modelling done on the subject before—anything and everything has become a part of the data set that the qualitative researchers must deal with now. Today, consumer is just one feed and not the singular source of data. As a result, qualitative researchers are no longer ostriches but have become aware and immersed beings connecting with people around them in every possible way and continuously analyzing this connection to understand what it means for the business. Some qualitative researchers now prefer to call themselves "human strategists" as they now solve human-centric problems that also provide opportunities for businesses to grow. Tools such as focus group discussions, in-depth interviews, etc., constitute a small component of the entire universe of qualitative research today and they, in fact, may not even appear in some of the projects at all.

One of the implications of this is the skillset that the qualitative researchers need today. Qualitative researchers have always been great at connecting the dots, structuring the unstructured data, and finding meaning in observations. As it was described to me once, qualitative research is like a stream of river that's meandering through a landscape, and it changes the size and shape according to what it encounters, but equally gives a new meaning and depth to the landscape. I would argue that qualitative researchers are better equipped and skilled than anyone else to be able to create that kind of meaning with the unstructured data. They may not understand how search analytics works or how statistical modelling is done, but they have an inherently honed intuitive ability to look at the output and connect with other observations coming from other sources and come up with an insight that no other expert can. And hence qualitative research would never be dead, it would only keep evolving and, arguably so, would be the only stream that would survive because it can subsume everything under it.

With evolving client roles, business problems, and methodology, qualitative research industry that was once only about building a strong relationship with consumers, has further evolved to include real humans at the heart of it:

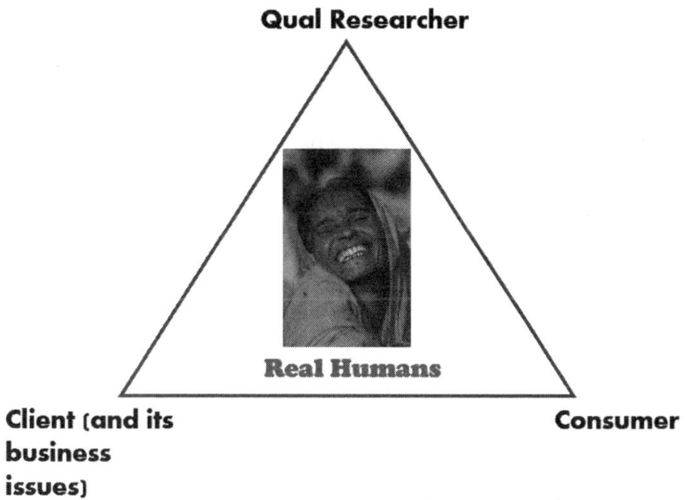

4. The Role of Technology

I will not go into technology that was used for research in previous centuries—it would suffice to say that the days of strapping people on to chairs and giving them electric shocks are well past us. At the beginning of the twenty-first century, the use of technology in qualitative research still largely meant watching or listening to video and audio tapes of fieldwork conducted and analyzing them for insights. We have now come a long way from there. Technology has now become an integral part of life for researchers. However, interestingly, qualitative researchers see technology both as an enabler as well as a hindrance.

It's an enabler because:

1. Qualitative research was earlier considered incomplete if you "weren't there". Technology now enables you to be

with people anywhere and anytime, whether physically or virtually.

2. It makes life "seamless"—from carrying out recruitments to working on conversations and observations, recording them and pulling out parts for further use, transcribing interviews, etc.
3. Preliminary content analysis—such as identifying themes, sentiments or trends—gets done through technology, allowing the researcher to focus and dig deeper on important issues.
4. Availability of big data adds different perspectives and depth to the analysis. It not only provides context but also allows you to flesh out hypotheses.
5. Technology massively enhances efficiency by reducing grunt work. It is good for heavy lifting on things like information and project management.

But it's also a hindrance because:

1. Holding focus group discussions virtually is emotionally exhausting. You cannot assess body language, or get a sense of the vibe of the room; you have to over-emote to get the energy going because respondents are multitasking.
2. Technology hasn't fulfilled all its promises yet. You can't really leave entire analysis to artificial intelligence despite all the promises that the providers make. While video analytics does not exist for all practical purposes, image analytics is only just maturing as a field now.

3. Technology companies make tall promises without really understanding the nuances of human behaviour and emotions. Researchers fall for them because they don't understand technology.
4. It can often provide false confidence about the insight it provides, and doing this risks discouraging people from really thinking and 'joining the dots'. Researchers become less involved in what they're seeing or hearing, and the relationship gets more transactional.
5. Big data, today, is available everywhere and you can get it free or access it at low cost. But it's often difficult to figure out the profile of people generating this data, their social contexts, and their lives. Without that depth of understanding, the data can be meaningless or prone to misinterpretation.

The World of Qualitative Research Post COVID-19 Pandemic

As per estimates quoted by researchers of large global qual agencies I interviewed, before the COVID-19 pandemic, around 70% of fieldwork or research globally was already being conducted virtually; it only increased to 100% during the pandemic. Technology has come to the front and centre during this time, if it wasn't already there and provided both ease and difficulty during COVID-19. With the advent of digital communication, young researchers in particular, have lost the art of accessing culture, seeing real people, developing intuitions about them, and dealing with them with a personal touch.

Interestingly, while talking to some of the world's leading qual researchers about the impact of COVID-19, there was a sense among the researchers that since they weren't physically with the respondents during the research in pandemic, some consumers felt less vulnerable and, therefore, were able to open up better. This allowed researchers to get a peep into the real human side of the 'consumers'. However, some respondents could hide their insecurities quite well because of the exact same reason—the researcher wasn't physically present at their homes or shopping with them so they couldn't peek at the real vulnerabilities. For some respondents, the lines between social media and virtual qualitative research blurred and they felt that they were creating social media content while responding to questions—as if they were influencers. All this added a lot of complexity and required an additional layer of analysis to decipher what was real and what was being projected.

Therefore, post the COVID-19 pandemic, researchers were itching to get back to real life and do some real work. But, on the other hand, the pandemic did reduce travels significantly, improving the researchers' work-life balance. So, now they are a lot more careful in choosing when they can travel and when virtual connects using technology can give good insights.

What Does the Future Look Like?

No one really knows what will happen going ahead, but I will try to extrapolate recent trends a bit and imagine the future:

1. Generalists won't exist, but there will be a merger of all sorts of specialists like data scientists, semioticians, and ethnographers. Today, they already work together as a team in several organizations. In future, the awkwardness between them would reduce and mutual appreciation of their skills would increase, understanding of the limitations of different data sets would enhance, and that would result in broader transferability and applications of specialisms. Consumer insights can then truly be holistic through systemic solutions and not just by individual brilliance or by a fluke of chance.
2. Technology would allow us to do some real social experiments—not in a laboratory, but by conducting small interventions in societies and observing the difference it makes in human behaviour and emotions. For instance, think of introducing a tech gadget like laptop in a village with high illiteracy rate for a few weeks to see what happens, install cameras in kitchens capturing real-life cooking feed and impact of different food samples being sent to that household, and so on and so forth. These ideas are limited only by your imagination.
3. AI for research would start to grow exponentially and mature. Technology would eventually start delivering all its promises—be it in spaces like video analytics, cultural insights, or in processing big data to effectively understand human behaviour. It would not be something that you experiment with once in a while

or use only for modelling and forecasting purposes but it would play a significant role in coming together of specialists and experts. Technologies like ChatGPT would become an ally to the qualitative researchers.

4. People would learn to monetize their own data. The trend of self-measurement and quantification would merge with the value and privacy of personal data. This would make people monetize the data they capture about themselves on their own and at their own terms. Recruitment for research would be a lot more expensive than today; it would be the most expensive component of research and would also look and feel very different. Face-to-face research would become a premium practice and be renamed to something like 'Nuance Workshops' or something similar.

5. Human intelligence would come back into vogue. Physical fieldwork done by human researchers would never see its end because you would always want the real nuances, but there would be a recognition all over again of the human cognitive abilities and the natural ways to develop an intuition or gut feeling. AI has to be trained by humans. Yes, machines do learn by themselves, but we would learn to make technology our slave rather than be slaves to technology, and that would always require human ingenuity.

Implications for Marketing and Research Professionals

Qualitative research is a highly-specialized skill where experts are trained in gathering unstructured observations, connecting the dots on-the-go, and observing things that may not be obvious to an untrained eye. To the uninitiated, it could seem like having simple conversations with people and summarizing them, but there is years of practice that goes behind this. That's precisely why some organizations encourage employees (particularly marketers) to do their own qualitative research, but suffice to say that it could also lead to naïve or sometimes wrong conclusions. Technology is increasingly used to support the gathering of observations in an unobtrusive way and while people think only data scientists can analyze the 'signals' coming out of a tech system, there is a lot more need of 'dot connectors' and 'storytellers' to understand the unstructured information coming out of that data. Qualitative research is not dying as some dramatic proclamations go but would continue to flourish even more as we learn to gather a lot more information from different tech systems. A few tips to use qualitative research methods more effectively:

- Use qualitative research to seek the depth of insight and complement it with data science to peel the layers of increasingly complex consumer context.

- Identify areas where expert qualitative research would be used and areas where teams can do 'consumer connect' themselves and get the insights.
- Identify and work with a roster of same qualitative research professionals regularly—this would ensure they understand not just the context of your business, but also the way business likes to imbibe insights and use them to create solutions for consumers.
- Use the professional skills of connecting the dots and storytelling—the value of which can't be overemphasized.

CHAPTER 8

Analytics and Its Role in Growing Business

Analytics has come a long way in the last decade. From being the domain of 'statisticians' who spoke in jargons and were forever dreaming of getting more and better-quality data, to a place buzzing with 'data scientists' who have access to lots of data and new tech to churn out eye-popping analytical models. The work of great analytics is always a true combination of art and science—creativity is necessary to think of new data sources, new ways of using different data. For instance, while working on analytical modelling to forecast the growth of tea business by town classes at Unilever in India, we decided to use cement production and its flow to different cities as a variable. That's because the head of the tea business visited a few cities where tea category was growing and realized that those cities were undergoing a lot of construction (infrastructure and new buildings) and every construction site had a few tea shops selling tea to people working there. This little anecdotal observation made a significant difference to the forecasting of the tea business. As a result, the combination of the observation and analytical modelling led to a far more robust forecast.

Types of Models

Analytics is a broad field, and it can often be quite confusing for an organization to setup and use analytical capabilities of both the employees as well as existing tools. So, we first start by looking at different types of analytics based on how they are done and their use of cases or applications. Some of these are 'always on' and some of them are done as and when needed. The list below is by no means exhaustive rather it is indicative, and the classification into traditional and new age is more to separate the capabilities—traditional needs data science and new age needs data science and technology.

Given below are only some type of traditional and new-age analytics:

TRADITIONAL ANALYTICS (These models usually 'explain' the phenomenon, but also allow for 'forecasting'.)	NEW-AGE ANALYTICS (These often use unstructured big data with or without traditional data sets, and work with tech tools like machine learning.)
Measure value of different marketing levers (e.g., Market Mix Modelling or MMMs) and optimizing the spends.	Getting insights through analyzing online conversations, pictures, etc.

TRADITIONAL ANALYTICS	NEW-AGE ANALYTICS
Drivers of change (e.g., drivers of category upgradation, drivers of category penetration, etc.).	Predicting trends before they happen.
Drivers of brand purchase.	Measuring and optimizing performance of digital campaigns.
Drivers of product performance.	Attribution modelling.
Media and brand analytics—how to allocate media budget across different categories and brands?	
Price promo optimization.	
Retail analytics; working with the retailers for shopper upgradation analytics to drive sales at the retailer for Unilever portfolio.	
Growth scout: where to focus in order to increase category or brand penetration.	

This section looks at some of these analytics in greater detail.

Measuring the Value of Different Marketing Levers

There are different marketing levers that an organization has and all of them are under their control, but different levers have varying impact on the final results. It is important to know which levers to press and to what extent. It's like driving a car; you need to know which gear you should be driving the car in, depending on the terrain, and when to accelerate or when to break. Measuring the importance and sensitivity of each of the levers is typically done using Market Mix Modelling. These models have been in place for decades but have evolved with more quantity and quality of data coming in. MMMs typically use sales as the dependent variable and model it against independent variables like advertising (both quality and quantity can be used, including the split between traditional or digital), distribution, price discount, competition activities like ad spends, discounts, etc. This model uses historical data and works out not just the sensitivity of sales to each of the

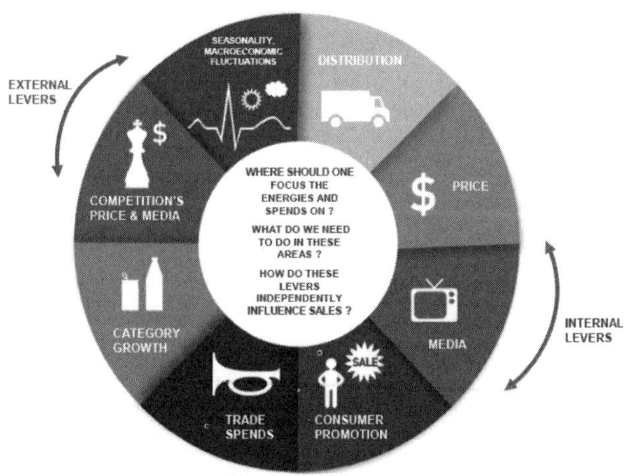

independent variables, but also the flexibility that exists for change in that variable, using optimization curves.

A good example of this is the MMM for 'regular' and 'premium' Knorr Soups range done for Unilever Turkey in 2011. Both the ranges showed sensitivity to different things:

REGULAR KNORR SOUP	ELASTICITY (% change in sales with 5% change in the dependent variable)	PREMIUM KNORR SOUP	ELASTICITY (% change in sales with 5% change in the dependent variable)
Average price	-4.0	RPI w.r.t. total regular soups in the market	-5.5
Knorr Regular Soups TV Gross Rating Points (GRPs)	0.4	Knorr Premium Soups Weighted Distribution	6.0
Knorr Premium Soups TV GRPs	0.7	Knorr Premium Soups TV GRPs	0.9
Bizim (Competitor) GRPs	-0.5	Knorr Cup-a-Soup GRPs	0.4
Spends on outdoor media	0.5	Bizim (Competitor) TV GRPs	-0.9

REGULAR KNORR SOUP	ELASTICITY	PREMIUM KNORR SOUP	ELASTICITY
Consumer promotion spends	0.3	Consumer ATL spends	0.6

This clearly shows what each of the soup range depends upon, but also shows the cross impact on each other. Regular Knorr soup was impacted by absolute price (sales went down with price increase) but was also impacted by the TV Gross Rating Points (GRPs) of both its own and premium range. Premium soups, on the other hand, were not impacted by absolute price but a lot more by the price relative to regular soups. The more premium they became relative to regular soups in the market, the more sales they lost. Similarly, on advertising, the competition GRPs had a negative impact on sales. While the brand can't do anything about it, this suggests continuously keeping an eye to counter the spends with own advertising. Interestingly, premium soups were impacted a lot more by distribution than advertising providing a clear lever for growth.

However, these relationships are never linear and hence increasing or decreasing the levels of independent variables doesn't cause same change in sales all the time. Hence, looking at the curve of the relationship and understanding optimum levels are equally crucial in using the model to predict the future sales.

For instance, look at the relationship between GRPs and sales often found in these models:

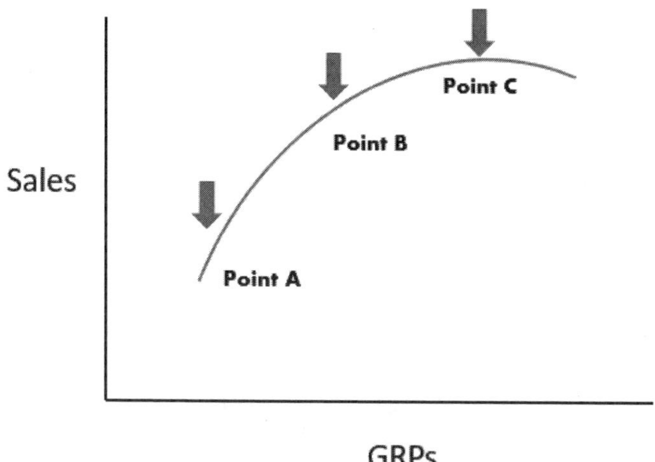

Sales do increase with the increase in GRPs but beyond a point the curve tends to flatten. Hence, if the current GRP levels of the brand are at point A, then increasing them results in a good increase in sales with promising returns. But if the GRPs levels are already at point C then increasing them further is unlikely to give any joy.

These MMMs are extremely insightful about the levers available to the business to increase sales. But they are also incredibly useful in deciding where and to what extent should the business be spending money on. At Unilever, these MMMs are often 'always on'—data comes in continuously and the model gets updated frequently. The business has access to understand the sensitivities at any point and can find the optimum spending levels. This 'always on' dashboard is also useful to see the impact of changes that the business makes on an ongoing basis providing continuous validation of the model.

An example of recommendation and the dashboard:

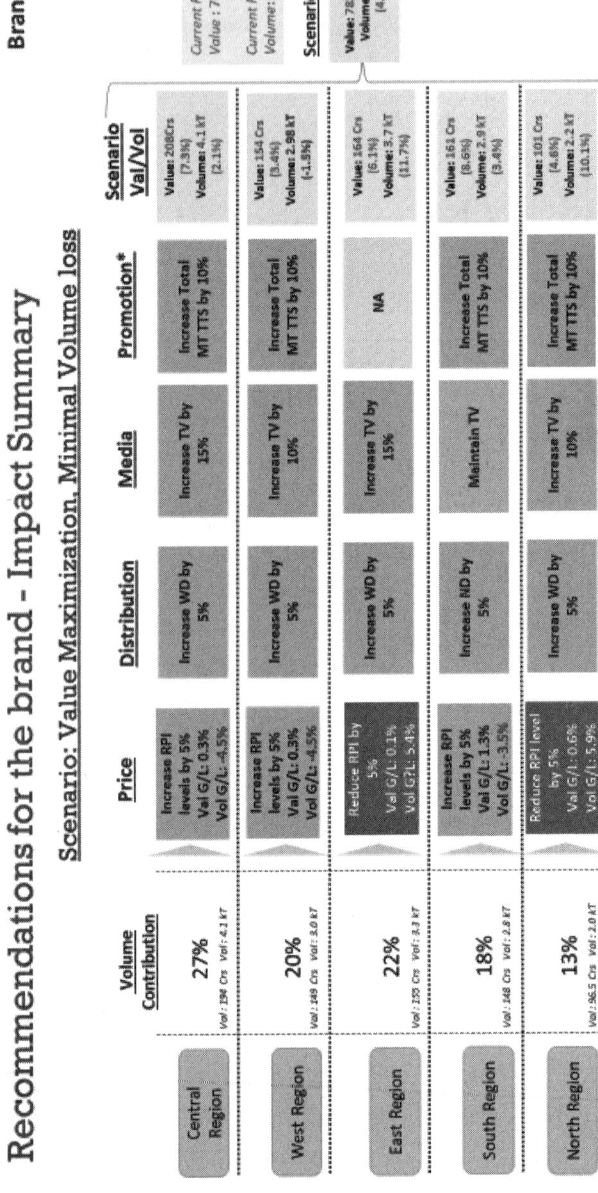
Recommendations for the brand - Impact Summary
Brand 2
Scenario: Value Maximization, Minimal Volume loss
Volume Contribution
Price
Distribution
Media
Promotion*
Scenario Val/Vol
Central Region
27%
Vol : 194 Crs Vol : 4.1 kT
Increase RPI levels by 5% Val G/L: 0.3% Vol G/L: -4.5%
Increase WD by 5%
Increase TV by 15%
Increase Total MT TTS by 10%
Value: 208Crs (7.3%) Volume: 4.1 kT (2.1%)
West Region
20%
Vol : 149 Crs Vol : 3.0 kT
Increase RPI levels by 5% Val G/L: 0.3% Vol G/L: -4.5%
Increase WD by 5%
Increase TV by 10%
Increase Total MT TTS by 10%
Value: 154 Crs (3.4%) Volume: 2.98 kT (-1.5%)
East Region
22%
Vol : 155 Crs Vol : 3.3 kT
Reduce RPI by 5% Val G/L: 0.1% Vol G?L: 5.4%
Increase WD by 5%
Increase TV by 15%
NA
Value: 164 Crs (6.1%) Volume: 3.7 kT (11.7%)
South Region
18%
Vol : 148 Crs Vol : 2.8 kT
Increase RPI levels by 5% Val G/L: 1.3% Vol G/L: -3.5%
Increase ND by 5%
Maintain TV
Increase Total MT TTS by 10%
Value: 161 Crs (8.6%) Volume: 2.9 kT (3.4%)
North Region
13%
Vol : 96.5 Crs Vol : 2.0 kT
Reduce RPI level by 5% Val G/L: 0.6% Vol G/L: 5.9%
Increase WD by 5%
Increase TV by 10%
Increase Total MT TTS by 10%
Value: 101 Crs (4.6%) Volume: 2.2 kT (10.1%)
Current Portfolio Value : 742 Crs
Current Portfolio Volume: 15.1 kT
Scenario Val/Vo
Value: 783 Crs (5.5%) Volume: 15.8 kT (4.2%)
*Values in brackets represent value and volume gains due to recommendations

Measuring the Impact of Drivers of Change

The growth of the business is not only impacted by the controllable levers but also by the factors that the organization can't control like economic growth or education levels of the population. Understanding what the external or uncontrollable factors are, along with internal or controllable factors (like marketing levers) provides an extremely useful insight to the business for prioritizing markets and long-term business forecasting. For instance, in the 90s, the facial moisturizers market development was dependent upon the per cap GDP of a country (which was proxy of income), and % of more than 34-year-old women population (older women have drier skin—so, more number of older women meant more sales), and the average temperature (lower temperature gave drier skin). The model also highlights emergent points—i.e., PPP per cap GDP and average temperature beyond which the market develops rapidly. This insight allows businesses to prioritize markets that are emerging or are on the verge of emerging but also develop products that could help skin care of women younger than 34 years of age.

There are different types of models in this space of drivers of change:

Market emergence models: These models look at what type of socio-economic conditions impact category sales. Examples of those would be drivers of premiumization within a category, identifying markers of development within cities or countries for distribution expansion, etc. Let's look at an example of premiumization within detergents category that identified

DETERMINANTS OF UPGRADATION

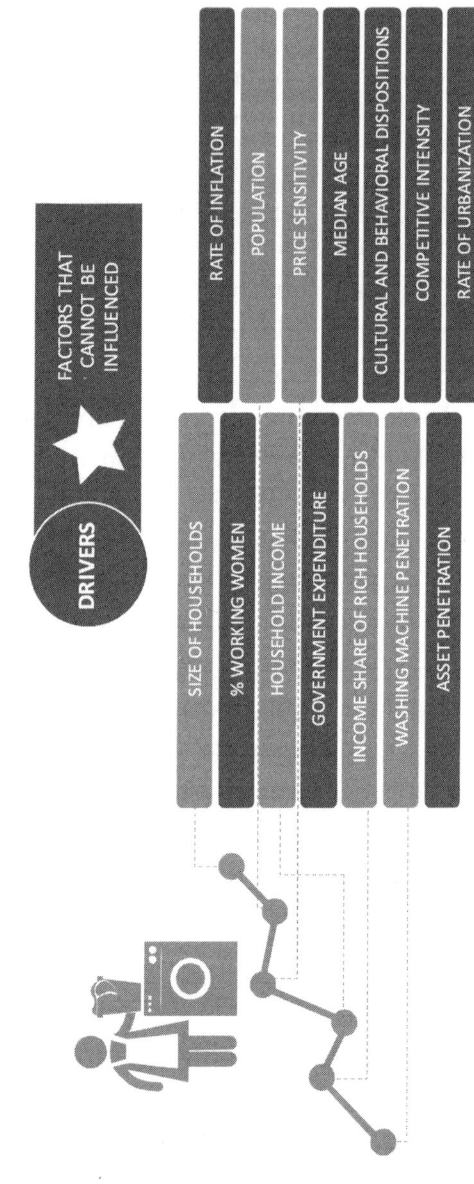

various 'controllable' and 'non-controllable' variables that lead upgradation from bars to powders to liquids.

Apart from obvious ones like the income and size of the household, this model provided an interesting insight—higher the % of working women in a market, higher was the chance of the market upgrading. While organizations like Unilever may not be able to do much directly about working women, it certainly can prioritize markets with higher education levels of women and higher work opportunities. But, more importantly, Unilever began working with several state governments and other agencies to improve education and employability of women, which further improves the economic conditions as well as the business prospects in the market. There are several award-winning initiatives in this space.

Growth scout: Tools like the driver analysis give an idea of 'how to play', but you also need ideas on 'where to play'. A proprietary bespoke tool developed within Unilever uses millions of data points across demographics, regions, and countries to identify potential value of deeper category or brand penetration. The results derived from this tool help the business prioritize growth opportunities and decide where it could most profitably invest additional marketing or product-development resources. The tool essentially prioritizes demographic segments with weaker penetration and usage and the size of prize.

For instance, analysis of face moisturizers in Indonesia suggested an opportunity of over €20 million for Pond's by increasing its market penetration. The question, then, is which segments should it focus on for increasing penetration (where

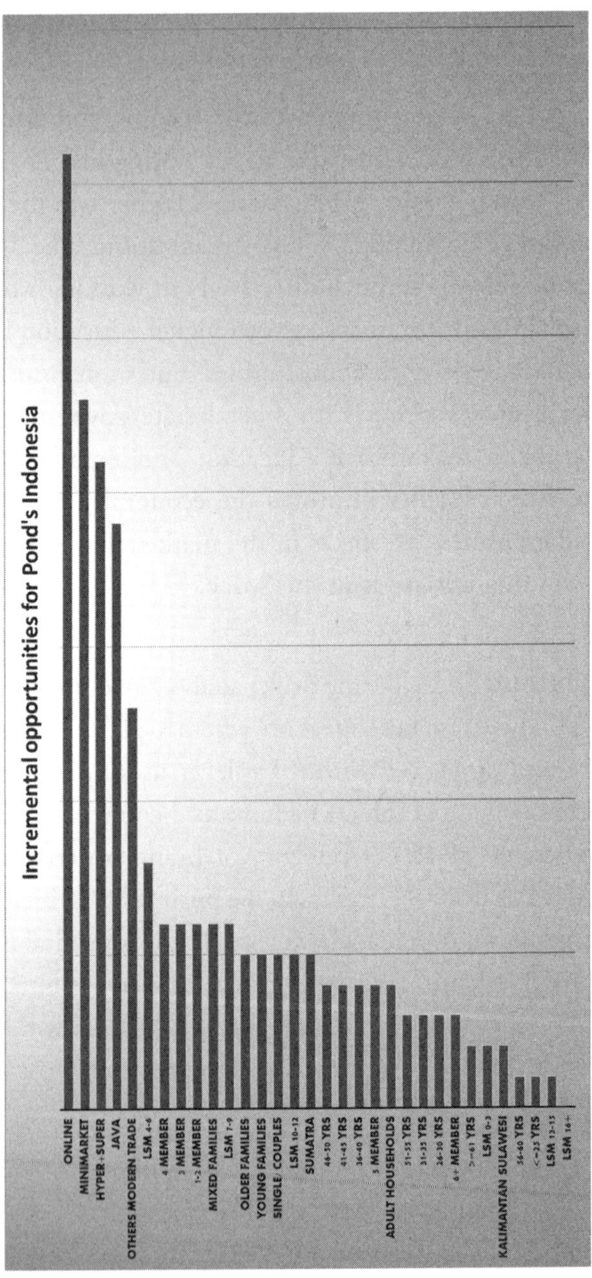
Incremental opportunities for Pond's Indonesia
ONLINE
MINIMARKET
HYPER+SUPER
JAVA
OTHERS MODERN TRADE
LSM 4-6
4 MEMBER
3 MEMBER
1-2 MEMBER
MIXED FAMILIES
LSM 7-9
OLDER FAMILIES
YOUNG FAMILIES
SINGLE/COUPLES
LSM 10-12
SUMATRA
46-50 YRS
41-45 YRS
36-40 YRS
5 MEMBER
ADULT HOUSEHOLDS
51-55 YRS
31-35 YRS
26-30 YRS
6+ MEMBER
>=61 YRS
LSM 0-3
KALIMANTAN SULAWESI
56-60 YRS
<=25 YRS
LSM 13-15
LSM 16+

to play?). Growth scout identified demographic segments and channels that should be the focus for increasing penetration.

Drivers of Brand Purchase

We have talked about brand drivers in the earlier section of Insights for Product Development or Innovation as well as in the Market Drivers section. To put it briefly, drivers are things that drive the brand preference in a category. The analysis not only shows drivers by importance but also how they ladder up to overall preference and the sensitivity of each of those. Look at drivers of ice cream brands in China (consumed in-home and out-of-home) about ten years ago. The analysis gave clear insights for the brands to work on:

1. Good value (in terms of price) and indulgence were key drivers of brand choice.
2. Emotional gratification was a lot more important than functional payoffs.
3. One of the key factors—indulgences—still had a lot of room to improve (sensitivity analysis).

The tea division in Unilever France used laddering analysis, which is a quantitative way of deriving the linkages of brand attributes to each other and to overall brand preference. Laddering uses brand perception data of several brands in the category and models them to see the impact of changing one attribute to other attributes and to overall brand preference. It's like playing different strings on xylophone – the pressure applied on the strings and the sequence of strings played impacts the sound that the xylophone produces. Laddering

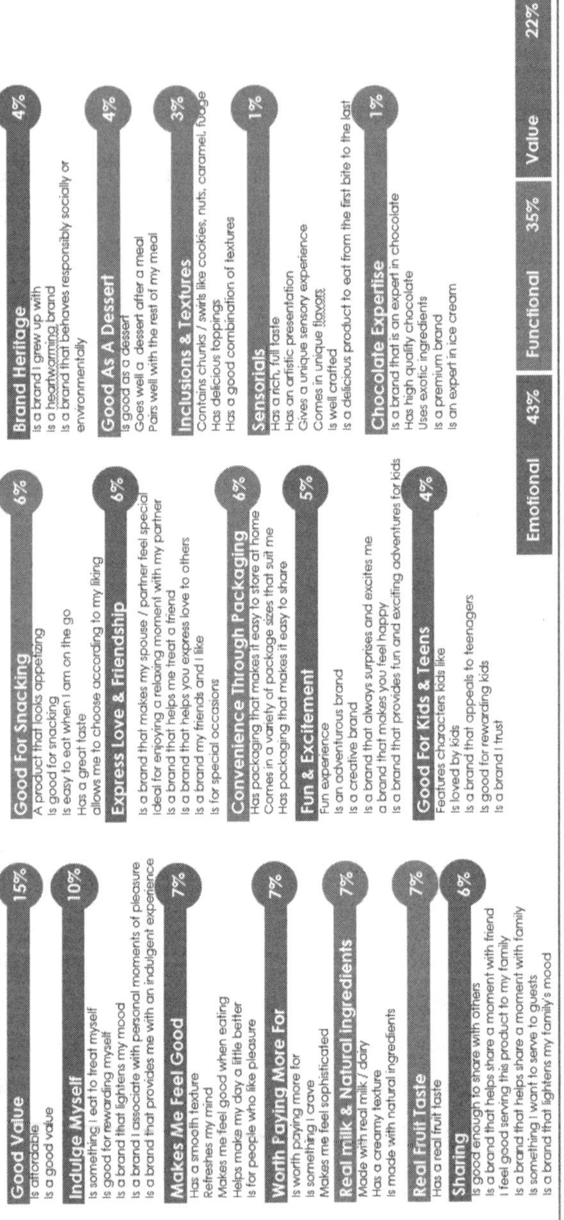
Good Value 15%
Is affordable
Is a good value
Indulge Myself 10%
Is something I eat to treat myself
Is good for rewarding myself
Is a brand that lightens my mood
Is a brand I associate with personal moments of pleasure
Is a brand that provides me with an indulgent experience
Makes Me Feel Good 7%
Has a smooth texture
Refreshes my mind
Makes me feel good when eating
Helps make my day a little better
Is for people who like pleasure
Worth Paying More For 7%
Is worth paying more for
Is something I crave
Makes me feel sophisticated
Real milk & Natural Ingredients 7%
Made with real milk / dairy
Has a creamy texture
Is made with natural ingredients
Real Fruit Taste 7%
Has a real fruit taste
Sharing 6%
Is good enough to share with others
Is a brand that helps share a moment with friend
I feel good serving this product to my family
Is a brand that helps share a moment with family
Is something I want to serve to guests
Is a brand that lightens my family's mood
Good For Snacking 6%
A product that looks appetizing
Is good for snacking
Is easy to eat when I am on the go
Has a great taste
allows me to choose according to my liking
Express Love & Friendship 6%
Is a brand that makes my spouse / partner feel special
Ideal for enjoying a relaxing moment with my partner
Is a brand that helps me treat a friend
Is a brand that helps you express love to others
Is a brand my friends and I like
Is for special occasions
Convenience Through Packaging 6%
Has packaging that makes it easy to store at home
Comes in a variety of package sizes that suit me
Has packaging that makes it easy to share
Fun & Excitement 5%
Fun experience
Is an adventurous brand
Is a creative brand
Is a brand that always surprises and excites me
a brand that makes you feel happy
Is a brand that provides fun and exciting adventures for kids
Good For Kids & Teens 4%
Features characters kids like
Is loved by kids
Is a brand that appeals to teenagers
Is good for rewarding kids
Is a brand I trust
Brand Heritage 4%
Is a brand I grew up with
Is a heartwarming brand
Is a brand that behaves responsibly socially or environmentally
Good As A Dessert 4%
Is good as a dessert
Goes well a dessert after a meal
Pairs well with the rest of my meal
Inclusions & Textures 3%
Contains chunks / swirls like cookies, nuts, caramel, fudge
Has delicious toppings
Has a good combination of textures
Sensorials 1%
Has a rich, full taste
Has an artistic presentation
Gives a unique sensory experience
Comes in unique flavors
Is well crafted
Is a delicious product to eat from the first bite to the last
Chocolate Expertise 1%
Is a brand that is an expert in chocolate
Has high quality chocolate
Uses exotic ingredients
Is a premium brand
Is an expert in ice cream
Emotional 43%
Functional 35%
Value 22%

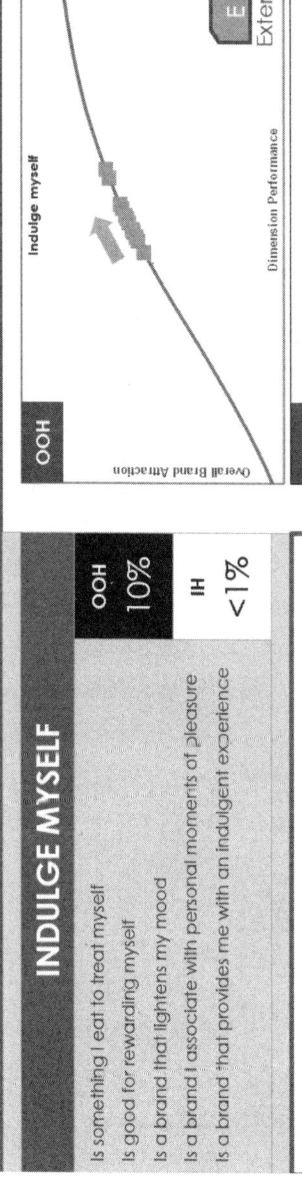
INDULGE MYSELF
Is something I eat to treat myself
Is good for rewarding myself
Is a brand that lightens my mood
Is a brand I associate with personal moments of pleasure
Is a brand that provides me with an indulgent experience
OOH
10%
IH
<1%
SO WHAT?
• Indulgence can be landed through themes of treating/rewarding as well as pleasure. It's a ME-moment!
• A top driver that still offers room for ownership – opportunity for Magnum.
• Indulgence is not as relevant a driver today for the IH space – a whitespace opportunity for the portfolio.
• All brands should at least reassure on this driver OOH.

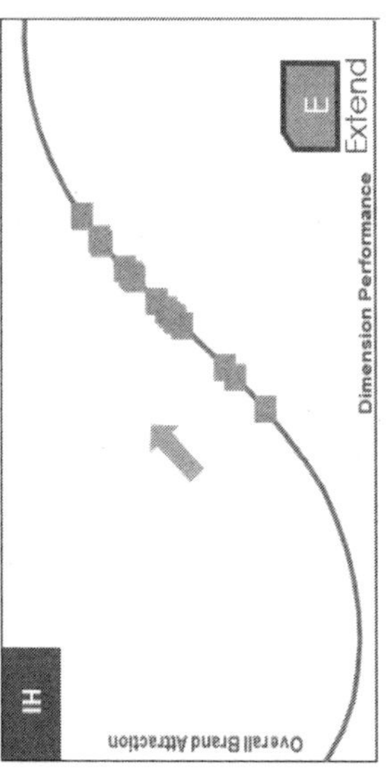
Indulge myself
OOH
Overall Brand Attraction
Dimension Performance
E
Extend
IH
Overall Brand Attraction
Dimension Performance
E
Extend

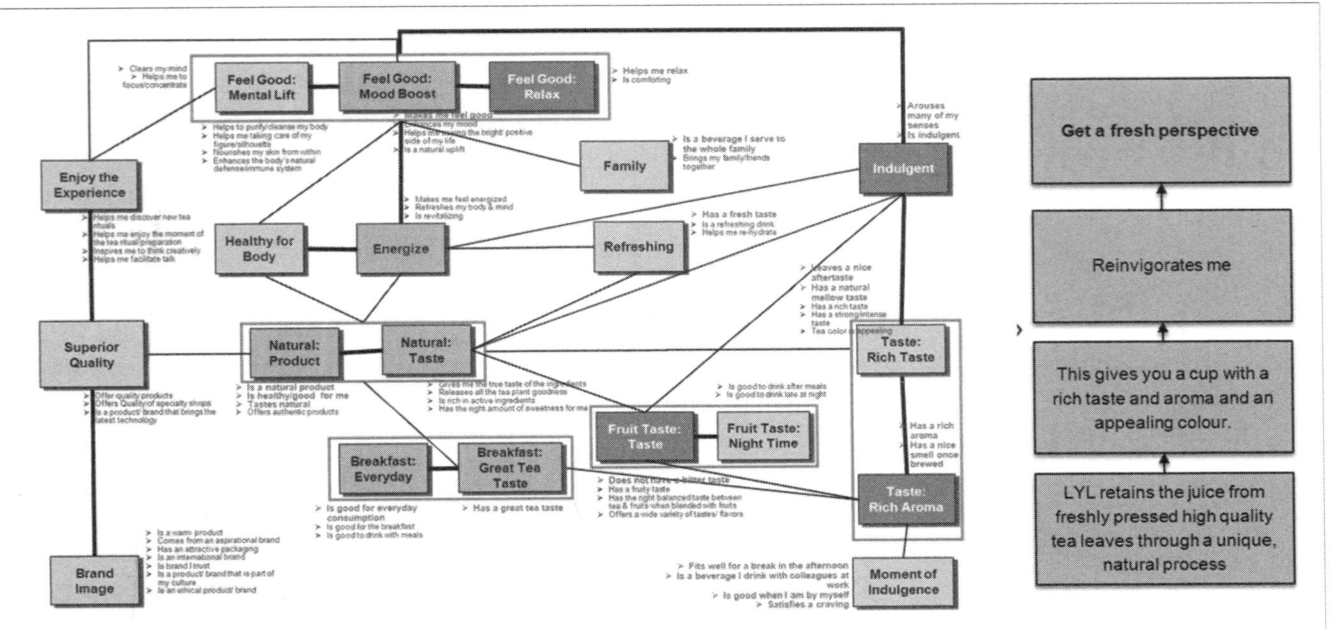
Feel Good: Mental Lift
Feel Good: Mood Boost
Feel Good: Relax
Enjoy the Experience
Family
Indulgent
Healthy for Body
Energize
Refreshing
Superior Quality
Natural: Product
Natural: Taste
Taste: Rich Taste
Fruit Taste: Taste
Fruit Taste: Night Time
Breakfast: Everyday
Breakfast: Great Tea Taste
Taste: Rich Aroma
Brand Image
Moment of Indulgence
Get a fresh perspective
Reinvigorates me
This gives you a cup with a rich taste and aroma and an appealing colour.
LYL retains the juice from freshly pressed high quality tea leaves through a unique, natural process

is finding out the optimum amount of pressure to be applied and best sequence of strings to produce the desired symphony.

The chart above shows the laddering analysis of tea on how the ingredients and process lead to the feeling of reinvigoration and freshness.

Drivers of Product Performance

This entails similar analysis to brand drivers but is done for products. Products are tested blind so that people can react just to the formulation without the halo effect of the brand and rate the products on various attributes and its overall performance. This is typically done for all the key brands in the market so that the results apply to the category rather than just the brand. But the analysis can pull out the drivers on which different products deliver better. Let's look at the example of soaps for the year 2005 in the US. The chart below shows what drives product performance and what drives those drivers. This insight helps the R&D and product development team to tweak the product exactly in a way that would drive product performance.

Let's now have a look at some of the new-age analytics that uses a lot of unstructured data, including big data collected through various sources.

Efficacy and "skin feel" are driving the positive opinion of Caress. Improving the overall fragrance opinion and moisturising feel on skin is the primary modification opportunity amongst those who dislike the bar

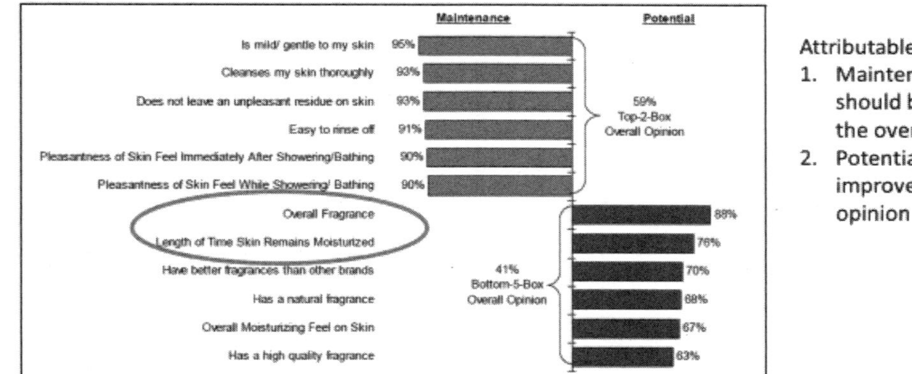

Attributable effects:

1. Maintenance: Positive performance should be maintained in order to retain the overall opinion
2. Potential: If perceptions on these are improved, it would improve the overall opinion

Overall, fragrance is the "gate keeper" – which means improvement in this would drive greater liking of the product. Modification of this fragrance needs to begin with the "root cause" – in other words having more natural and mild fragrances likely to result in pleasant and refreshing feel leading to perceived higher quality of fragrance and overall opinion

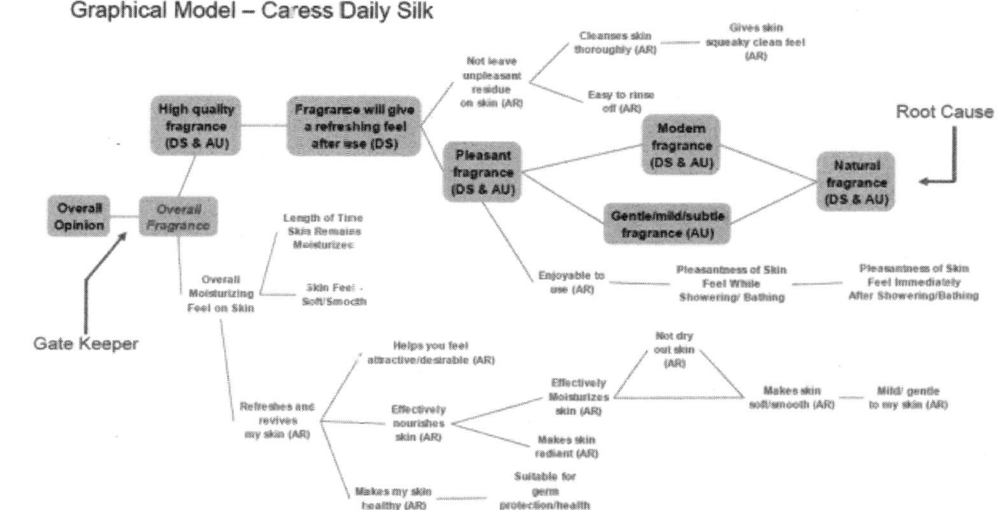

Getting Insights through Online Conversations

With the explosion of social media, there are millions of conversations happening every day on different forums where people are talking about their lives, their joys and sorrows, and sharing pictures to express their feelings. Some of the platforms on which they have these conversations are open for 'listening' in, i.e., third parties can see the conversations happening and analyze them and even participate in those conversations. Platforms like X (formerly Twitter), Reddit, Quora, etc., are largely public, so anyone can see the conversation and follow the entire thread. But some platforms like Facebook and Instagram give the option to users to make their posts private (in which case only their connections or followers can see them) or public, in which case anyone can see them. This allows listening to those conversations allowed by the users' privacy settings.

The reason these conversations provide useful insights for businesses is that these conversations are natural, spontaneous, and unprompted (unlike a market research setting, which is relatively more scripted). Arguably, there is a social façade that people have when talking in public and the analysis does need to factor that in. For instance, Facebook and Instagram are platforms where people like to show off their fabulous lives, while X is where they rant. But the kind of questions they pose can be quite insightful. For instance, if one is looking for beauty trends, a scan through social media is quite useful to understand current definitions of beauty and things that people are willing to do to attain beauty standards. Social conversations are quite useful even when trying to understand brand equity—people spontaneously express their opinions about brands and that can be extremely insightful on the dimensions they are using for talking about the brand, the context in which brand is being referred to, and, of course, what they are saying about it.

While it sounds quite easy, there is a need to apply a contextual lens to this. There are some brands and categories that lend themselves quite easily to social conversations. For instance, there are a lot of conversations about beauty, food, family, travel, etc., but there aren't enough conversations about cleaning toilets or washing clothes and utensils. So, brands like Lakmé and L'Oréal can mine a lot of social conversations, but Surf (Omo or Persil) and Ariel won't have it that easy. Similarly, people talk a lot about teeth whitening but not enough about bad breath. In situations like this, it is important to see the conversations in a broader context, which can actually provide an interesting and strategic perspective. So, while people don't talk about bad breath or toilet cleaners, they do search for solutions to these problems. People may not talk about detergents, but they do talk a lot about fashion and the clothes they are wearing, and the ease or difficulty of caring for them. The 'listener', therefore, needs to listen more intelligently and use different aspects of the big data for analysis to gain an insight.

For instance, at Unilever, we were looking for ideas of new formats of detergents that could be launched in the future. When we looked at the lives of hyper-connected urban population across the world, we realized that convenience was the ultimate currency, because it brought in a lot more efficiency and gave people space to get more out of their lives.

...the real problem is *having to do* laundry instead of spending time on relaxing, exercise, entertainment and other social activities

A convenient solution is "cheating" at home care tasks: when not finding the time for a deep-clean, consumers are looking for ways to make their homes/clothes *seem* clean instead

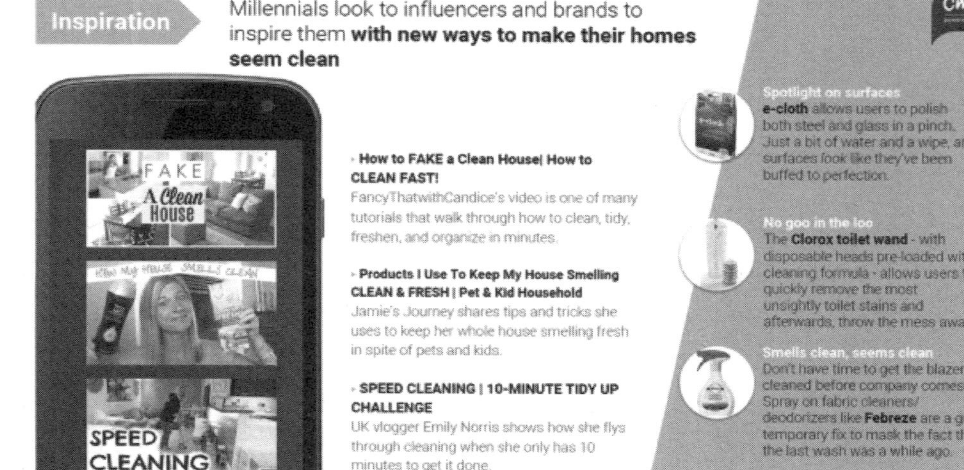

The question then emerged: What does 'convenience' mean when it comes to doing the laundry? You can find answers to such questions through social media conversations and searches quite easily than trying to understand what people need from a detergent or how they wash clothes. And this discourse also allows for the conversation to be elevated to a higher strategic level giving a far better insight into innovations that are likely to be developed in the future.

Gaining insights through images is becoming another big source—estimates suggest that over three billion images are uploaded every day. Not every image is accompanied with an explanatory text, and images themselves are capable of conveying a lot more about the mood and setting than the context and the caption accompanying it (an image does speak more than a thousand words).

Unilever CMI teams developed a proprietary in-house capability (called 'Pixel') that uses Computer Vision Technology and cloud computing solutions for analyzing images at a large scale and to extract valuable insights from image-heavy social media platforms, such as X (Twitter), Instagram, and Pinterest.

An interesting and successful use case for this was developing an ad for an Indian tea brand Taj Mahal. The brand had a long heritage of using music maestros enjoying the tea and performing their best ("Wah Taj!" ads), but in recent times, these ads weren't being as appreciated as before. The team decided to look at pictures of how people drink tea, in order to understand different moods and settings associated with tea, and here is what they found:

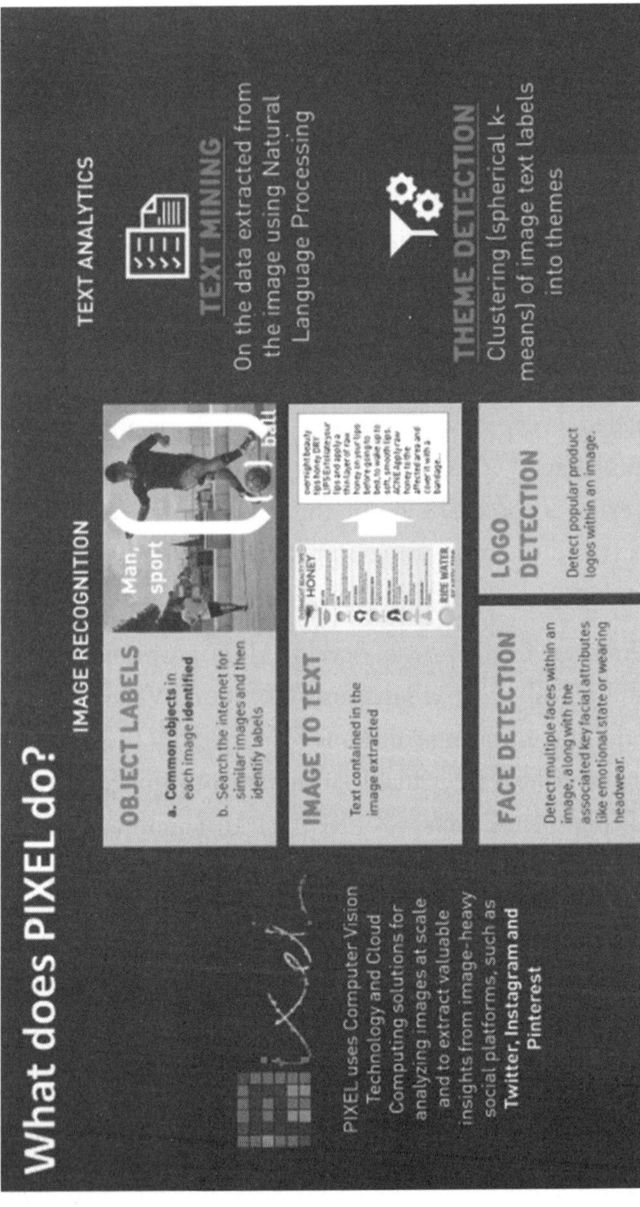
What does PIXEL do?
PIXEL uses Computer Vision Technology and Cloud Computing solutions for analyzing images at scale and to extract valuable insights from image-heavy social platforms, such as Twitter, Instagram and Pinterest
IMAGE RECOGNITION
OBJECT LABELS
a. Common objects in each image identified
b. Search the internet for similar images and then identify labels
Man, sport
ball
IMAGE TO TEXT
Text contained in the image extracted
FACE DETECTION
Detect multiple faces within an image, along with the associated key facial attributes like emotional state or wearing headwear.
LOGO DETECTION
Detect popular product logos within an image.
TEXT ANALYTICS
TEXT MINING
On the data extracted from the image using Natural Language Processing
THEME DETECTION
Clustering (spherical k-means) of image text labels into themes

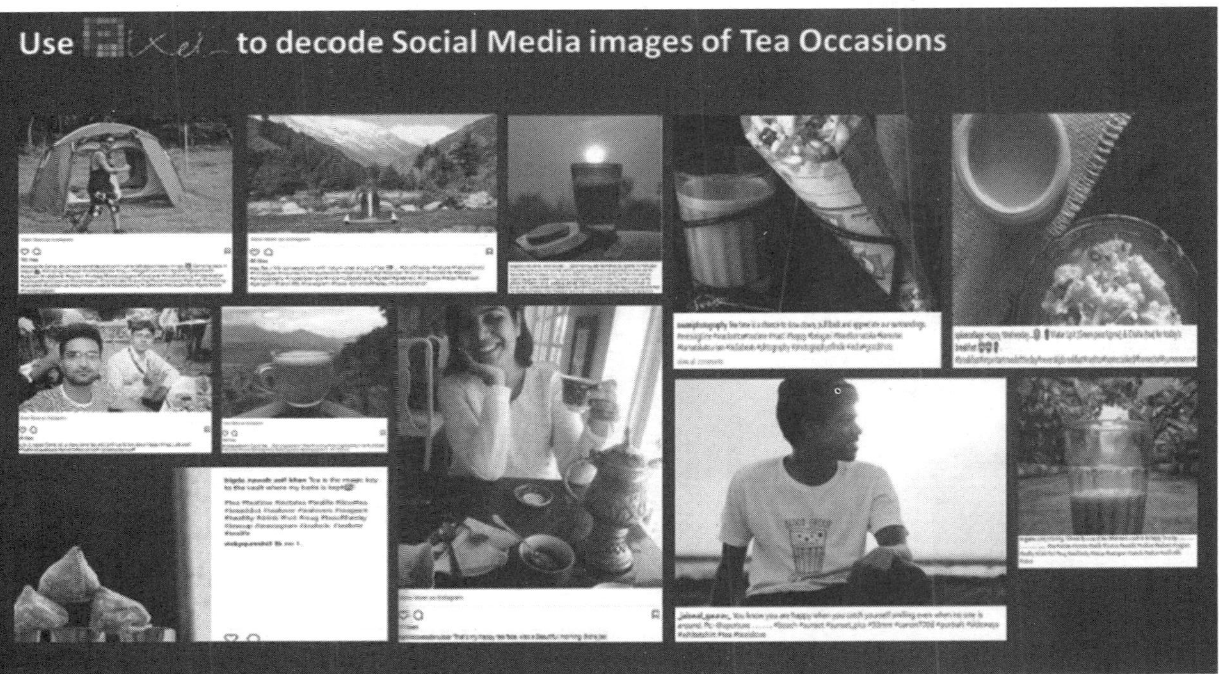
Use
to decode Social Media images of Tea Occasions

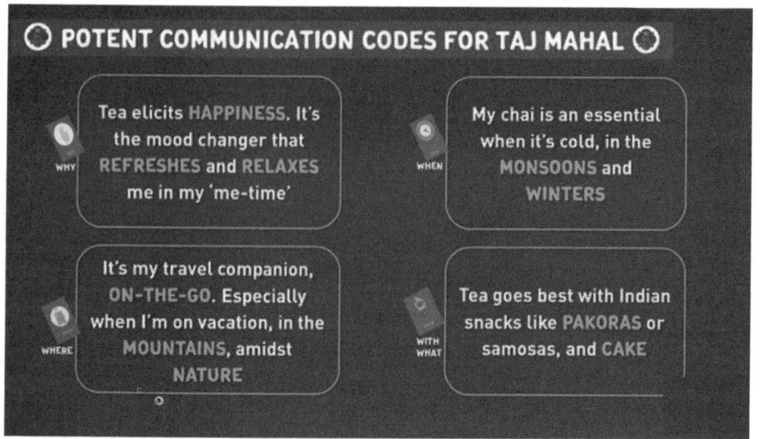

The team used these insights to produce an ad with a music maestro playing music outdoors (with a beautiful backdrop of Dal Lake in Kashmir) inspired by the tea that enhanced the mood of everyone around him. Thus, the brand used its heritage combined with the insights to make a new ad which worked brilliantly in pre-testing and post-launch of the product This gave a new direction to the advertising for the brand.

Predicting Trends before They Happen

As consumer lifestyles and choices undergo rapid shifts, 'fast' moving consumer good companies need to keep pace with them in order to offer the right products that are 'in trend'. Unilever CMI developed a proprietary tool (an award-winning tool in different forums across the world) to predict the trends in a market. Conceptually, the way it works is as follows:

1. Identify current category trends in the market: Using Google search analytics, YouTube videos, Pinterest

Prioritization Matrix

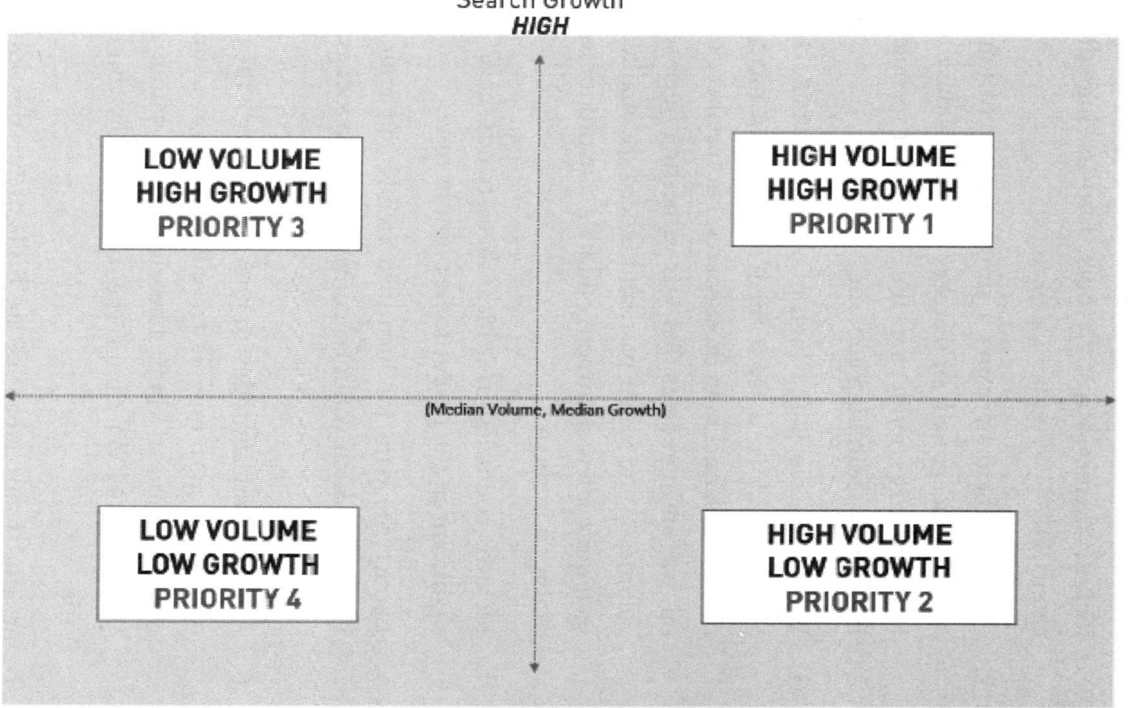

boards, databases like Euromonitor, Mintel, etc., to identify themes across flavours, formats, ingredients, claims, etc.

2. Prioritize them by using a simple matrix: Volume of searches and growth of searches on each of the theme. High-priority trends are the ones that people are increasingly searching a lot for.
3. Validate to see if the high-priority ones make sense: Simple check is to see if there has been an increasing number of launches in those spaces. For instance, 'onion oil' was an ingredient that was witnessing huge search volumes in the recent past, and indeed the market had seen quite a few shampoos and hair care products with onion oil in them.
4. Identify countries in which these trends have been significant in the past at some point in time.
5. Extract the data for identified trends and countries: Data like search volumes, conversations, launches, and so on.
6. Apply statistical models to understand where the trend originated and how it travelled in those countries over a period of time: Theories like Dynamic Time Warping (DTW), Graph theory, etc., allow you to do this.

Beauty and food categories are brilliant for this kind of trend mapping. Imagine looking at new things rolled out in Paris Fashion Week in summer and using this tool to predict when and which of these patterns and fabrics would appear in the wardrobes of women in small towns of US, Brazil, India, or China. Knowing this in advance gives a huge space for businesses to prepare and nurture the offerings in identified spaces well before they actually occur.

Hindustan Unilever Ltd. (in India) has a brand called Lakmé which is one of the leading-edge beauty and fashion brands in the country. It has a long-standing heritage of being India's first cosmetic brand and has introduced most Indian women to their make-up regime. As the most trusted make-up brand in India, it plays a role of democratizing trends for Indian women by bringing them to India. Lakmé was, therefore, the right brand to use this capability to identify the innovations it should introduce in the Indian market.

The established trends considered for this analysis were—matte, prime, nude, winged eyeliner, lip lacquer, coloured eyeliner, contouring, highlighter, bronzer, and make-up setting spray. Around 20 countries were shortlisted where these trends were big at some point in time and the analytics were applied to understand leading markets, transmitter markets, and follower markets for these trends.

This methodology showed that 'matte' lipstick was trending in the U.S. and the UK in 2017 and it was predicted to become big in India between 2019 and 2020.

This helped Lakmé to activate the matt trend in India and they used it on the Lakmé Absolute range in the Lakmé Fashion Week in 2019.

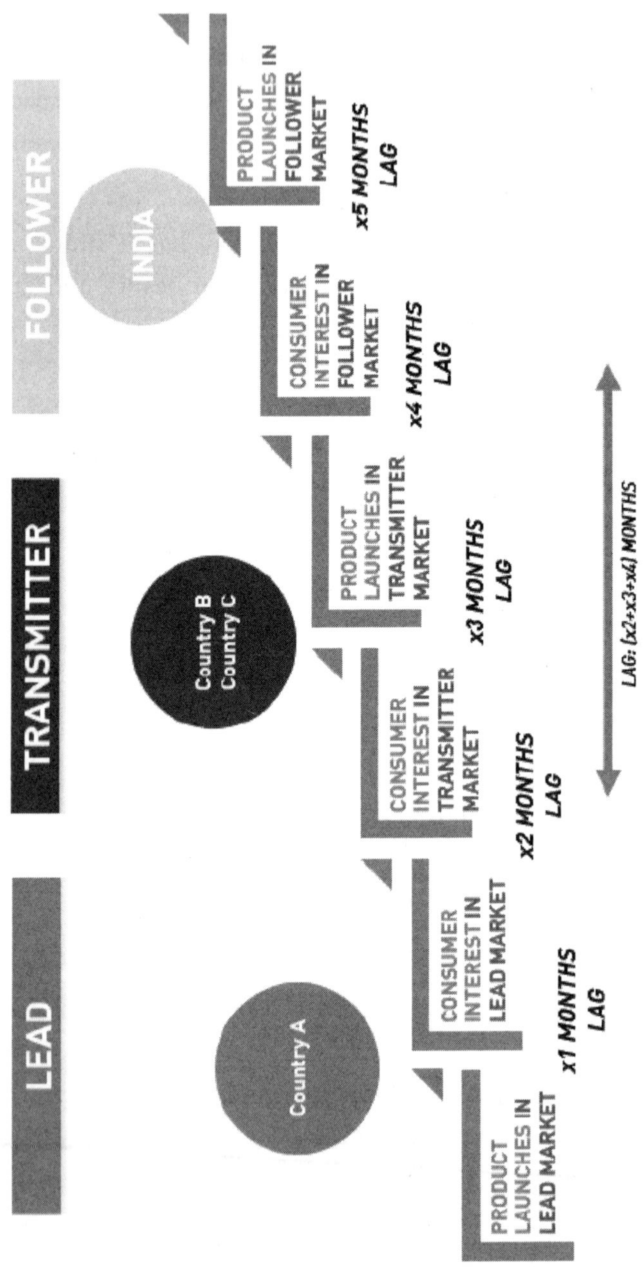
LEAD
TRANSMITTER
FOLLOWER
Country A
Country B
Country C
INDIA
PRODUCT LAUNCHES IN LEAD MARKET
x1 MONTHS LAG
CONSUMER INTEREST IN LEAD MARKET
x2 MONTHS LAG
CONSUMER INTEREST IN TRANSMITTER MARKET
x3 MONTHS LAG
PRODUCT LAUNCHES IN TRANSMITTER MARKET
x4 MONTHS LAG
CONSUMER INTEREST IN FOLLOWER MARKET
x5 MONTHS LAG
PRODUCT LAUNCHES IN FOLLOWER MARKET
LAG: (x2+x3+x4) MONTHS

Country X
Country Y
INDIA
Country Y and India Search Volumes
0
5000
10000
15000
20000
25000
30000
35000
40000
45000
50000
Country X Search Volumes
0
20000
40000
60000
80000
100000
120000
140000
160000
Jun-14
Jul-14
Aug-14
Sep-14
Oct-14
Nov-14
Dec-14
Jan-15
Feb-15
Mar-15
Apr-15
May-15
Jun-15
Jul-15
Aug-15
Sep-15
Oct-15
Nov-15
Dec-15
Jan-16
Feb-16
Mar-16
Apr-16
May-16
Jun-16
Jul-16
Aug-16
Sep-16
Oct-16
Nov-16
Dec-16
Jan-17
Feb-17
Mar-17
Apr-17
May-17
Jun-17
Jul-17
Aug-17
Sep-17
Oct-17
Nov-17
Dec-17
Jan-18
Feb-18
Mar-18
Apr-18
May-18

Several other brands like Dove, Pond's, TRESemmé also use this method extensively to prioritize innovations for their portfolios.

Measuring and Optimizing Performance of Digital Campaigns

This is one of the 'always on' kind of analytics that allows the teams to optimize the spends on the right asset in almost real time. This is usually a dashboard that shows the impressions (or completed views of videos), clicks, engagement, costs, and comparison over a period of time to enable benchmarking. The details by vehicle (Facebook, You Tube, etc.) and by audience are

Key Metrics

Metric Indicators: ▲ or ▼ related to the performance of the selected date range compared with the same number of days immediately prior - allowing for week-on-week, month-on-month, etc. comparisons

COST	IMPRESSIONS	Engagement Rate
XXX EUR	7bn	5.92%
EUR Prior Period	(Blank) Prior Period	(Blank) Prior Period
▲ Growth Rate	▲ Growth Rate	▲ Growth Rate
CTR	**Avg. CPM**	**CPV**
0.49%	XXX EUR	XXX EUR
(Blank) Prior Period	EUR Prior Period	EUR Prior Period
▲ Growth Rate	▲ Growth Rate	▲ Growth Rate
Clicks	**Completed Views**	**Video Completion Rate**
37M	2bn	43.07%
(Blank) Prior Period	(Blank) Prior Period	(Blank) Prior Period
▲ Growth Rate	▲ Growth Rate	▲ Growth Rate

Digital Media Performance Tracker (DMPT) dashboard provides continuous insight on the digital campaigns that helps optimise investment on an on going basis

Social Media Platform over Time

cement Type ● Facebook ● Youtube

Select Metric

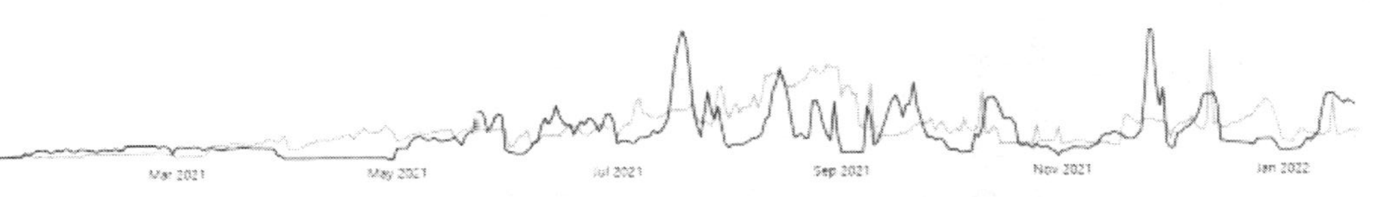

also provided to see the effectiveness of campaigns across them. This enables the teams to regularly compare the performance of each campaign and optimize the spends on the go.

An example of the part of this dashboard for a category for first few months in 2021 is given above:

Framework for Analytics Capabilities

Some of the examples talked about in the section above illustrate different analytics used in businesses. But how does a business think about them strategically and create a plan to create and prioritize different models? In my view, there are two ways to look at it:

The first framework provides an organization with a broad view of the kind of analytics it should be setting up. This framework looks at the models from the view of providing strategic inputs that can be used for long-term planning against those for managing an ongoing performance. When juxtaposed this with the ability of the model to give a wider cross-category view against a narrow brand or category view, it provides a good strategic guidance as shown in the chart below.

Any organization needs to have each of these quadrants but depending on the priorities, some would need to be emphasized over others. For instance, an organization looking at inorganic growth via acquisition needs to have enough models in the first quadrant, whereas several models operate at any point in time to make an organization perform and deliver on 'business as usual' in the performance management for core category quadrant.

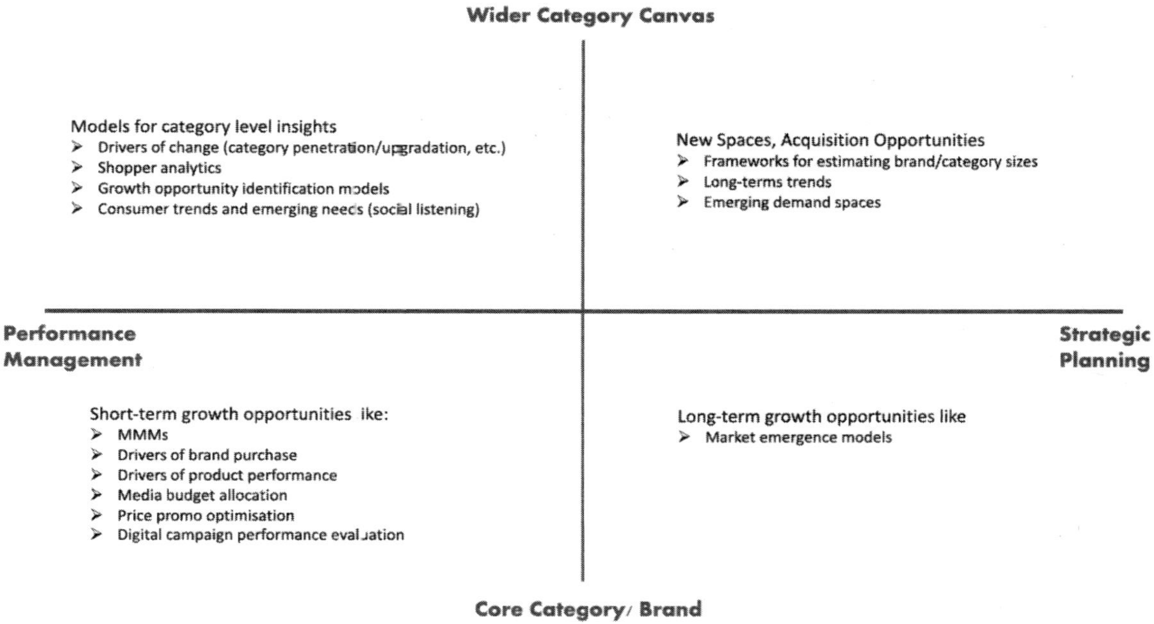

Wider Category Canvas

Models for category level insights
- Drivers of change (category penetration/upgradation, etc.)
- Shopper analytics
- Growth opportunity identification models
- Consumer trends and emerging needs (social listening)

New Spaces, Acquisition Opportunities
- Frameworks for estimating brand/category sizes
- Long-terms trends
- Emerging demand spaces

Performance Management

Strategic Planning

Short-term growth opportunities like:
- MMMs
- Drivers of brand purchase
- Drivers of product performance
- Media budget allocation
- Price promo optimisation
- Digital campaign performance evaluation

Long-term growth opportunities like
- Market emergence models

Core Category/ Brand

Second framework is primarily more for the analytics team to understand the kind of models that need to be developed to meet the needs identified above. The technology and capabilities needed are quite different for different models. So, one axis is about traditional modelling methods (like MMM), while new-age ones is about social listening or analytics. The resources needed, on the other hand, also differ on whether the model is a one-time exercise or an 'always on'.

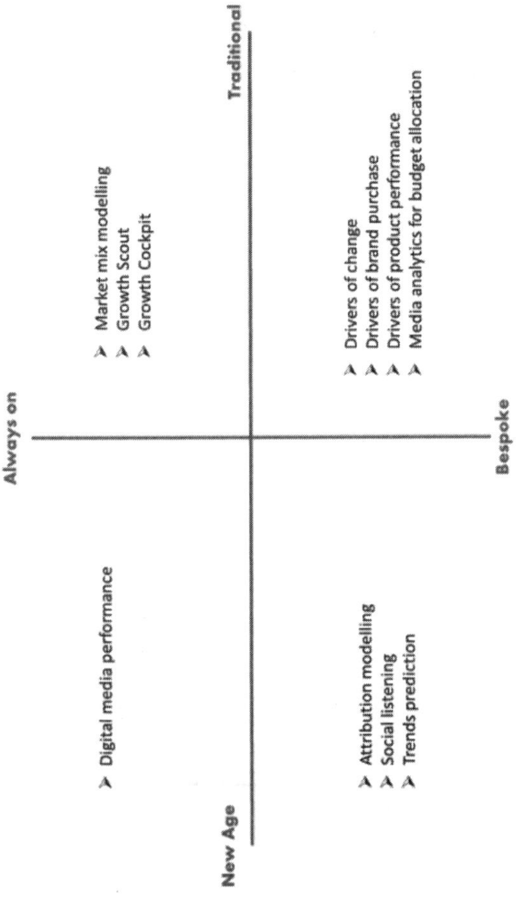

Implications for Marketing and Insights Professionals

Analytics as a field has existed for several decades but the capabilities have exploded with processing speed of computers and AI coming into the fray. Every organization has tons of data that it can analyze to improve the speed and efficiency of serving its customers. The framework in this chapter is meant to give ideas on what kind of analytics should an organization be using and how should it go about building analytics capabilities. The implications for the marketing and insights teams looking into this are:

- Identify the data or information that the organization has.
- Create a clear data strategy: what data do we have, what can we do with it, how do we gather more, how should it be organized and analyzed. And here, by data, the reference is not just to consumer-first party data, but data about everything consumer behaviour data, purchase data, sales data, or it could also be supply chain data or even employees' data.
- Based on the data available and data strategy, the frameworks and examples in this chapter can be used to identify the role of analytics in helping grow the business.

- Then comes building analytics capabilities—decision to develop it in-house or in partnership with analytics firms (depending on the nature of data, capabilities needed, etc.).

Analytics, when combined with insights, can indeed be that engine that is capable of powering the growth of the business more than any other lever. But, it could also become an untamed beast, and, therefore, needs to be nurtured with care, skills, and expertise.

CHAPTER 9

Talent Development in Insights

What are the skills that are needed to be a part of an insights team (or a marketing team looking after insights) of an organization and how are they evolving over a period of time? There is often a debate on the skills needed to be in research and analytics companies that provide services to organizations, as against the skills needed for insights and analytics team in the client or user organization—people think it's the same job, just on different sides of the table. The chapter on evolution of an organization towards consumer centricity provides information on the way insights team operates along the evolution. However, there is merit in articulating those separately, as the organizations looking to enhance consumer centricity and people looking to make their careers in the client organizations would need to know what it takes to embed insights in the decision-making process.

Unilever looks at the talent development on two dimensions—skills and competencies. The skills are about 'what' people do in their jobs, while competencies are about 'how' people do their jobs. Applying that thinking to the talent in insights industry:

1. **Skills:** These are the capabilities that people need in order to do their job. These are developed through training and experience over time and needs refreshing every few years, just like we sharpen tools regularly. In the insights space, the skills needed are in the area of statistics, psychology, research methodologies, and processes. In analytics, on the other hand, the required skills are in data science which involves statistical modelling, creating algorithms for analytics and tools needed for that. The broad area of skills for an insight manager are:

    a) Underlying principles of market research
    b) Analysis and interpretation of data
    c) Understanding and appreciation of face-to-face interactions, qualitative research, and digital methodologies
    d) Understanding and appreciation of strategic research
    e) Design and manage research projects
    f) Design and manage research programs for a brand or category or market
    g) Maximize value from the research partners
    h) Understanding of idea generation and development
    i) Understanding of product and pack tests

j) Understanding of mix screening and tests (STMs)
k) Understanding pricing research
l) Understanding communication research
m) Understanding shopper research
n) Understanding in-market performance tracking and evaluation
o) Understanding application of analytical modelling
p) Understanding data mining, etc.

Arguably, these are also the skills needed for individuals working in research companies that service clients. They would need to understand the methodologies and analysis in order to offer the best solution to their clients.

So, what differentiates a client insight manager from a manager at a research agency? In my experience the two roles, while being on different sides of the same table, are actually quite far from each other. There is a sort of a bridge that a person needs to cross in order to come to the other side of the table. The client insight managers obviously needs to have good skills for research, but they also have a seat at the table of the brand or category or market that they are working for in their organizations. This means that they need to understand the business ambition and the strategy of their business unit and should be able to create an insights plan that would help the business meet their ambition. And they need to find the right research agency and analytics partners to be able to generate the insights needed, which isn't as simple as it sounds. Additionally, once they get the insights, they need to be able to communicate those to the business and influence the right decisions—this requires stakeholder management. In many ways, the client insight manager's job begins where the research agency manager's job ends. In Unilever parlance, these are defined as 'competencies' and are about how things are done.

It's not that the research agency managers don't need these competencies, they do need them in order to partner with their clients on the best solutions. But the emphasis tends to be a lot more on the skills than competencies in an agency because it's their skills that get them the business. And the competencies they need are different from the competencies required for an insight manager that are described below:

2. **Competencies:** Some of the competencies used in Unilever are in the following areas, though they do evolve over a period of time:

    a) **Passion for growth:** The ability to understand how the business would grow; being passionate about finding ideas that would lead to growth and bringing those ideas to life; possessing entrepreneurial ability to some extent to reach for the new possibilities.

    b) **Breakthrough thinking:** Understanding business opportunities and obstacles and being able to come up with insights, trends, new ideas, and concepts, and having the conviction to try and implement those.

    c) **Organizational awareness:** The ability to understand organizational culture; formal and informal networks; ways the decisions are taken and the ability to influence them.

d) **Change catalyst:** Being receptive towards new things; being able to set a clear vision for the change needed; propagating the change through own and team's actions.

e) **Strategic influencing:** Recognizing the need to persuade different stakeholders at different points in time; drawing upon the insight on how individuals and teams think and decide; ability to build support and energy behind the right project and so on.

f) **Nurturing talent:** Actively seeking opportunities for self and team development; identifying right talent and supporting them in their growth through coaching, experiences, etc.; creating a mindset of development across the business; identifying right talent in external partners who can support the business and groom them over a period of time.

These skills and competencies work hand in hand, and both are needed for success. Typically, as the individual rises to a senior position in the organization, the competencies become a lot more important for success, but without losing the skills. Competencies—or 'how' a person works—defines the leadership style and the way the individual is able to collaborate with the business for the insights to be most impactful.

How do these skills and competencies change and what is needed to future-proof insights professionals (so that they always remain relevant)? Given the in-roads that artificial intelligence and machine learning have already made in this field, it is important to upgrade the skills as the machines have already taken over a lot of manual work. In my view, some of

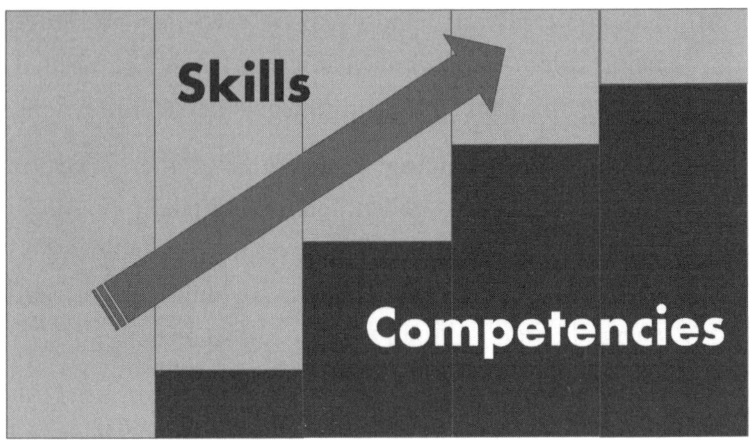

the capabilities that would keep insight managers relevant in the future are:

a) **Creativity and originality:** Creativity is still the domain of human beings and would remain so for a long time, even though machines can now create music and paint. It is the ability to think logically and go on a path evaluating different hypotheses that is still valid and will remain the right way of approaching a problem.

b) **Critical thinking and analysis:** This is not in contrast to creativity, rather complements it. It is the ability to think logically and go on a path evaluating different hypotheses is still and would remain right way of approaching a problem.

c) **Being technodexterous:** The ability to work with technology comfortably and adapting it to suit the needs. Technology needs to be our ally, instead of us being slaves to it. But that requires some understanding of changing tech and how it can be of use.

d) **Leadership and social influence:** The ability to influence the right stakeholders and take charge in different situations would always be needed, in every sphere of life.

e) **Emotional intelligence:** Enough has been said about this in the corporate literature but suffice to say that the ability to understand and empathize with others enhances the human connections and influence.

Implications for Marketing and Insights Professionals

Insights professionals need to constantly keep upgrading themselves not just on the new and upcoming methodologies and technologies but also on the new management practices of partnering the business in the right manner. Insights professionals should aim to be 'thinking partners' for businesses—as they can strategically influence the decisions and decision-makers—and that requires regular upgradation of skills and competencies. McKinsey & Company has identified 13 skills and competencies that professionals should have to future-proof themselves; I believe all of these apply to insights professionals as well:

Cognitive

Critical thinking
- Structured problem solving
- Logical reasoning
- Understanding biases
- Seeking relevant information

Planning and ways of working
- Work-plan development
- Time management and prioritization
- Agile thinking

Communication
- Storytelling and public speaking
- Asking the right questions
- Synthesizing messages
- Active listening

Mental flexibility
- Creativity and imagination
- Translating knowledge to different contexts
- Adopting a different perspective
- Adaptability
- Ability to learn

Interpersonal

Mobilizing systems
- Role modeling
- Win–win negotiations
- Crafting an inspiring vision
- Organizational awareness

Developing relationships
- Empathy
- Inspiring trust
- Humility
- Sociability

Teamwork effectiveness
- Fostering inclusiveness
- Motivating different personalities
- Resolving conflicts
- Collaboration
- Coaching
- Empowering

Self-leadership

Self-awareness and self-management

- Understanding own emotions and triggers
- Self-control and regulation
- Understanding own strengths
- Integrity
- Self-motivation and wellness
- Self-confidence

Entrepreneurship

- Courage and risk-taking
- Driving change and innovation
- Energy, passion, and optimism
- Breaking orthodoxies

Goals achievement

- Ownership and decisiveness
- Achievement orientation
- Grit and persistence
- Coping with uncertainty
- Self-development

Digital

Digital fluency and citizenship

- Digital literacy
- Digital learning
- Digital collaboration
- Digital ethics

Software use and development

- Programming literacy
- Data analysis and statistics
- Computational and algorithmic thinking

Understanding digital systems

- Data literacy
- Smart systems
- Cybersecurity literacy
- Tech translation and enablement

Source: Defining the Skills Citizens Will Need in the Future of Work: McKinsey article dated June 25, 2021.

CHAPTER 10

New Product Development in Customer-Centric Organizations

Developing new products and innovating current ones is an imperative for all organizations, irrespective of the industry they operate in. There are several reasons why constant innovation and refreshing ideas are necessary for a customer-centric organization:

1. **Changing market circumstances:** The conditions in which businesses and customers operate often change. For instance, in the times of low inflation (when oil prices are low as well), several local and unbranded detergent bars pop up in developing countries like India because the technology barrier to enter the category in such categories is low (in other words, anyone can make the detergent bars

relatively easily). So, when oil prices are not high, several local entrepreneurs make those bars and start selling them thereby tapping into the opportunity provided by low and affordable oil prices. But when the inflation goes up, the margins of those businesses dry up and they can't increase prices because they sell their products as commodities, and hence these local products disappear from the shelves. Consumers are then hit by the double whammy of cheaper products disappearing from the market and branded products becoming more expensive because of inflation. This changes the market and consumer dynamics; and detergent manufacturers need to have innovative ideas to deal with such situations.

2. **Technological changes in the way the products or services are used:** Think about the way content is consumed today as opposed to the appointment-viewing on TV ten years ago. Or, the way banking has changed with smartphones thereby reducing the need to visit the banks physically. In the FMCG world, technology brings in not just new products, but also the way they are bought by consumers. For instance, body washes offer a superior bathing experience than bar soaps, or detergent capsules wash clothes better than powders in the same washing machine. Similarly, as consumers move towards e-commerce for buying their groceries, brands need to adapt to the new purchase environment and learn to compete on virtual shelves. While leading-edge brands and businesses introduce the change, rapid adoption by consumers forces other brands to follow as well, resulting in complete change of market.

3. **Changing consumer context:** People get older, their incomes change, their household size changes, their kids grow up and start influencing the consumption at home, and so on. When these changes happen at a broader level, they bring massive changes in the way products and services are consumed. Consider some interesting facts about per capita GDP (nominal) growth in four markets across the world and growth in the number of cars in these markets:

   The per capita GDPs of India, Indonesia, the U.S., and the UK show that Indian per cap GDP (nominal) grew over 200% from mid 1990s to mid 2010s, while Indonesian per cap GDP doubled and both the U.S. and the UK went up by 40% (Source: IMF, Nominal per cap GDP at current prices). Please see the table below:

	UK	INDIA	US	INDONESIA
1994	$21,460	$346	$27,674	$1,116
1995	$23,171	$374	$28,671	$1,254
1996	$24,433	$400	$29,947	$1,394
1997	$26,773	$415	$31,440	$1,308
1998	$28,283	$413	$32,834	$572
1999	$28,768	$441	$34,496	$830
2000	$28,338	$442	$36,313	$870
2001	$27,917	$450	$37,101	$834
2002	$30,127	$469	$37,946	$1,003
2003	$34,480	$544	$39,405	$1,186

	UK	INDIA	US	INDONESIA
2004	$40,411	$624	$41,642	$1,280
2005	$42,144	$711	$44,034	$1,404
2006	$44,590	$802	$46,217	$1,766
2007	$50,420	$1,023	$47,943	$2,064
2008	$47,884	$994	$48,471	$2,417
2009	$38,892	$1,097	$47,102	$2,469
2010	$39,642	$1,351	$48,586	$3,177
2011	$42,107	$1,450	$50,008	$3,690
2012	$42,502	$1,434	$51,737	$3,740
2013	$43,470	$1,438	$53,364	$3,667
2014	$47,468	$1,560	$55,264	$3,533
2015	$44,979	$1,590	$57,007	$3,368
2016	$41,115	$1,714	$58,180	$3,605
2017	$40,618	$1,958	$60,293	$3,886
2018	$43,275	$1,974	$63,165	$3,946
2019	$42,713	$2,050	$65,505	$4,193
2020	$40,246	$1,916	$64,367	$3,919
2021	$46,704	$2,250	$70,996	$4,358
2022	$45,730	$2,366	$77,192	$4,799
2023	$49,099	$2,500	$81,632	$4,942

The per capita GDP of India remains lowest among these international markets (because of high population) even though India ranks among the fourth-largest in the world today in terms of absolute GDP. This has meant more than doubling of average income for families in India. This has resulted in increased consumption of expensive good and services and improving the lifestyle of people. This is reflected quite appropriately through the growth in the number of cars sold (in millions) between 2010 to 2020 in these markets.

CARS SOLD (MILLIONS)	2010	2020	GROWTH
India	127.70	295.80	132%
Indonesia	15.80	22.60	43%
United States	250.00	276.00	10%
United Kingdom	30.30	32.70	8%

4. **Brands become outdated and need to periodically reinvent themselves:** This can happen due to several reasons: changing consumer trends (e.g., people taking photos on smartphones affect the sales of digital cameras); competition offering newer functional and emotional benefits (e.g., shampoos offering hair colour protection for people who colour their hair, making this a hygiene factor for all the brands to have this feature in a short span of time); refreshing brand's positioning (e.g., in India, the skin cream brand changed its name from Fair & Lovely to Glow & Lovely to keep in line with the evolving codes of beauty); and so on.

While the reasons for innovation may vary, it is clear that businesses need to have an innovation engine that enables them to develop new products (under new brand names or brand extensions of existing brands, depending on the context) and refresh, modernize, evolve, or improve existing ones, so that they don't become obsolete. However, the way the new product development or innovation ecosystem is built within an organization, depends on the fundamental DNA of the organization. In my view, there are four different types of organizations, and they have very different approaches to the way they create products or services:

1. **Product-centric organizations:** A product-centric company is the one that focuses primarily on developing new and advanced products, irrespective of its demand in the market. There was a time when most of the large organizations were primarily product-centric. Remember the famous statement of T. Ford "You can buy Ford car of any colour you want, as long as it's black"—that is a reflection of a typical product-centric sentiment. These companies spend heavily in R&D and have real expertise in the products they make and innovations around them. Companies like automobile companies, white goods manufacturers, non-banking financial companies (those into mutual funds, insurance, etc.) tend to be product-centric organizations, though that's a broad generalization. Tech companies like Apple and Google are also said to be heavily product-centric since they understand the 'product' and its technicalities more than anyone else. Furthermore, true visionary product-centric companies also tend to be 'market-driving' companies. With their vision of what the products could be, they drive the

market and bring in changes that no one else could foresee. Apple and Google are good examples of market-driving, product-centric organizations.

These product-centric organizations typically innovate their products using their own expertise and technical know-how. They truly understand how a product can perform better or how a mutual fund can deliver better returns for that matter. And, hence, in the past, they used to focus more on the product than consumers or customers. Their innovations usually had a pipeline of product improvements for years in advance. Think of Intel chips; they had a plan for the enhancements in their chips years in advance. Their assumption being: consumers are always looking for new and improved products. Bringing in consumer centricity in these organizations ensures that they are looking at consumer needs in tandem with the product improvement. For instance, when a refrigerator brand introduced vegetable tray on the top shelf of the fridge and freezer at the bottom shelf, it was based on the observation that people used vegetable tray a lot more often than the freezer. Therefore, placing it on the top shelf made it convenient for them.

As an organization, 3M prides itself on being product-centric, but has also taken several steps towards being customer-centric. Having an insights team that works closely with the designers and bringing in effective methods to gain consumer insights has helped them move along that journey. A lot of work done by them is exploratory in nature (rather than being evaluative). The emphasis is on listening to the voice of the consumer early on in the product development cycle rather than applying standard protocols of research at the later stage of development. This kind of early exploration work opens the eyes of people on the customer feedback about the idea being developed or the real issues they face in the problem that is being attempted to solve by the designers. Therefore, it's not about large sample sizes but about finding the right people, often 'super' users of the category (those who are heavy users and are highly involved in the product), and asking them the right questions. Often, it's also about understanding what people can't articulate or reading between the lines.

Before Apple came out with iPod (their portable media players), consumers would have never said that they miss having such a device or that they would want one with a touch screen. But designers who know the tech capabilities and what people really want can combine the two to create successful products. Product-centric companies have to walk a tight rope balancing what consumers want and what the technological or service possibilities are. The insights teams usually play the role of creating that balance and bringing in the voice of consumer to influence the product decisions at the right stage.

2. **Finance-centric organizations:** These are also called revenue-driven organizations as they are a lot more driven to maximize revenue (sales and profit). Product-driven companies prioritize creating great products, but finance-driven ones are naturally more focused on the financial growth. Both can't happen without each other, but finance-driven companies would put in a lot of emphasis

on identifying growth opportunities first and then creating the right products and services around it. The opportunities are usually identified by looking externally at the competitors and other markets to draw inspiration. These companies tend to involve all employees across functions in cutting costs, boosting profits, and growing customer base (to increase the revenue). Every business initiative like new launches, new activities, etc., must justify itself on its contribution to the bottom line and anything that's not paying off is mercilessly done away with. For such organizations, financial transparency is a must. And, hence, there is a lot of emphasis on analytics that provide details of how much things cost and how much money they bring in.

Feels like a bit of a cliché, but, generally speaking, banks and non-banking financial companies tend to be finance-focused (not that others aren't). A bank's emphasis is on increasing their deposits and securing a large customer base that it can lend to at lowest possible cost. Therefore, they tend to look for opportunities to get new customers to deposit their money and take loans by expanding their branches, making more accessible ATMs, and so on. There hasn't been too much of innovation on how banks make money; this hasn't changed for centuries because basic principles have remained the same. The banks' act of collecting and lending money is very different from understanding consumer needs for money which include: having an insight on the aspirations of what people want to do with the money, or difficulties they face in understanding a lot of financial jargons and processes around their money, or what makes people risk averse as opposed to trusting someone with their money. A little bit of that insight would help banks add a human touch while designing their products, branches, and their customer recruitment programs rather than treat it as a mechanical and transactional activity, the way customers often feel when they interact with bankers.

Venture Capital firms are another set of organizations that tend to be finance-driven—chasing multiplications in the valuations of the companies they invest in. Investment decisions are based on the financial trends of the business and credentials of the founders, but not so much by understanding the real consumer needs that those founders are trying to meet. They make an assumption that if a business is successful, it must be meeting some consumer need, but for a business to be successful in the long term, it needs to be based on real consumer needs and evolve as needs of the consumers evolve.

There is obviously nothing wrong with the objective of revenue maximization. That, indeed, is the goal of the businesses operating in capitalist societies, but losing sight of what customers really want that would keep driving revenue growth is a problem. Customer centricity and new product innovations in these organizations are more about seizing different opportunities, identifying the way these opportunities can be maximized, scrutinizing analytics to forecast the demand and estimate future growth, etc. There is perhaps an opportunity in these organizations to 'humanize' the data and look at numbers in the form of consumer stories—how are people using products and services and how are they making a real difference in their lives. For instance, an online stock broking platform would need to know what really draws non-investors in the stock market to start investing, the baby steps they take, the hand-holding they need, the anxieties they have, and how they decide on which broking platform to trust. This understanding could lead to different features of the platform and different customer 'recruitment' advertising or programs than what you see in the markets today.

3. **Marketing-centric organizations:** These organizations rely heavily on marketing to drive their growth, which is different from 'sales-driven' organizations. In sales-driven organizations, the sales or business development team focuses on selling existing products and services to potential customers. These are typically the companies where the process of sales involves a long evaluation—think of car dealers, tech companies, or software providers. Marketing is a 'support' to the sales team providing leads via direct marketing, SEO, and SEM kind of initiatives.

   Marketing-driven organizations, on the other hand, rely on the marketing activities, branding, innovations, etc., to drive sales. FMCG or CPG companies tend to be marketing-driven since the products are usually low-priced and the differentiation between them can be quite low as well. Therefore, they need a 'brand' to create a unique position in the minds of the consumers as entry barriers are quite low allowing possibility of competition entering in the market, and so on. Marketing, therefore, is a key lever that creates unique brands and advertising to generate salience and preference for the products to gain an edge in the market. Sales team supports the marketing activities by ensuring wide distribution and right retailer incentives that can translate the marketing activities into sales.

Such organizations tend to regularly use market research and consumer analytics to understand consumer preferences, design new products and innovations, as well as to create and strengthen brands. The insights team is, therefore, focused on having a robust set of protocols to develop and test new initiatives as well as track their performance in the market. These organizations tend to be at the second or third of the insights function evolution stage (as discussed in chapter four).

Interestingly, several product-driven organizations are now being more marketing-centric, where they merge their strong muscles of product development with the newly-developed marketing muscles. Automobile companies are an excellent example; they are equipped with the research and development and technical know-how of creating great vehicles, but they also make use of marketing to create unique brands in the minds of consumers. And as they evolve, the brand positioning drives product development further. For instance, an SUV by Mercedes-Benz would obviously look and perform differently from the SUV by Toyota, and that's driven by what the brand stands for.

4. **Customer or consumer-centric organizations:** Arguably, this is the next stage of evolution for the marketing-centric organizations. These are the companies where every decision is taken keeping benefit of consumers front and centre. What consumers need, how are they presently meeting their needs, what are their anxieties and tension points, the broader role of products or services in their lives, and so on, are some of the talking points that lead to innovation of new products and renovation of existing products. All the functions, including R&D, supply chain, finance, etc., are geared towards prioritizing and meeting the needs of the consumers and leaving the internal complexity aside for decision making.

   Marketing tends to play a lead role in such organizations as they are usually tasked with translating the consumer understanding to product or service offerings. Consumer insights teams work hand-in-hand with marketing, like two sides of the same coin. Hence, you often see talent moving between marketing and insights function over a period of time. The insights teams tend to be at Stage 3 or 4 of the evolution model as discussed earlier (in chapter 4) and their job is to go beyond protocols and established methods; their real role lies in making everyone within the organization consumer-centric. 'Bringing the consumer to the boardroom' is what they essentially do. And it means making the real consumer stories come alive—at every stage of development and decision-making—by helping the team develop a gut feeling about products and consumers, making information available and accessible, and everything that has been described in earlier chapters on how to make organizations insightful.

Interestingly, no company is only one of the above—the best ones are a combination of all. Unilever puts consumers at the centre and aligns all the internal functional capabilities to meet the needs of the consumer. This ensures that the needs of the consumer—that's being addressed—dominates the conversations and is used to drive revenue growth, design new products, manage supply chain, and so on.

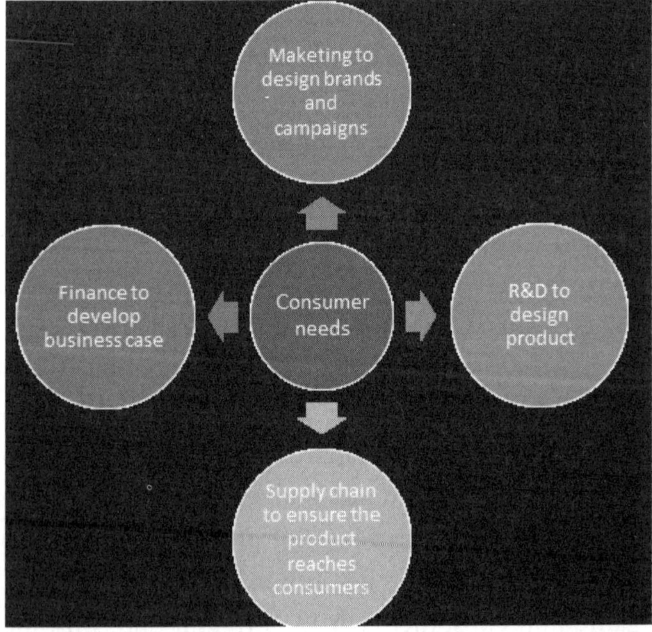

In Unilever, the R&D teams continuously work on developing new products and bring in new technology to enhance the performance of existing ones. This requires keeping an eye on the latest tech and product trends, just like product-centric companies. However, the conversations are rarely about launching a new face cream; for instance, that might have been developed with the latest technology. Rather, the conversations are about evolving benefits that consumers are seeking from face creams and whether the new cream can deliver on those benefits and perform better than other product formulations and competition as well. Functions like R&D are, therefore, continuously renovating their 'ammunition' so that they are able to design the right product to suit consumer needs, once the need has been identified. This way the role of R&D never diminishes but stays relevant and actually is further enhanced by being more consumer-centric. Similarly, finance teams understand the profit and loss of different products and brands intimately so that they are able to partner with the marketing teams to find a potential solution for consumer needs which can maximize revenues (sales and profits)—in other words, create a business case to see the financial viability of the new solution.

This kind of work in a consumer-centric environment requires a firm grip on evolving consumer needs and often an empathetic understanding of unstated or unspoken needs. In other words, reading between the lines of what people say as against what they mean. And, hence, the role of consumer insights is pivotal in this space.

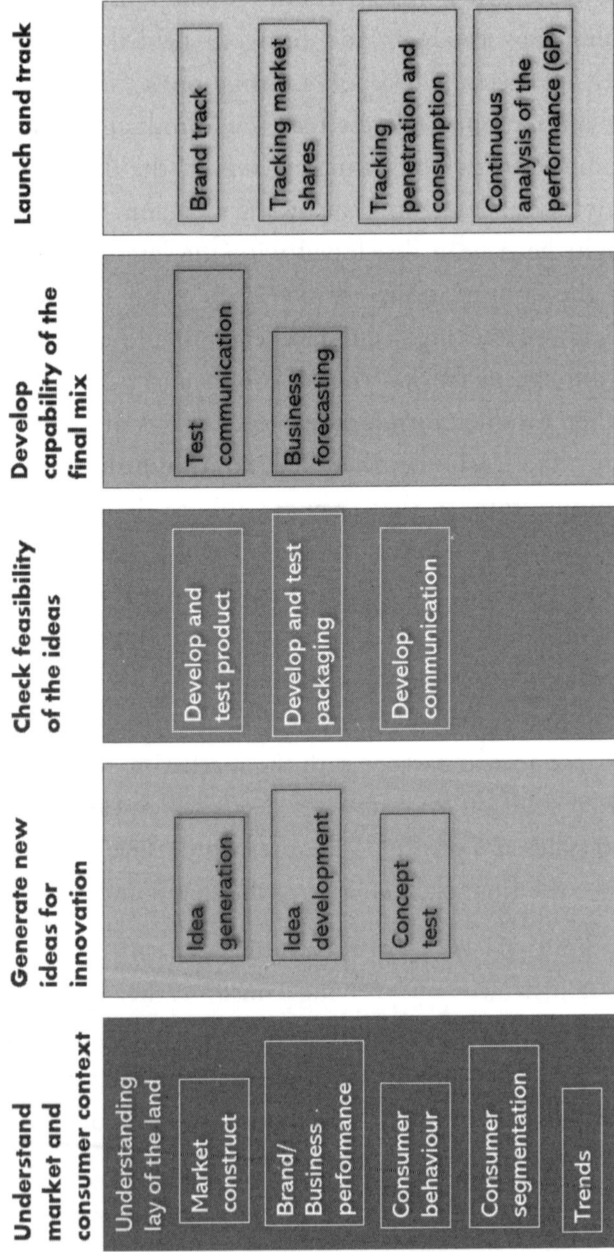
Understand market and consumer context
Understanding lay of the land
Market construct
Brand/ Business performance
Consumer behaviour
Consumer segmentation
Trends
Generate new ideas for innovation
Idea generation
Idea development
Concept test
Check feasibility of the ideas
Develop and test product
Develop and test packaging
Develop communication
Develop capability of the final mix
Test communication
Business forecasting
Launch and track
Brand track
Tracking market shares
Tracking penetration and consumption
Continuous analysis of the performance (6P)

In a consumer-centric organization, the usual journey of new product development looks like a version of the chart shown above. This chapter further elaborates each of these pillars more from FMCG point of view (using Unilever examples in several cases), however, the learnings that you will draw from this chart can apply to any industry.

Understanding the Market and Consumer Context

It all begins with understanding of the context: how the market is changing, how consumer behaviour is evolving, what the emerging trends are, etc. It can be an exploration based on a client brief or a problem or an issue that the brand or business might be facing. For instance, the sales or market share of our iconic body lotion brand is declining and you need to understand how you refresh the brand. For that, there is a need to bring the 'outside in', so to speak. In other words, understand what has changed in the market and consumer context which is making our brand less favourable than before. But it can also be an open-ended exploration to spot new opportunities that might be emerging with the changing context. This may require a bit more effort on creatively connecting the dots and gaining deeper consumer insights to pick out latent needs. And it may also need observing emerging trends not just in your category but also in the consumer environment. For instance, soap and body wash category teams should always keep an eye on trending fragrances and ingredients and also the emerging ones in the market. Similarly, they should keep tabs on fragrance and ingredients that are passé and may need to be replaced with new and more interesting ones. This doesn't apply to consumer packaged goods alone but any category that the business teams are working in. Whether you work in tech industry that sells products like TVs, printers, and mobile phones, or in service industry like retail or car servicing, it is a good practice to observe emerging trends because they can change consumer preferences and behaviour quite rapidly.

But how do you go about gaining that contextual understanding? It can feel quite ambiguous and, therefore, daunting—where do you begin and how do you create a path for an insightful exploration?

One of the ways to do that is to give a structure to this exploration and have information available for the organization in different buckets, so that people can tap into that information when needed. Given below is one way of structuring that information (12 boxes of insights). Since it can be time-consuming and heavier on the pockets to collect this huge amount of information, it makes sense to have a strategic 'program' in place that strategically fills the gathered information in these boxes over a period of time with regular frequency. That way the budgets get assigned and information is available to all the stakeholders for using on different projects. The next few sections detail out each of these 12 boxes of insights.

MARKET CONSTRUCT			
	Market Landscape	Market Behaviour	Market Drivers
CONSUMER BEHAVIOUR			
	Consumer Lifestyle and Trends	Shopping Behaviour and Changing Patterns	Media Behaviour – Current and Evolving
BRAND PERFORMANCE			
	Brand Positioning	Brand Equity	Brand Communication
CONSUMER SEGMENTATION			
	Benefit Segmentation	Needstate Segmentation	Consumption Segmentation

Market Construct

Market construct is about understanding the current 'lay of the land' in the marketplace. The market landscape, behaviour of consumers and retailers, and drivers of the market together paint a complete holistic picture. It is also very useful to generate new ideas for innovation (and understanding the performance of your business in the market).

Market landscape

This is about understanding the category size, growth, category penetration, the segments (geographical or social, economic, needs-based, etc.) where the category is more penetrated, the extent of fragmentation that exists (are there lots of brands that compete for consumers' attention or only a couple of large ones dominating the mind and the market), how developed the market is and how much more can it be developed (e.g., based on per cap consumption, or the frequency and loyalty levels), category substitutes and to what extent can they compete, etc. For example, a pen manufacturer would have personal laptops and phones as competition because people may simply stop writing with the pen and paper and use the devices instead.

This information is usually available through syndicated service providers like NielsenIQ (Retail Measurement Service), Kantar World Panel, GFK, etc. But it is important to have it organized and analyzed in a bespoke manner that suits the organization and the way people can see it, understand it, and effectively use it.

Let's look at an example of understanding the 'lay of the land' using category fragmentation analysis (shown in the table below). This analysis explains a lot about the category and consumer behaviour but is often overlooked. Kantar World Panel provides invaluable consumer behaviour information, which in my view, if analyzed well, could negate the need of doing a lot more consumer research. Product categories can be segmented based on consumer behaviour in these 'behavioural' groups because the marketing strategies needed to succeed in each group are distinct from each other. The table below shows the category landscape based on consumer behaviour and how that behaviour impacts the performance of the businesses (and hence the strategy needed to be successful). The framework used here is the fragmentation of the category in terms of number of brands consumers use—the more the brands they use, the more fragmentation it causes and lesser tends to be the consumer loyalty, and vice versa.

For instance, categories where consumers are highly loyal to their brand(s), tend to be quite consolidated, and very few brands form the top 80% of the market. Whereas categories where consumers easily switch brands, each brand has a relatively smaller share and the top 80% of the market is highly crowded with several brands. Take bar soaps, for example. People buy soaps about eleven times a year; and if they are truly loyal to a brand, they would at the most buy it four out of eleven times, but remaining seven times they would buy different brand, just so that they can experiment with different fragrances and avail offers on soaps in the market. A soap brand, therefore, is deemed successful if it gets about 0.75% of market share—one because that also translates into huge volumes, and second because in a crowded market, getting close to 1% share is a great start. If you look at a highly-consolidated category– like jams in India, the leading brand, on the other hand, occupies about two thirds of the market and the loyalty is very high. A new brand there can get about 8-10% share relatively easily to start with; but would struggle to go beyond that as consumer loyalty would create a huge barrier.

Fragmentation	Highly-fragmented but fiercely loyal consumers	Highly-fragmented but consumers are open to change	Category is getting consolidated, but consumers are open to change	Highly-consolidated category but consumers have some openness to change	Highly-consolidated category but fiercely loyal consumers
	Dating multiple partners without commitment	Living together but flirting with others	Engaged but flirting with others	Open marriage	Married and committed
No. of brands in top 80% of the market	13	13	6	3	1 or 2
Frequency of buying the category (per year)	Medium to low	Very high	High	Low	Low
Loyalty to brands	Very high	Very low. Consumers flirt with a lot of different brands	Medium	High	Very high. Consumers don't want to switch from their loyal brand

Examples	Deodorants, tea	Soaps detergent bars	Toothpaste, face creams, shampoos	Coffee, ketchup	Jams, soups, noodles (in India)
Ease of a new brand getting acceptance	Medium to low	High	Medium	Low	Very low
Key marketing strategy for brands	Sharp differentiation on one of the key category drivers + Regular refresh of the brand and keep giving tempting offers	Sharp differentiation on key driver(s)	Superior product performance on key category driver but emotional differentiate on other drivers (e.g., sun protection cream should be very good in protecting your skin, but can have a different range of fragrances or skin feel).	Start with the segment that's willing to experiment (innovators) and use their credentials to build the brand (testimonials).	Brand should not be very different from leading brand(s) on the main driver, but offer differentiation on other unique but relevant drivers. Plus, offer good deal to make people try (and thereby block the shopping window for other brands).

Market behaviour

This is not so much about consumer behaviour, but market behaviour and the behaviour of the brands within the market, given the existing market dynamics. In other words, it's about the finer nuances and idiosyncrasies and quirks of the category and the brand, which could be because of the way market is structured, or the way retailers behave, or the way a brand is positioned or the sourcing of the raw material or any other such factors. This, therefore, is a wider scan and requires historical perspective and sometimes analytical modelling. Here are a few examples:

1. When oil prices go down, there is an emergence of low-cost detergent brands from the unorganized sector (particularly in developing markets). The low cost of oil and relatively low technology barriers gives them enough margins to come out in the market with cheaper alternatives. But they disappear equally quickly when the prices go up.

2. When the commodity price of tea goes up, it increases the cost of production for tea companies. This increase in cost may be passed on to the consumers through higher retail prices, which may result in a decrease in demand for branded tea products. This can have a negative impact on the sales and revenue of branded tea companies, as consumers may switch to cheaper alternatives or reduce their overall consumption.

3. In markets where there is a stronghold of retailers (e.g., Walmart in the US or Tesco in the UK), retailers in some categories have their 'store' brands (also referred

to as private labels) that look and feel similar to other well-known brands in those categories and are given higher shelf space. This presents a different dynamic of competition and requires a measured response because retailers are also partners to manufacturer brands for selling.

Understanding these category dynamics is critical for the business to operate in those categories. One of the ways to deal with it is to estimate the 'sensitivity' of different variables to the sales of the brand or category. Let's look at an example of market mix modelling for one of the Unilever brands that gives insights on what impacts brand sales:

The brand in the charts below is highly responsive (elastic) to its own advertising spends but also equally shows negative elasticity to the ad spends of its competitors. Which means the brand not only needs to maintain certain levels of advertising but also needs to keep an eye on the spends of competition brands and its own share of voice (calculated on the spends of all the brands in the category). It is moderately elastic to distribution, promotion spends, and relative price index (RPI which is the ratio of brand price vs. category average price). Brand is priced slightly lower than the optimum price point of value maximization but increasing RPI to that level would mean lower volumes. The distribution of the brand has been going up and so are the volumes as per the elasticity to distribution. Given this 'behaviour' of the brand (or it's elasticity to its levers), it would make sense for the brand to prioritize ad spends and not increase promo spends or increase spends on distribution.

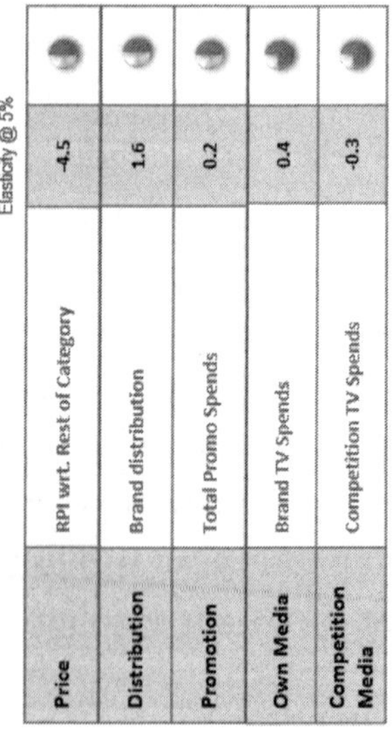

		Elasticity @ 5%	
Price	RPI wrt. Rest of Category	-4.5	
Distribution	Brand distribution	1.6	
Promotion	Total Promo Spends	0.2	
Own Media	Brand TV Spends	0.4	
Competition Media	Competition TV Spends	-0.3	

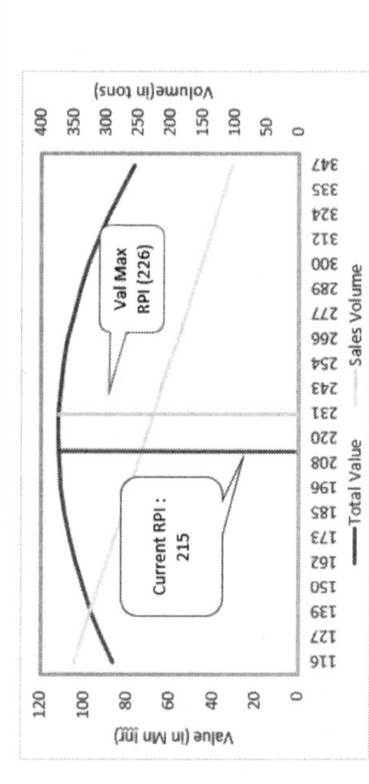

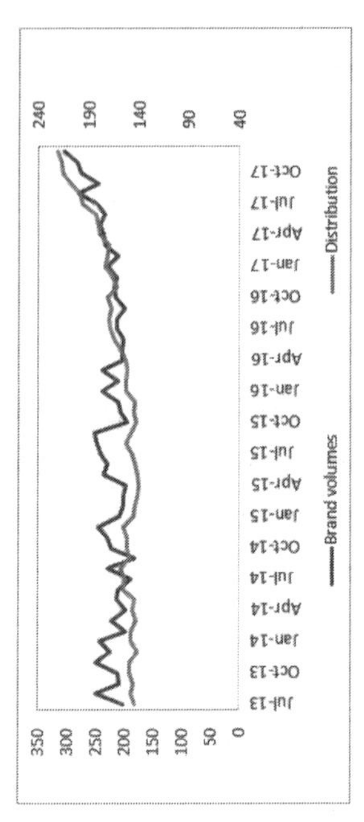

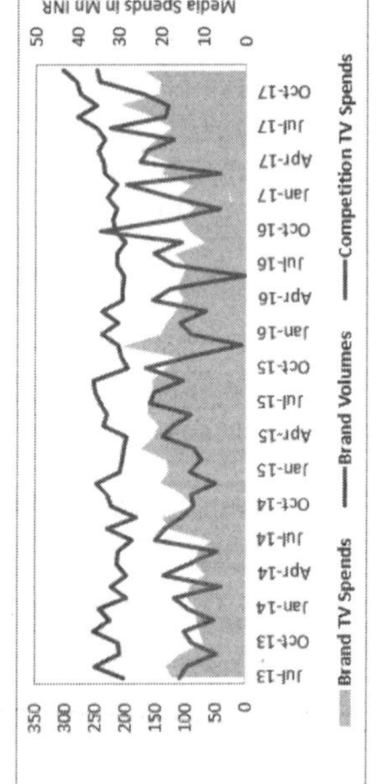

Market drivers

Above example of elasticities indicates what drives the market for a brand. Similarly, it is imperative to understand what drives the market—in other words, what causes an increase in the penetration and consumption of a category. Usually it is done through analytical modelling, however, sometimes good qualitative conversations with consumers can give an insight on what makes people consume a category more (though qualitative would make it difficult to create a baseline of the drivers and brand performance at regular intervals).

There are two ways Unilever looks at market drivers:

1. Category penetration growth drivers, i.e., what would make more people consume the category if the category is relatively under-penetrated; or, what would increase the consumption of the category for the highly-penetrated ones. Modelling historical data is a good way of arriving at the insight for category drivers of this nature. Byron Sharp's principles of brand growth, in this context, are extremely useful as well. They outline the normative behaviour and are very powerful in understanding the reasons for penetration, gain and loss, and identifying the right strategy for brands of different sizes. These drivers vary a lot depending on the category landscape, whether the category is nascent or established, fragmented or consolidated, etc. This driver analysis gives a great insight on what brands need to do to grow the penetration and needs data from different sources (retail audits, household consumption, brand or ad track, spends on advertising and promotion, etc.).

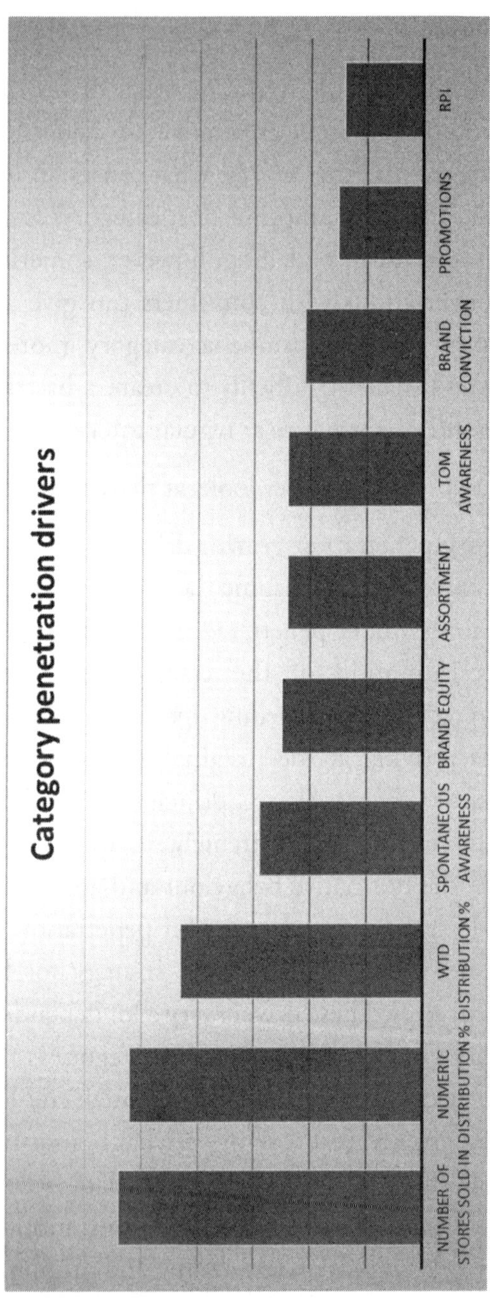
Category penetration drivers
NUMBER OF STORES SOLD IN
NUMERIC DISTRIBUTION %
WTD DISTRIBUTION %
SPONTANEOUS AWARENESS
BRAND EQUITY
ASSORTMENT
TOM AWARENESS
BRAND CONVICTION
PROMOTIONS
RPI

An example of drivers of category penetration for one of the FMCG categories, based on modelling done across sources, is shown above. This suggests that the category sales are dependent a lot on physical availability of the products—the number and type of shops the brands are available in—followed by mental availability variables like salience and brand equity.

2. Brand growth drivers within a category or, in other words, what makes people choose a particular brand over others. Arguably, these could be called brand drivers, but this is done for all the key brands in the market and aggregation of those becomes market drivers. This gives an insight on how consumers choose one brand over another. This obviously is dependent on the category landscape (are there several, established brands in the market vs. a few, price tiers of the brands in the market, brand differentiation, clearly-established needs in the minds of consumers etc.).

   An example of drivers is given below for shampoos in the USA in 2009, carried out by the BASES team of NielsenIQ. This analysis outlines what is important to consumers in making a brand choice (drivers), perception of various brands on those drivers, and finally, the elasticity available to each brand on each of the drivers (how much can a brand improve on it and the difference it would make to that brand being chosen). This not only gives an insight on the brand performance but also is an excellent tool for identifying new opportunities for the brand.

In the example below, it is clear from the analysis presented in first chart that consumers choose their shampoo based on its price (the most important driver with 43% weight) followed by the functional and sensorial benefits provided by the brand (41% weight). Furthermore, among the sensorial benefits, brand that protect and moisturize hair are preferred over others, followed by those which are suitable for everyone in the family and the products being gentle in cleaning.

The analysis in the next chart details how different brands perform on those drivers. For instance, it is clear that two brands (Brand 1 and 2) stood out and were perceived to be doing well on moisturizing and protecting hair (the most important driver), while the rest of the brands were seen to be good for everyone in the family and everyday use (no differentiation on that attribute). Interestingly, none of the brands were doing well on dandruff and scalp protection—all were perceived to be bad on that driver—and it was not seen to be a very important driver. Therefore, it might present an opportunity for differentiating new products by highlighting the importance of scalp protection. And indeed, that's what happened in the next few years. The brands picked up that benefit and highlighted its importance to consumers through advertising and product, consequently raising the importance weightage of this driver in the brand choice.

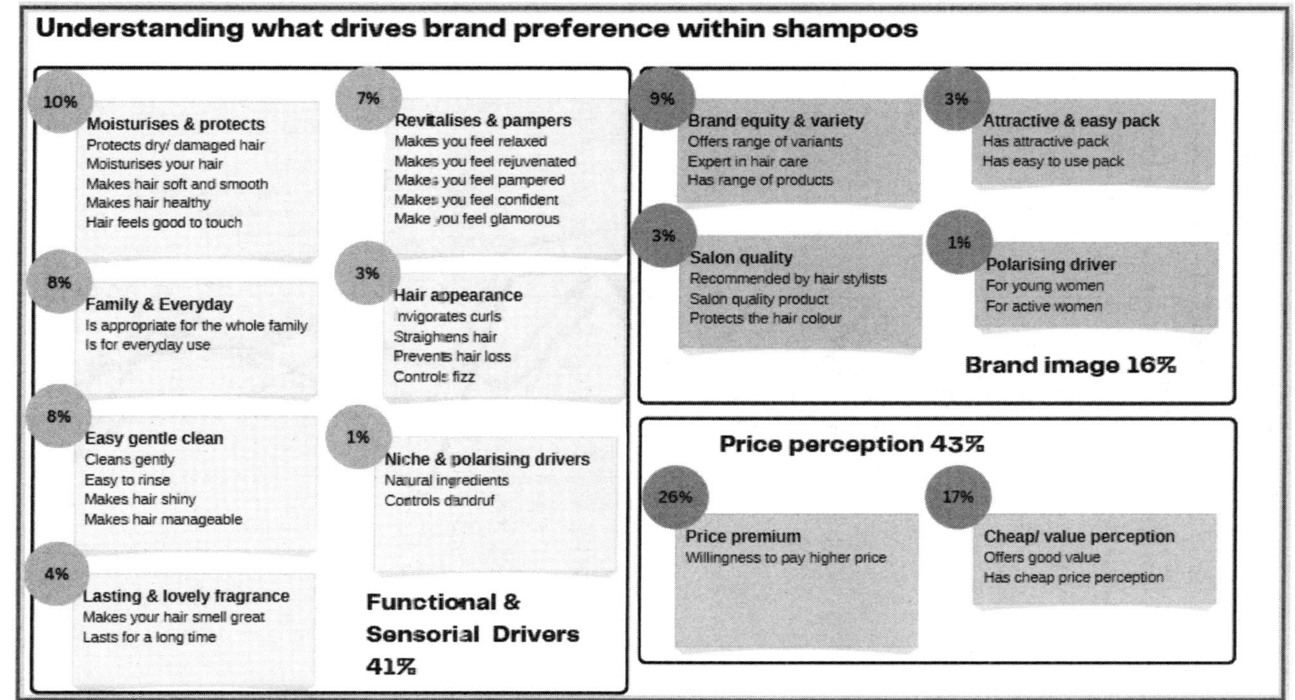
Understanding what drives brand preference within shampoos
10%
Moisturises & protects
Protects dry/ damaged hair
Moisturises your hair
Makes hair soft and smooth
Makes hair healthy
Hair feels good to touch
8%
Family & Everyday
Is appropriate for the whole family
Is for everyday use
8%
Easy gentle clean
Cleans gently
Easy to rinse
Makes hair shiny
Makes hair manageable
4%
Lasting & lovely fragrance
Makes your hair smell great
Lasts for a long time
7%
Revitalises & pampers
Makes you feel relaxed
Makes you feel rejuvenated
Makes you feel pampered
Makes you feel confident
Make you feel glamorous
3%
Hair appearance
Invigorates curls
Straightens hair
Prevents hair loss
Controls fizz
1%
Niche & polarising drivers
Natural ingredients
Controls dandruf
Functional & Sensorial Drivers 41%
9%
Brand equity & variety
Offers range of variants
Expert in hair care
Has range of products
3%
Attractive & easy pack
Has attractive pack
Has easy to use pack
3%
Salon quality
Recommended by hair stylists
Salon quality product
Protects the hair colour
1%
Polarising driver
For young women
For active women
Brand image 16%
Price perception 43%
26%
Price premium
Willingness to pay higher price
17%
Cheap/ value perception
Offers good value
Has cheap price perception

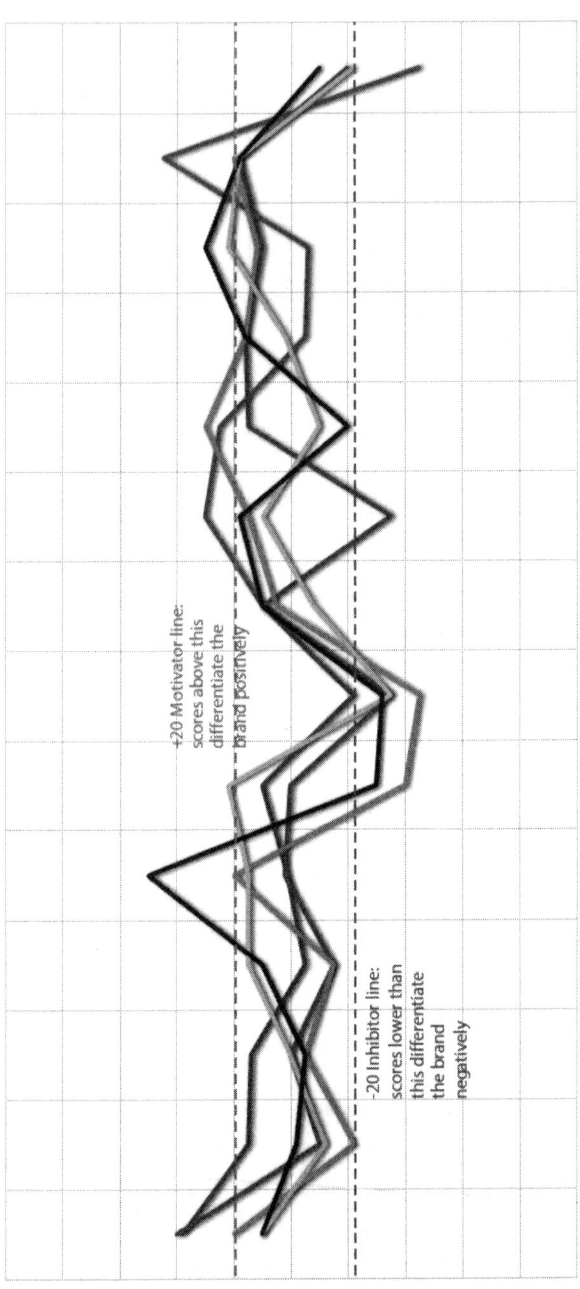
+20 Motivator line:
scores above this
differentiate the
brand positively
-20 Inhibitor line:
scores lower than
this differentiate
the brand
negatively

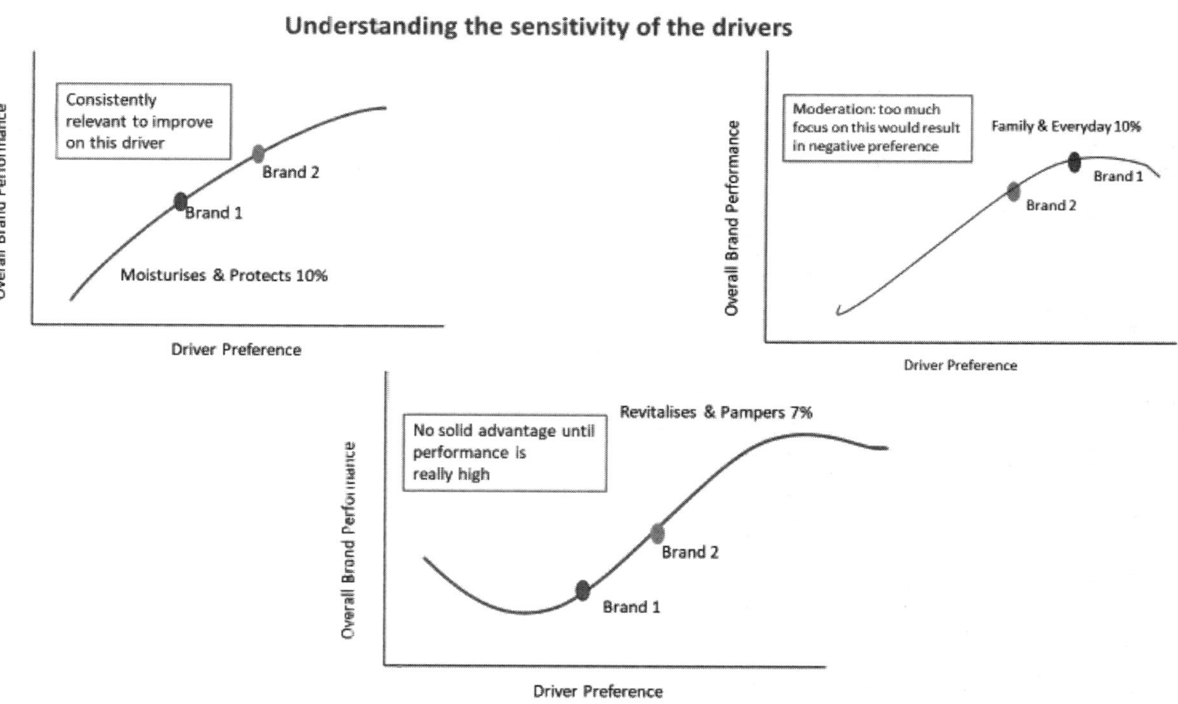
Understanding the sensitivity of the drivers
Consistently relevant to improve on this driver
Brand 2
Brand 1
Moisturises & Protects 10%
Overall Brand Performance
Driver Preference
Moderation: too much focus on this would result in negative preference
Family & Everyday 10%
Brand 1
Brand 2
Overall Brand Performance
Driver Preference
No solid advantage until performance is really high
Revitalises & Pampers 7%
Brand 2
Brand 1
Overall Brand Performance
Driver Preference

The importance of drivers in decision-making and the performance of brands on those drivers provide useful insights while deciding a way forward for the brand. But what I find truly interesting is the elasticity of these drivers—in other words, the scope for a brand to improve on a driver and what returns it can provide in terms of increasing the brand preference. As the chart above shows, Brand 1—though already performing well and standing out on the first driver of 'moisturizes and protects'—still has a lot of scope for improvement and further increasing its preference. While being suitable for 'family and everyday use', it is already on top of the curve and any further increase would not result in brand preference.

Consumer Behaviour

This section is about understanding consumer behaviour in detail. Some of the category consumption behaviour comes in from the previous 'market construct' section; this section, however, is more about general consumer behaviour that directly or indirectly impacts product categories.

Consumer lifestyle and trends

Given the rapid change in consumer environment, it is always critical to observe consumer trends and how their lives are changing, its impact on the product category, brand consumption, and so on. For instance, technology, today, is present in every aspect of consumer lives and that's making a difference in the way people shop for products and even consume them. Sustainability is another such huge dimension. These larger forces, which are beyond the control of manufacturers and brand teams, can dramatically impact consumer behaviour. Unilever looks at such consumer trends from three levels:

1. **Macro forces:** These are the larger forces comprising social, economic, political, technological, etc., aspects that impact the world. These are not under the control of the companies and brands, but they are massively impacted by them. Typical horizon (which the typical duration for these broad macro forces would be relevant in shaping the consumption patterns) for these is five to ten years which is highly useful for strategic planning of the business. For instance, one of the macro forces typically identified by marketers is 'environment under stress'—this is no longer an issue that is restricted to a few environmental groups, but is affecting the way people are choosing brand and consuming categories. This, in turn, is impacting the way companies are creating and marketing brands. The full impact of this force is yet to play out and would continue shaping consumer choices for another decade or more.

2. **Category or people trends:** This is the second level of trends. These are changes that you see in categories and people behaviour driven by macro forces (or by the changes caused by the macro forces). The horizon for these trends is medium term (two- five years) because they change relatively faster than the macro trends. They are highly useful for identifying brand innovation and communication strategies. Let's take an example of Unilever's food category. The team at Unilever identified a trend called 'positive impact choices' in the

said category as a result of the microforce 'environment under stress' where consumers make choices that are environmentally conscious. Some of the manifestations of these trends visible in the market are:

a) Meatless entering the mainstream (more people are becoming vegetarian and vegan, and avoiding meat).

b) Rise of social enterprises (people choosing brands from enterprises that give back to the environment either in terms of money flowing for help or products that help fringe communities).

c) Environmentally-friendly packaging (the one that's either recyclable or has been made without harshly impacting the environment).

3. **Product and shopper trends:** This third level of trends show up on the product shelves in the market as a result of the macro forces and category or people trends. These trends are short-lived, can change frequently, and are hence huge (in numbers) to follow. In continuation with the above chain of thought on 'environment under stress' and 'positive impact choices' trends, you would see products on the shelf that are more 'organic' than before, are vegetarian or vegan, offer a lot more transparency on where or how they are produced with details of their carbon footprint, products with different types of packaging, the ones that allow you to track their journey from farm to fork, and so on. These products on the shelf can change relatively faster with evolving technology in this space, but the new products

would still be underpinned by the higher driving forces. In other words, the manifestation of these forces can change relatively faster.

There are several companies that enable organizations to track this level of trend. For instance, Mintel tracks launch of every product in the market with complete details of brand or company: name, SKU, price, claims, functional benefits, and so on. This can be an extremely useful source of monitoring the shopper trend. Google search trends is another good source of monitoring these trends, especially in categories where consumers journey is a combination of online and offline tracks. Unilever not only tracks the launch of new products in every category of interest, but also closely keeps an eye on the benefits offered, claims made, ingredients, fragrances or flavours of the brand, and so on. In a simplistic example below, you can see from Google trends that consumer interest, globally, has picked up in 'onion oil' as an ingredient for hair care and is driven by South Asian and African countries (Argon Oil, on the other hand, has lost its sheen).

To summarize, observing trends by only looking at what is available on the shelves and what people are buying can provide a very narrow (and, therefore, potentially misleading) perspective as it is subject to rapid change. It is important to look at broader categories or people trends and macro forces that are driving these changes in order to gain real insight and, arguably, foresight as well. These trends enable companies to keep an eye not only on forever-evolving market situation, but also generate ideas for new innovation and renovations of existing products.

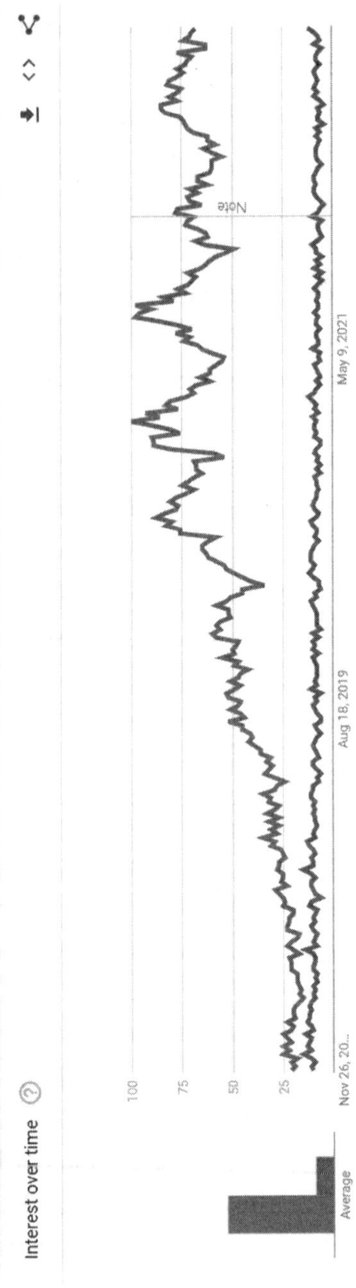
Interest over time
Average
100
75
50
25
Nov 26, 20...
Aug 18, 2019
May 9, 2021
Note

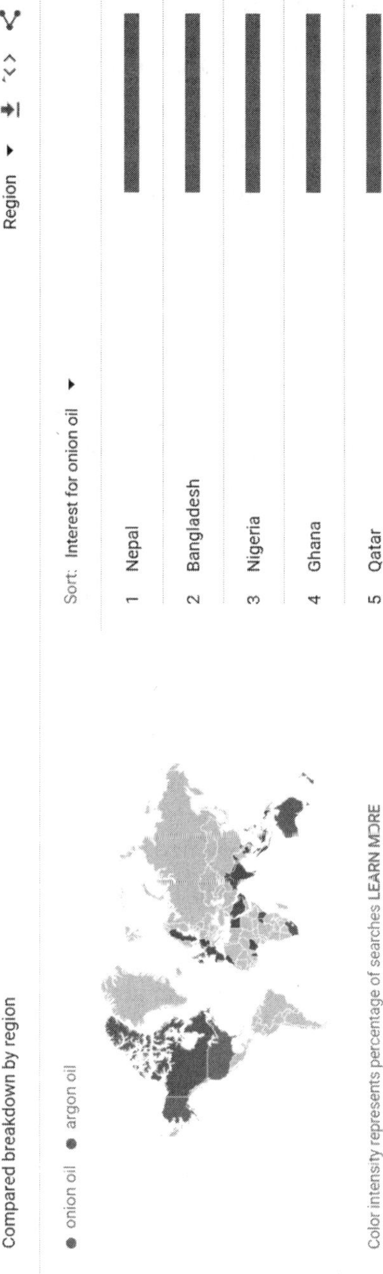
Compared breakdown by region
Region
onion oil
argon oil
Sort: Interest for onion oil
1 Nepal
2 Bangladesh
3 Nigeria
4 Ghana
5 Qatar
Color intensity represents percentage of searches LEARN MORE

Shopping behaviour and patterns

Companies like Unilever spend a lot of time observing and understanding the way people shop for consumer products. Product availability is one of the key drivers of sales in consumer products, but the way the product is made available (we call it quality of distribution) makes a massive difference in its sales as well. And that is all about behaviour of consumers as shoppers. It is well known that when retailers play pleasant music in their outlets, the sales go up; or when bakeries are filled with the aroma of freshly-baked bread, it results in an increased sale of its goods. All these mentioned above are the factors that retailers can influence; now let's look at some of the several factors that the brands have the power to influence the sales:

1. The physical or literal position of the brand on the shelf (to be placed in the center or on the side, at eye-level or higher or lower than eye-level, and so on).
2. The font sizes on the pack.
3. The colour of the brand or variant.
4. The distinctive assets owned by the brand in terms of colours, logo, pictures, and how visible are they from a distance.
5. Point of sales (POS) material and how visible it is, etc.

Arguably, these factors are equally relevant in the physical and the digital environment of an e-commerce platform. Understanding the influence of these factors on purchases and optimizing them for the maximum impact is an area of specialization in itself within the insights work stream. There are broadly two streams of insights in this space:

1. **Pre-testing of material before deployment:** This involves shelf test of packaging (to see the product stand out in different retail environments), POS material, etc. Several digital and physical methods available for pre-testing involve cameras, live feeds coming through shops, simulated digital shelves, eye-tracking mechanisms, and so on. Unilever, in some countries, also has full-fledged physical shops of different types of outlets (grocery store, pharmacy store, etc.) and hi-tech simulated digital shops created in the office as a cutting-edge facility for shopper insights. These facilities work with retailers to design their shelves and are used for extensive packaging tests before product launch, giving an edge to the organization in the market place.
2. **Evaluation post-launch:** This involves regular auditing of the shelves in different environments post the product launch with tailor-made score cards that inform the business of its on-shelf performance and impact on the shopping behaviour. Advanced technological solutions using image recognition offered by companies like Parallel Dots and Imagevision.ai have now made real-time shelf assessments possible. This has replaced deploying huge research and field teams, making it cheaper and faster to make changes on shelves than ever before.

The stream of shopper insight has come a long way in the last decade and has evolved in the similar way consumers shopping has. There are now full-fledged methods available to map the 'consumer journey', which involved understanding what triggers the purchase, what influences it, the process consumers follow to ultimately choose and buy a brand. These steps in a consumer's journey are quite dynamic and, therefore, mapping has to account for the ways in which the journey can change with different triggers.

One of the ways in which Unilever looks at different consumer journeys is explained below. The same can be adapted for different categories, as the principles remain the same, but specifics change.

There are four axes or dimensions of the consumer journey:

1. **Personas:** This is not a 'person' per se, but more of a needstate that drives the person to behave or shop in a certain way. This also means that the same person can have different personas on different purchase occasions. Some of the examples of personas are:

    a) Deal seeker: someone who is looking for a good bargain. This doesn't say anything about their affordability but about what they are looking for during a purchase. An example would be someone buying airline tickets looking for the cheapest flight as opposed to shortest flight, or a flight at a convenient departure time.

    b) Eternal optimizer: someone looking for better ways of doing the same thing, particularly a chore, but in better ways while optimizing the cost and product performance. For example, a person looking for better ways of doing laundry that minimizes the effort but gives great result without incurring higher costs.

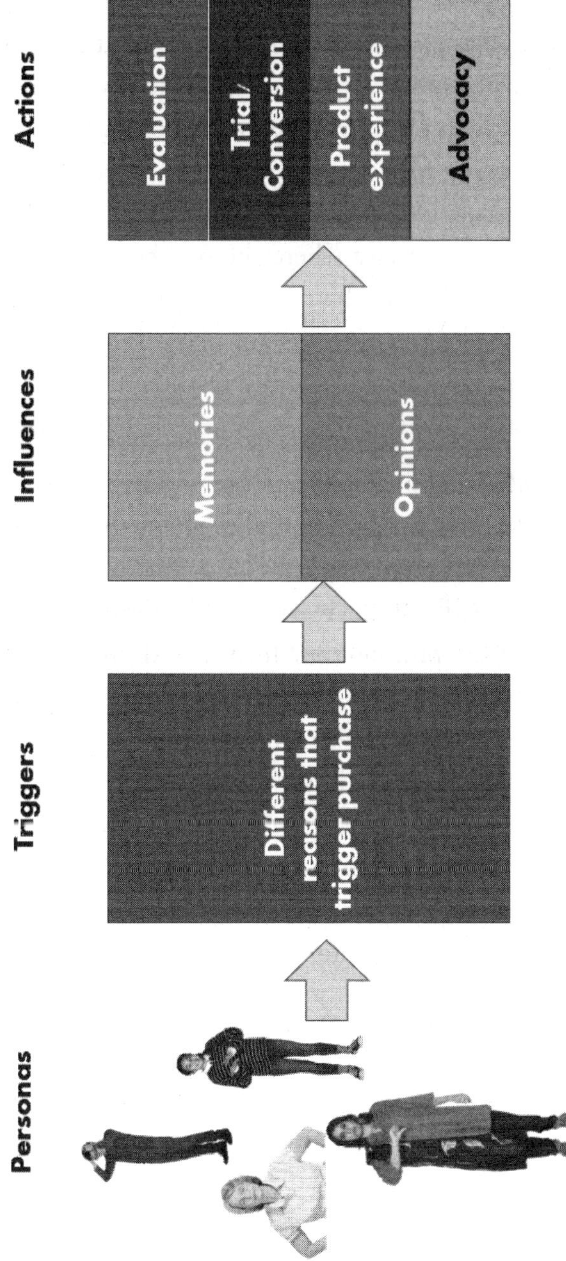
Personas
Triggers
Different reasons that trigger purchase
Influences
Memories
Opinions
Actions
Evaluation
Trial/ Conversion
Product experience
Advocacy

2. **Triggers:** They are the reason an individual starts its purchase journey in the first place. It reflects the need for a product. It could be an immediate need (e.g., I have run out of shampoo), a short-term need (e.g., I'll be going for a wedding, so need a shampoo that makes my hair look good), or a long-term need (e.g., I have moved to a city where the weather is lot more humid that makes my hair frizzier and need a shampoo that can help me manage my hair). People with different personas react differently to these triggers and, hence, the two are linked to each other intrinsically.
3. **Influences:** These are the moments that affect the decisions the person makes about the purchase. These could be what they know and remember about different brands from their exposure in the past. It could also be the opinions they form based on the 'influencers', which could be the friends they trust, people they see on media talking about related issues, advertising they remember liking or disliking, what retailers say about the brands while purchasing, the subliminal influences of brand semiotics (colour, fragrance or flavour, design, service offered for service brands), and so on. Understanding and managing these influences are important for a brand to nudge people in the right direction.
4. **Actions:** Finally, these are things people do at the end of journey: from buying products, using them to recommending them to others (if they like the experience). This may involve visiting physical stores,

talking to people who offer the service (in case of service industry), trying free samples or using the product or service during free trial, and so on.

The journey that consumers take is now increasingly physical and digital (phygital) and both are quite intertwined. A brand needs to understand the journey in full detail so that the 'touch points' can be identified for the brand to initiate the right conversation at the right point of intervention. For instance, if the sales staff at a TV store are trained to identify cues of whether the customer visiting the store is ready to buy a TV or just exploring options can either 'influence' them on the brand that's right for them or offer the right deal that helps them get off the fence. Similarly, search engine optimization and marketing can be tailored to provide the information depending on what consumers are searching for in the product.

Media consumption and patterns

Unilever spends about 14% of its turnover on 'Brand and Marketing Investment' (Source: Unilever Annual Report, 2020) making it one of the largest advertisers in the world. Therefore, understanding media consumption and changing trends within it is the key to optimize these spends. Media agencies working with Unilever obviously use the measurement services provided by agencies across the world in order to manage media spends, but having insights on consumer preferences enables the organization to create the content that moves in line with the trends as well.

Consider an example of reach of different media in 2017 (pulled out and aggregated from different sources across the world). Often brand managers assume that digital channels would provide them greater reach for their campaigns (probably driven by the fact that they themselves spend a lot of time on digital media). Media Insights about the reach and profile of different vehicles are necessary for the business to understand the media landscape of their consumers.

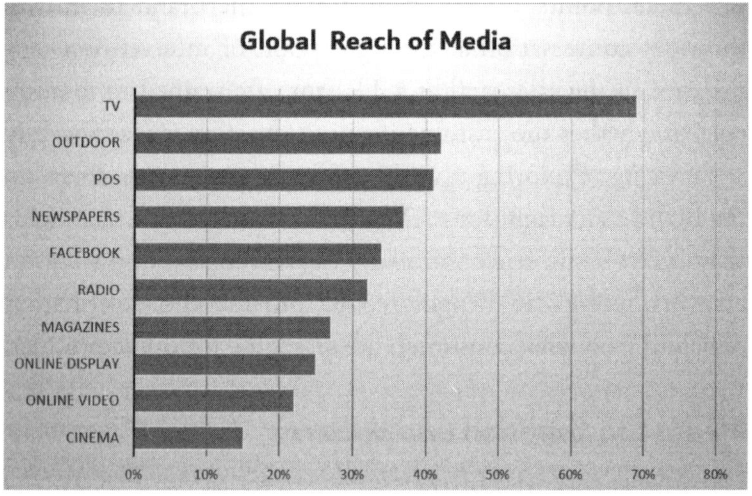

This suggests that TV does bring in more reach than other media. However, only TV would never suffice as it would reach saturation point at about 50% reach. Saturation point is the point beyond which additional spends only generate frequency but not additional reach. In the US, saturation point is at about 40% reach with TV; in Brazil, it's at about 60%; while in India, it's at 50% (this is 2017 data sourced from Mindshare which uses different sources for measuring TV reach in these countries). The implication of this is that beyond TV, other media need to be added that would bring unduplicated reach; in other words, reach amongst audiences who have not been exposed to TV ads. Some digital platforms do tend to bring in additional unduplicated reach (depending on the target audience), particularly those who are light TV viewers and no TV viewers.

Understanding this kind of broad landscape of media is critical for marketing teams to know how they can reach their audience and the kind of creatives they would need.

Then there are events that force change in consumer behaviour—like how a football World Cup would make people switch to (sport) channels they may not be regularly watching. Or, an unprecedented event like COVID-19 pandemic that forced people across the world to stay indoors for an unpredictable amount of time. That was bound to change the media consumption—not just during the lockdown period but some changes are likely to sustain even post the lockdown. Understanding not just how the consumption patterns are changing but why they are changing would allow advertising to shape accordingly. Consider some interesting facts around the media behaviour change during the pandemic:

1. As per Nielsen Digital Rating sources in different markets, the time spent on news and current events increased dramatically in March 2020 vs. March 2019 (chart below shows data for some of the markets). This has straight implications on the media buying for large advertisers.

2. Nielsen studies showed that home-bound consumers led to a sharp 60% increase in the amount of video content watched globally. One thing that was consistent across markets was the time spent per viewer watching news

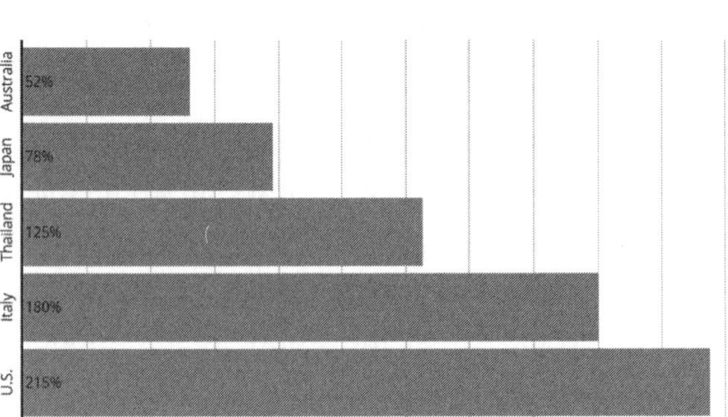
n
PERCENTAGE DIFFERENCE OF TIME SPENT ONLINE ON MOBILE DEVICES ACCESSING CURRENT EVENTS AND GLOBAL NEWS, MARCH 2019 VS MARCH 2020
Australia
52%
Japan
78%
Thailand
125%
Italy
180%
U.S.
215%
%

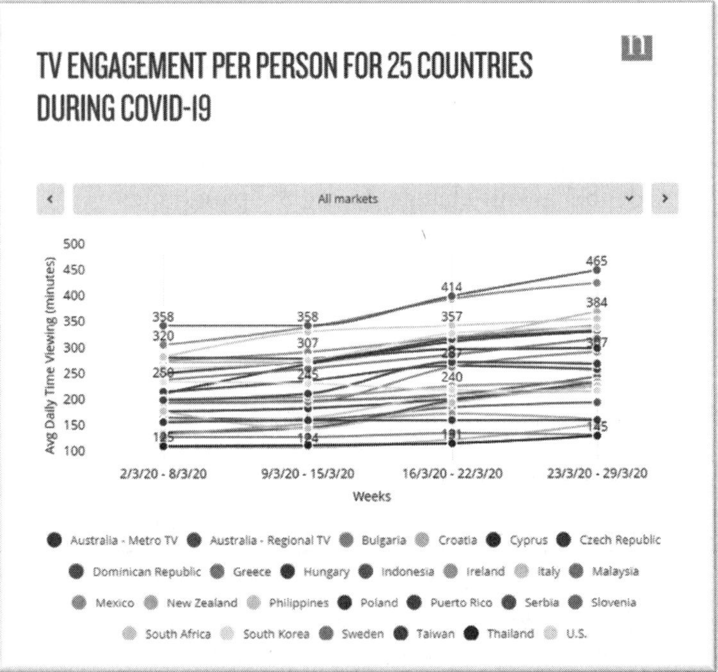
TV ENGAGEMENT PER PERSON FOR 25 COUNTRIES DURING COVID-19
All markets
Avg Daily Time Viewing (minutes)
500
450
400
350
300
250
200
150
100
2/3/20 - 8/3/20
9/3/20 - 15/3/20
16/3/20 - 22/3/20
23/3/20 - 29/3/20
Weeks
Australia - Metro TV
Australia - Regional TV
Bulgaria
Croatia
Cyprus
Czech Republic
Dominican Republic
Greece
Hungary
Indonesia
Ireland
Italy
Malaysia
Mexico
New Zealand
Philippines
Poland
Puerto Rico
Serbia
Slovenia
South Africa
South Korea
Sweden
Taiwan
Thailand
U.S.

and entertainment was going steadily up as the spread of COVID-19 virus was worsening.

Understanding the changing media trends not only requires tapping into the system of TV viewership and print readership in different countries but also into real-time 'always on' media trackers that monitor the digital behaviour and time spent on different media.

Brand Performance

This pillar is about holistic and granular understanding of the brands within company's portfolio. In Unilever, this forms a part of the strategic understanding of the insights' agenda so that it is regularly carried out and always available (as opposed to doing an ad hoc brand evaluation once in a while) for identifying opportunities for the brand and any potential emerging threads.

Brand positioning

While performance of the brand in terms of sales, market share, penetration etc., are monitored closely and often linked to performance evaluation of the business teams, it is equally important to understand the drivers of that performance; in the sense, to see if the brand stands for what its intended positioning is in the minds of the consumers. This says a lot about positioning attributes that the brand 'owns' in absolute sense and relative to competition. For instance, if Coke is competing with all the beverages, then it is important to look beyond the 'share of throat' (in other words, share of Coke in all the beverages that a person drinks in a day) and understand what consumers seek from beverages and how Coke delivers on those attributes.

This typically builds on the analysis of drivers done for the category every couple of years (see 'Market Drivers' under 'Market Construct' section). These drivers indicate the attributes that consumers use to differentiate one brand from another. The same analysis also provides the performance of all the brands in the market on the attributes. However, it is important to track the performance of the brand on key attributes over a period of time and attribute the changes in the performance to different marketing activities being carried out.

In Unilever, this is typically done as a part of the brand track globally with Kantar Millward Brown. The driver analysis usually has 30 to 40 attributes, but the track has a reduced set of 10 to 15 (derived analytically to have a shorter list that represents the broader list). A careful consideration is needed, therefore, to select those 10 to 15 attributes for the track. Those attributes must include:

1. Attribute(s) that the brand is positioned on (e.g., good for tough stains for Surf Excel or Persil or Omo).
2. Attributes that direct competition brands are based on.
3. Attributes that are important in the category (e.g., fragrance, amount of lather, etc., for detergents).
4. Emerging important attributes in the category (e.g., sustainability).

Qualitative research is also used extensively to understand the attributes consumers use to make brand choices, particularly the new emerging ones. However, tracking the performance of a brand over a period of time can be challenging with qualitative research.

Share of endorsement (SOE) and brand image profiles (BIP) are the typical analyses used in this case. SOE is the share of a brand on the endorsement it gets on a particular attribute, while image profile for a brand is deviation from the average performance on each attribute. Simply put, SOE is what the brand is good at, while BIP is what the brand is famous for. If you think of Julia Roberts, the actress, she is known for many things—a great actor, good choice of movies, commercially successful, beautiful personality, and so on, but what she is most famous for is her charming, genuine smile. Julia Roberts would, therefore, have high SOE on all attributes of an actor, her BIP would be highest on the smile.

Let's look at an example of anti-bacterial brand from one of the developing markets:

This clearly indicates that the brand is good for several things—better fragrance, cleansing and refreshing the skin, improving the health of the skin, etc. But what differentiates this brand from others (what it is famous for) is that it protects from germs and, therefore, it also is known to be recommended by health experts (dermatologists) and improving the health of the skin. If this is in line with the intended brand positioning (i.e., germ protection) then this attribute performance in turn, reflects positively for the brand. Furthermore, its monthly or yearly tracking would indicate whether the brand managed to remain strong on these aspects and, equally important, if

PRODUCT | PERFORMANCE | SKIN | BRAND PROFILE BEAUTY

SOE Q2'14	SOE Q3'14	SOE Q4'14	SOE H2'14	SOE YTD'14		BIP Q2'14	BIP Q3'14	BIP Q4'14	BIP H2'14	BIP YTD'14
12	15	15	15	15	Better fragrance	-5	-6	-7	-6	-6
13	17	17	17	17	Cleanse the skin deeply	0	1	0	0	1
16	21	21	21	22	Protect effectively from germs	14	14	14	15	14
12	15	16	16	16	Moisturize the skin better	-3	-5	-3	-4	-3
13	17	16	17	17	Refreshes/ Revives your skin	-2	0	-1	-1	-1
13	16	16	16	16	Leave skin soft and smooth	-3	-3	-3	-3	-3
12	16	16	16	16	Gentler and milder	-4	-2	-3	-3	-3
13	16	16	16	16	Makes your skin fairer/lighter	-2	-4	-4	-4	-3
14	18	19	19	19	Improves skin health	5	6	7	7	7
13	16	16	16	16	Make you look and feel beautiful	-4	-4	-4	-4	-4
13	16	17	17	17	Are brands I trust more	1	0	1	0	1
16	21	21	21	21	Brand recommended by health experts	12	13	14	13	13
14	18	18	18	18	Are suitable for the whole family	3	3	3	3	3

not more, it would help understand the impact of different marketing activities on the brand.

Let's look at the example below. A hair care brand (competing with Unilever) was trying to position itself on 'making hair strong' for several years, however, wasn't able to make a successful mark in the market. They then brought in a clutter-breaking ad campaign focusing on this specific attribute. As the ad recall went up, so did the association of the brand with 'strong hair'. This is an exceptionally clear case study where the impact of the new ad was directly visible on the attribute. But there are other times when modelling (attribution analytics) is needed to isolate the impact of different activities on different brand attributes.

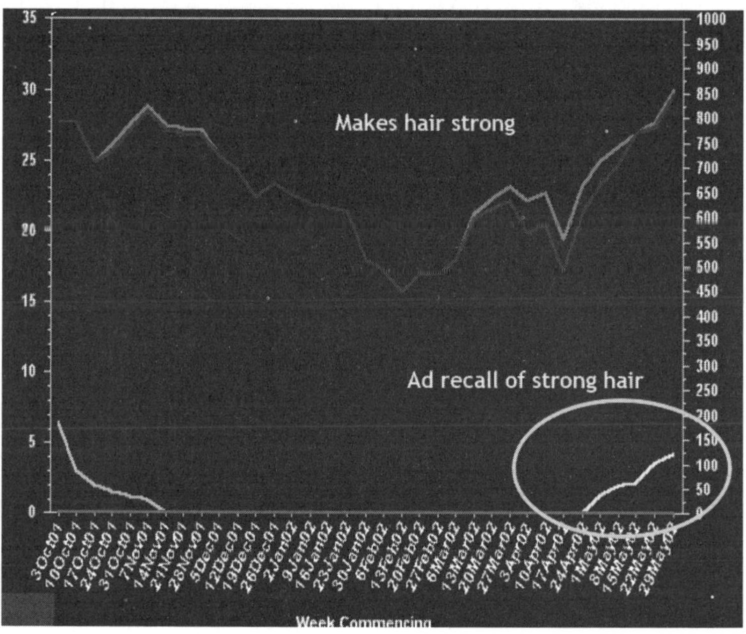

Qualitative research can be used effectively to understand the finer nuances of brand positioning. It is particularly useful when the brand is trying to change its position, or if a new brand is attempting to create a unique position for itself. Qualitative research gets real in-depth insights on how people use the brands in the category, how they make choices, what do they really think of the brand, the imagery of different brands, the colours or symbols or signs, etc., that go with the imagery which should (and shouldn't) be used in advertising and packaging and the imagery, the flavours or fragrances that would complement the brand position, etc. This requires real expertise in conducting and analyzing the results provided by the experienced professionals in the qualitative research world.

Unilever uses a tool called 'Brand Key' to express the positioning of a brand. Several organizations across the world use similar tools to define their brand and that serves as the reference document for all the activities the brand undertakes. One of the key foundational pillars of a brand key is 'consumer insight' or 'human truth' or 'consumer reality' as it is called in different versions. However, that insight is what the brand is based upon and it then addresses the need or aspiration or anxiety expressed in the insight. Qualitative research, as described above, is used extensively to articulate that insight.

An example of Dove shampoo brand key below shows how the brand coherently manages to address the pressure women feel due to the high standards of beauty decided by the society and portrayed by most beauty brands (this is precisely the insight on which Dove brand is based).

8) Brand Discriminator:
- Only Dove can nourish and repair damaged hair and inspire women to feel truly beautiful.

6) Functional Benefits:
- Skin care: keep skin nourished, smooth, soft
- Hair care: reduce hair fall & breakage (95%), nourish hair from the inside → strengthen hair

5) Product Truth:
- Skin care: Body wash has Nutrium Moisture → nourish hair from inside. Soap bar contains of ¼ moisturizing cream
- Hair care: Micro Moisture Serum + Fiber Actives → repair damaged hair from inside; Trichazole Actives nourish hair roots

1) Roots:
- Strong & well-known global brand (Unilever is the No.1 brand owner - Brand Footprint 2015, Kantar World Panel - Link)
- Strong R&D, talent human resource & wide distribution channel
- Dove is the top riser in Health & Beauty Care sector (BrandFootprint 2015, Kantar World Panel)
- Diverse product lines which meet all of segments (Beauty bar, body wash, shampoo, conditioner, treatments); dove; white; moisturizing; soft product shapes; normal women (no celebrities) and their testimonials

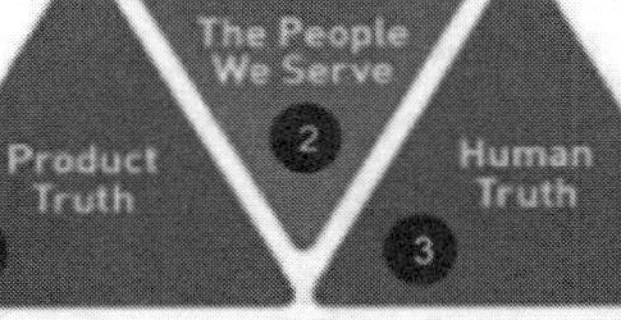

10) USLP:
- Dove's Self-Esteem Project aims to help young people to improve self-esteem through educational programs → Over 11 million people have received help since 2005. Over 2 million participated in 16 countries in 2012

9) Brand Personality:
- Natural beauty, soft, feminine, sophisticated, purity, inner confidence

7) Emotional Benefits:
- Empower women by increasing self-esteem; make them feel more confident, optimistic about their real beauty; more feminine

4) Purpose:
- Re-define true beauty & deliver real care

2) The People We Serve:
- Natural & Confident women seeking "Real Beauty"; want to look and feel optimistic

3) Human Truth:
- Beauty standards of a woman is decided by the society → Being beautiful is a pressure, instead of something natural that women would enjoy

Source: Slideshare.net

Brand Equity

The equity of a brand is a net sum of what the brand is capable of. This comes from the brand's legacy and its strengths in the marketplace as well as consumers' minds. The word 'equity' is derived from the financial world to add a sense of 'worth' to this concept. However, in the marketing world, brand equity is not measured so much in terms of actual or potential sales or what the brand would be financially worth, if sold. This poses an interesting challenge on the measurement of brand equity. It needs to indicate what the brand is worth in the minds of the consumer; in other words, what they think the brand can really deliver. Take the case of Apple, for example. Apple has great equity in terms of being an innovator in tech products that make its consumer's life simple and convenient. But is the equity strong enough for Apple to start manufacturing cars for instance? If they could move from desktops to laptops, iPods to iPhones, and so on, can they take the next leap towards making cars? While it has an equity of being innovative and simplifying tech for people, can it make a complex machinery with several moving non-electronic parts required in a car? This section looks at various ways in which organizations like Unilever look and measure brand equity in order to answer the question posed for Apple.

Qualitative research is used extensively to understand different associations and determine the strength of these associations. The agility of this research method is well-suited for navigating the nuances of the brand and gives a crystal clear picture. One of the equity models used at Unilever is the one offered by the organization Quantum Solutions. Their proprietary model shown below looks at the brand holistically in terms of values that are core to the brand, values that are peripheral, supporting, missing, and distracting. This model is, therefore, quite useful in terms of understanding what the brand is capable of and the attributes it may need to own or enhance in order to do new things in the market. An anti-bacterial soap, for instance, may have germ protection and health as the core values of the brand, and would have 'suitable for whole family' as its supporter value, 'affordability' as peripheral value. However, if it is perceived to be harsh on skin, it may be a detractor and 'providing luxurious beauty bath' maybe a value that's absent (for the right reasons).

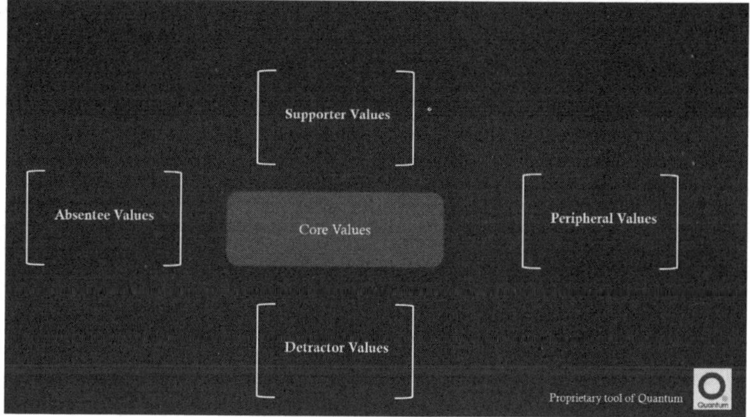

The issue with the qualitative model is that it can't be used to track and make direct comparisons over a period of time and correlate it with the input variables like advertising spends or other marketing activities. Needless to say, it is very effective in understanding the core values of the brand and how those are evolving over time, if the same qualitative research is repeated every couple of years.

For quantitative measurement and tracking, there are couple of other syndicated models used by several organizations, which usually are coupled with complimentary qualitative research to enhance the understanding about the brand.

1. **Interbrand's Best Global Brands:** They look at the financial analysis (which looks at the financial return to the investors), role of the brand (the portion of the purchase decision attributable to the brand as opposed to other factors like price, availability, etc.) and brand strength (ability of the brand to create loyalty). Details are given on their website Best Global Brands 2020: Methodology - Interbrand. Using this methodology, they publish the list of brands globally. For 2022, the top brands were:

01 Apple +18% 482,215 $m	02 Microsoft +32% 278,288 $m	03 Amazon +10% 274,819 $m	04 Google +28% 251,751 $m	05 Samsung +17% 87,689 $m
06 Toyota +10% 59,757 $m	07 Coca-Cola 0% 57,535 $m	08 Mercedes-Benz +10% 56,103 $m	09 Disney +14% 50,325 $m	10 Nike +18% 50,289 $m
11 McDonald's +6% 48,647 $m	12 Tesla +32% 48,002 $m	13 BMW +11% 46,331 $m	14 Louis Vuitton +21% 44,508 $m	15 Cisco +14% 41,298 $m
16 Instagram +14% 36,516 $m	17 Facebook -5% 34,538 $m	18 IBM +3% 34,242 $m	19 Intel -8% 32,916 $m	20 SAP +5% 31,497 $m

This is a great tool to understand the 'worth' of a brand from a holistic perspective. The trouble is, if your brand is not in it, then you don't get the worth; and, more importantly, it doesn't give a detailed understanding of what has created the value for the brand in order to act on those learnings.

2. **BrandZ Score from Kantar:** One of the world's largest research companies, Kantar, is also a leading research organization on advertising and marketing measurements. They run brand and ad tracks for several brands across the world, and, as a result, have a huge understanding of what makes a brand valuable. Using those learnings, they have created BrandZ Score that they publish every year. The methodology and other details can be found on their website (kantar.com). You'd be able to discover the BrandZ Top 100 Most Valuable Global Brands. The top global brands as per their 2022 report were:

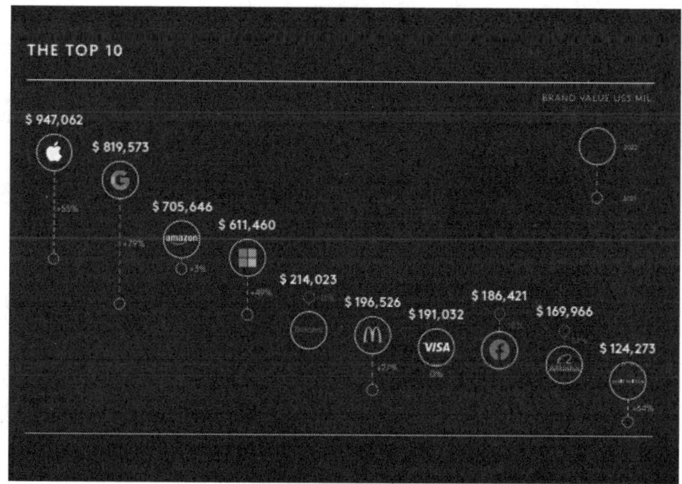

This has similar advantages and limitations as the Interbrand report.

The best way to get a detailed equity understanding for a brand—that can be compared over a period of time and with relevant set of competitors—is to have a bespoke measurement; usually included in the brand tracking. Unilever looks at the brand equity score in two ways—one is via brand pyramids or signatures, and the other one is via brand equity score.

Brand pyramids—derived from the Kantar Millward Brown tracking questionnaire (done every week across markets for all categories globally)—indicate the strength of the consumer relationship with the brand. It is usually in the form of a pyramid which indicates that the relationship tends to be like a ladder where a large solid base shows good reach for the brand, and it keeps narrowing down as consumers move up from being unaware to trialists to regular users to being fans of the brand. A typical pyramid looks like this:

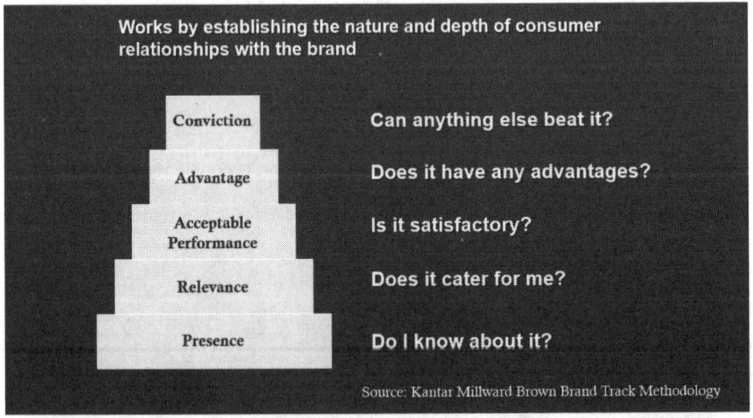

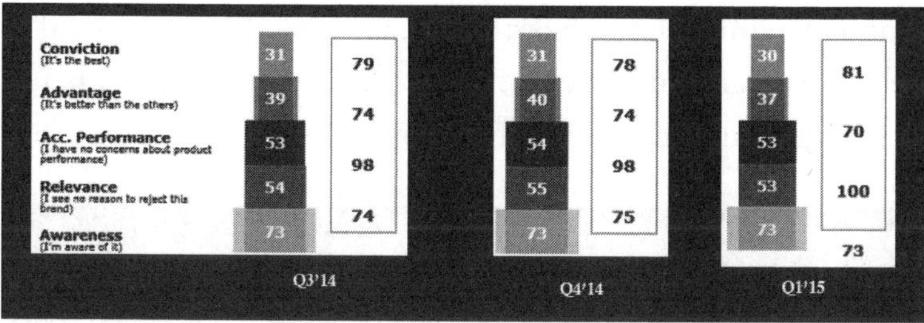

Brand signature, on the other hand, is about conversion from one level to the other. The idea is to calculate average conversion in the category (for all the key brands in the market measured during tracking) and compare the conversion for your brand with the average. Obviously, higher the conversion the better, because it means your brand is converting consumers from a basic relationship to a more involved one at a faster pace than other brands. The reason it is referred to as 'signature' because the shape of this data indicates what kind of brand it is and its strength. Here are the signature typologies from Kantar Millward Brown studies:

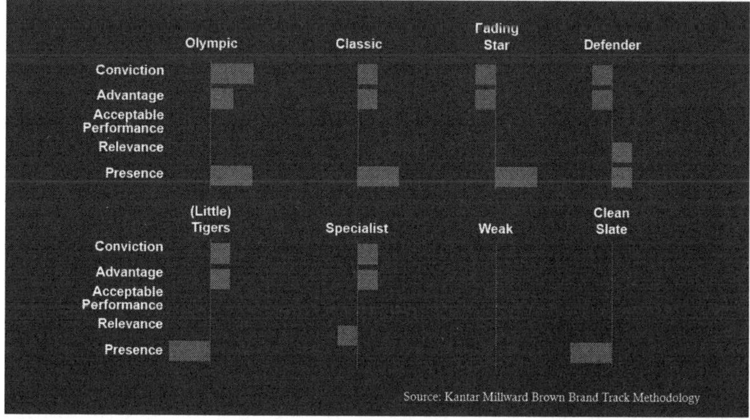

Source: Kantar Millward Brown Brand Track Methodology

As an example of the application or use case, look at the brand pyramid and signature of Omo in Thailand in 2010 below. It clearly indicates a strong master brand, which is not as strong in all the variants that it operates in:

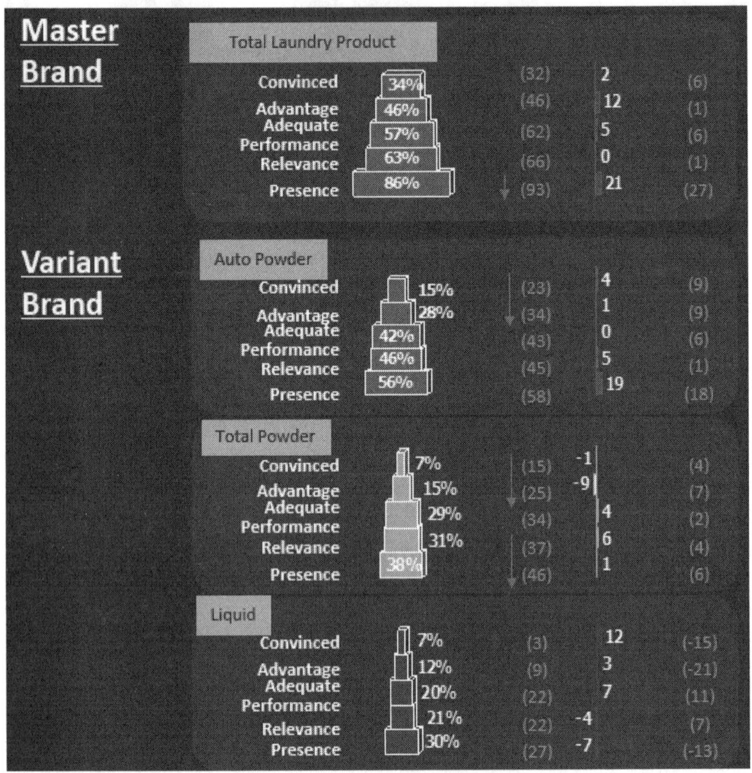

The pyramids, signature calculations, and usage have evolved over a period of time and have become simpler. However, conceptually, they remain the same and give a fantastic picture of what a brand is capable of.

The other way of looking at brand equity that has gained popularity in the last few years is through its brand equity

(BE) score. While the pyramids and signature are a great pictorial representation of the brand strength, they turn out to be a little impractical when used in analytical modelling to understand the reasons for the change or even to summarize the trend over a period of time in a crisp fashion. BE Score meets those requirements quite well, though it lacks the depth of understanding that a pyramid or signature can provide. Therefore, it's best to use both. There are two ways in which BE score can be derived:

1. **Weighted average:** The weighted average of the brand's scores on all the attributes on which the brand positioning is evaluated during the tracking. The weights can be derived in various ways but, conceptually speaking, they are done by regressing the attribute performance scores of the brand with the overall brand sales or opinion or any other similar overall measure of the brand included in the tracking. The weights remain constant for couple of years but the brand scores change with every track giving dynamic agility to its BE score. The limitation of this method—though it was quite popular in Unilever for a few years and used by several other organizations—is that it assumed that the equity of a brand is primarily measured by those attributes alone. It ignores other 'facets' of equity like ease of availability, salience, etc. It is further limited by the attributes included in the study; if some critical attributes are missing in the list, then the attributes don't correlate well with the overall measure. Statistically speaking, the variance in overall measure is not explained by the variance in attribute

scores. Therefore, while it provides a BE score, it can be a relatively narrow view of the brand performance.

2. **Pyramid Score:** The other way is to make use of attribute statements further used to define the pyramid and aggregate them in a score. This method uses weights for these statements (that information is proprietary to Kantar Millward Brown) and derives the score. This takes care of the limitations in the previous method and provides a more holistic view of the equity.

   One of the use cases of this kind of BE score comes from analytical modelling relating the BE score data calculated this way, for several categories across markets, with brand penetration. That model suggests that the changes in this score over a period of time also correlate well with the changes in brand penetration thereby greatly validating this score. Given below is an example of drivers of penetration for one of the Unilever brands, which has a strong equity. This suggests that the change

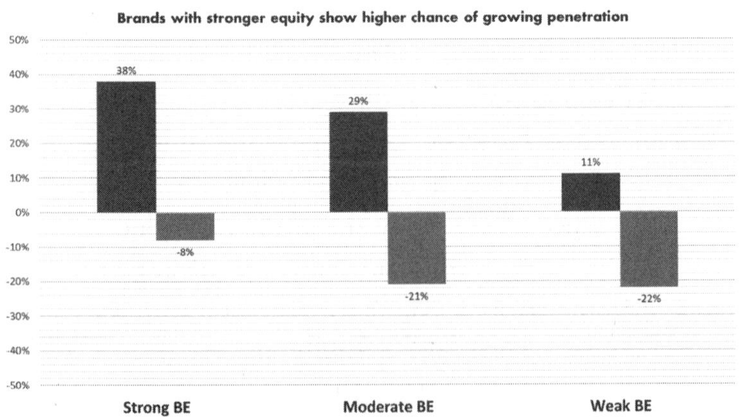

in BE score for the brand can impact penetration two quarters down the line (lag effect) as against another brand with moderate equity that can impact penetration immediately.

Brand communication

Consumer good companies like Unilever spend substantial amount of money on advertising. Around 14% of the organization's turnover is spent on brand and media investments, according to Unilever's annual report 2020. Therefore, understanding if an ad is right for the brand—both strategically (to see if an ad is in line with brand strategy), as well as on execution (to see if a specific creative would deliver on expectations)—is a high priority for marketing and insight teams.

Ad pre-testing is used extensively to 'judge' the creative's ability to deliver on air before the ad actually goes on air. And an on-air performance is evaluated through brand and ad tracks, which form the 'post-launch evaluation'. While those are a lot more about evaluating specific ads and their performance, to have an understanding of what has worked historically in all the aspects of the brand's communication is a critical part of the strategic understanding of a brand. Arguably, it is not only what has worked for the brand in the past but also an understanding of the changing codes of communication of the category, changing consumer preference on the nature of the preferred communication, and the mode of receiving them should also form a part of this area of the strategic understanding. Let's look at these aspects separately.

1. What communication works for your brand?

Kantar Millward Brown, the world's largest communication testing agency, has a model called Link™ that is widely used by brands across companies for pre- and post-testing. The construct is fairly intuitive and has been validated consistently across the globe to show that an ad classified as 'good' by this framework would more often than not deliver on the expectations when launched.

In the classic version of this model, it brings down the performance of the ad to two dimensions, viz., Awareness Index or AI (which is a validated measure of the ad's engagement) and persuasive ability of the ad (measured by the persuasion score). In other words, it evaluates if viewers would engage with the ad to create a memory in consumers' minds (in other words, the ad is likely to stand out in a clutter); and if it would persuade the non-users to buy, and tempt their existing users to repeat purchase, and so on.

The work done by Kantar Millward Brown and advertisers like Unilever has shown that these two drivers of success are independent factors with little correlation between them. The best prediction of the short-term sales potential of advertising comes from combining AI and persuasion into a composite measure called the Link Short-Term Sales Likelihood (STSL) value. The STSL score shows a clear relationship with the in-market sales return: strong performing ads are four times more likely to generate a large sales return than the weak ads (says the press release by Kantar Millward Brown in the UK). The Short-Term Likelihood of Sales (STSL) can be provided with only the pre-test results. But with basic volume share data and simple pricing and media spend assessments, the probable magnitude of the sales increase could be predicted. With a more tailored approach for an individual brand, where full spend, pricing, and brand elasticity data is available, Link™ can provide specific sales volume predictions.

Ultimately, it's the holistic understanding of what's working in the ad (and what's not) that provides the clear guidance on its way forward. The diagnostic analysis elaborates what is making the ad persuasive and memorable and what is distracting it from making it memorable or less persuasive. Let's look at the Clinic All Clear celebrity ad referenced to in the 6P analysis in the earlier part of the book. The ad for the anti-dandruff shampoo featured two Indian celebrities who were dating at the time and the chemistry of their relationship was used to land the message of anti-dandruff component.

The ad, however, didn't do well in the pre-testing. It resulted in low awareness index (which is a reflection of less engagement with the ad) and high persuasion—suggesting that it would fail to break the clutter; however, those who would remember seeing it would be persuaded by it. It's not a great result for an ad as it could be quite risky to spend money behind an ad of this nature. The AI was low because consumers didn't really engage emotionally with the two celebrities playing basketball with each other, and to make things worse, they misappropriated the brand to that of a competitor. As a result, the clutter-breaking ability was poor, but it did land the message of being an anti-dandruff shampoo (probably because of the historical legacy of Clinic All Clear and the competition brand), resulting in good persuasion.

The ad went on air and it didn't deliver either an increase in the brand equity or sales. Furthermore, the performance was even worse in southern parts of India where people didn't recognize them as celebrities. It's the detailed diagnostics of this analysis that give clues on why the ad has landed at the position on the framework which leads to a change in the advertising.

While the pre-testing helps optimizing the creative before it is aired, evaluating its performance post the ad is aired on an ongoing basis gives valuable insights on maximizing the returns from the ad. It also facilitates the link between the performance of the ad and brand measures. This evaluation is part of the brand or ad track and the key measures it looks at are:

1. Did the ad get noticed on air (break the clutter)?
2. Do people remember what brand the ad was for? Sometimes, there is a misattribution to competition brand, particularly if the ad is not very differentiating.

3. What message did it land?
4. Did it persuade people to take action (try the brand or repeat purchase, etc., depending on the objective)?

The pre- and post-testing performance of the ads is highly correlated. In other words, an ad tends to perform in the same way in both (if the definition of the target sample is the same). This insight has led companies like Unilever to use the pre- and post-testing *in conjunction* to maximize the understanding of the ad performance. Ads with big spends tend to be pre-tested while others are evaluated directly post-launch (since the tracker is a continuous one). A combined analysis of the two for a brand also gives useful insights on the kind of advertising that works for the brand (next point in this section).

An example of summary of performance of aired ads of two hair care brands in post-tracking:

This analysis makes it clear that, in 2014-15, Brand 1 shampoo ads performed much better than Brand 2 shampoo ads. Brand 1 ads broke the clutter, were recognized to be for the Brand A and were generally quite enjoyable and engaging. Brand 2 ads, on the other hand, were engaging, but could have done better on clutter-breaking ability and being persuasive. A deeper analysis from the pre-testing and historical performance gave vital clues on the elements to change in the ads that could make Shampoo B ads perform better.

Communication performance 2014 - 2015

Brand 1

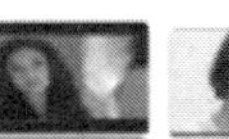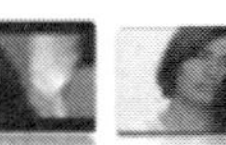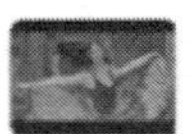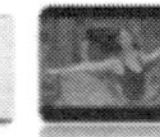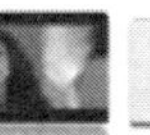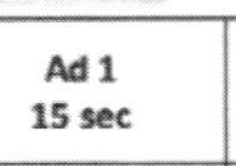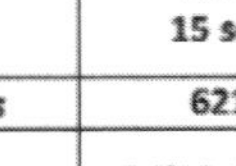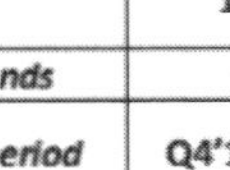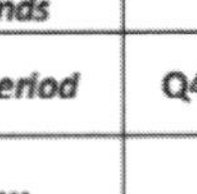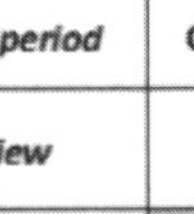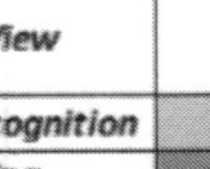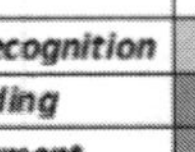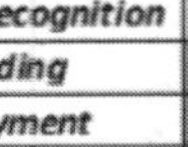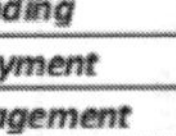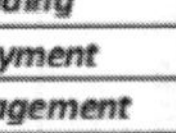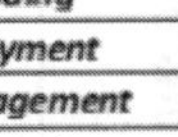

TVC Name	Ad 1 15 sec	Ad 2 20 sec	Ad 3 30 sec	Ad 4 15 sec	Ad 5 20 sec	Ad 6 30 sec	Ad 7 30 sec	Ad 8 20 sec	Ad 9 30 sec
GRP Spends	621	527	1,161	635	826	474	834	854#	446#
Airing period	Q4'13-Q1'14	Q1' 14	Q1-Q3'14	Q2'14	Q2-Q3'14	Q2-Q3'14	Q4'14-Q1'15	Q1 2015 - *	
Post View	-	24/03/2014- 06/04/2014	05/05/2014 18/05/2014	07/07/2014 - 20/07/2014	4/8/2014to 17/4/2014	18/08/2014 31/08/2014	17/11/2014 14/12/2014	27/4/2015 10/5/2015	20/04/2015 - 03/05/201
Ad Recognition									
Branding									
Enjoyment									
Engagement									
Persuasion									
Main Point									

All India data * GRP data not available # GRP data till Q1 2015

Communication performance 2014 - 2015

Brand 2

TVC Name	Ad 1	Ad 2	Ad 3	Ad 4
GRP Spends	708	1,027	758	247[#]
Airing period	Q1'14	Q4'14	Q1'14 – Q4 '14	Q1'15 - *
Post view Date	07/04/2014 – 04/05/2014	01/09/2014 – 21/09/2014	19/5/2014- 01/06/2014	09/02/2015 - 22/02/2015
Ad Recognition				
Brand Linkage				
Enjoyment				
Engagement				
Persuasion				
Main Point				

2. Understanding codes of communication for your brand through meta-analysis of historical performance

This brings us to the meta-analysis of the historical performance of the ads for a brand. If the same ad agency has been working on the brand for years, they usually become the default 'custodians' of the brand advertising and have an excellent perspective on what has worked for the brand in different markets. The insights team in an organization can also be the other custodian as they can bring the objective analysis from pre and post tests on what has worked for the ad to stand out and impact the brand performance. This conversation is critical to understand the codes the brand should continue using that are familiar to consumers and have made its ads memorable in the past.

When you usually see the ads for brands like Pepsi, Coke, Dove, and Nike, you know what brand it is for even before the brand appears in the film. That is because they keep the style of the storytelling consistent. Additionally, the colours used in the background, the personality of the characters, celebrity if used etc., are always consistent and in line with the brand values. The historic analysis puts to rest the debate on the elements that the brand can't afford to drop and the elements that can be changed or modernized or evolved. This usually comes from mining the previous ad tests (pre and post) and good qualitative research with the users and non-users to get sharp insights on what a brand should retain in its communication and what it can afford to lose.

An interesting example of such meta-analysis carried out by the Advertising Standards Council of India (ASCI) helps

Part B
Analysis of cross-category advertising content reveals that a significant proportion and the most widely viewed cache of advertising seems to continue to borrow from an inventory of stereotypes

Women trapped in a loop of portrayals: Content analysis of advertising reveals oddly persistent images that appear repeatedly. Every category seems to have its own 'key image' frames that appear across different brands. Whether it is a woman holding a tray of food, young girls wearing monochrome costumes in beauty and fashion ads, women being instructed by male voice-overs in detergent ads, young women gazing anxiously into the mirror in skin care ads, women being cheerful and carefree while washing dishes or cooking multi-course meals for the whole family - these images keep making a consistent appearance.

Much of the stereotyping lies in the subliminal background of a film or image: Stereotypes reveal themselves when one sees between the frames. It is in the general body language, appearance, attire, task-pairing, spaces in which women are set in, that a gender bias makes its appearance. For e.g., women wearing traditional clothing are often cast as being less aware than western attired ones, food advertising typically distances the woman from moments of life by placing her in the kitchen, skin care ads show groups of young women moving and mouthing jingles in sync.

Women's empowerment-oriented advertising pins new stories on existing cultural stereotypes of women: Even as advertising scripts show women being more successful, more independent - they stay loyal to existing cultural stereotypes. Women are increasingly shown to be independent but rarely to be free of the social behaviours typically attributed to them. E.g., new attributes like entrepreneurial zeal are still shown alongside the woman being caring and continuing to fulfil domestic duties or the emotional care-taking of her family.

New stereotypes load women with burdens they may not seek to bear: Old stereotypes are being replaced by some new ones. The 'working woman', the woman who 'balances work and home', the 'cool' or 'bindaas' teenage girl are part of a new set of representations. Though each of these are meant to reflect the new lives and choices of women, they are also stereotypical new ways of being. We must ask ourselves if women want to be celebrated for bearing more burden at home and work, or for their fashion and style to be interpreted as an invitation to flirting.

The male celebrity has coercive power over women in ad narratives: Several categories like food, home cleaning, detergents - seem to use the male celebrity in a particularly authoritarian mould - evaluating, rejecting and then correcting a woman's actions or choices. A surprising factor of this coercion is that it usually plays out in the domain of the woman's home, where the male celebrity/movie star usurps power and space that should not be his to claim.

A tendency to infantilise men, not normalise their partaking in domestic and emotional labours: Though brands seem to want to show more equitable division of labour or more non-gendered attitudes to domestic duties or child-rearing, there is a common misstep. More often than not, such male characters are written to appear inherently incapable or inexperienced in basic tasks. This tends to reinforce stereotypes of both genders, keeping the burden squarely on women even though brands might intend to connote the opposite. The fact that men in this situation are typically written and depicted as 'cute' and childlike in their bungling of simple tasks, the ad builds in a reason to absolve them of the new duties they are being asked to shoulder.

Typically, male oriented categories are slowly including women in the frame, but very often without agency: Finance and automobile advertising is seeing more women present in imagery than ever before. However, women are still framed as silent on-lookers or receiving the benefits of good male judgment without seeming to have their own, or having weaker contact with or control over with the product than men have been shown to possess.

Beauty is represented along very narrow definitions: There seems to be an implicit code of beauty that women are measured against. This becomes visible in the casting of female actors in advertising. Not only is this code visible in beauty and fashion categories, where skin colour and tone, weight and height seem to be strictly defined, but is one seen across advertising. Implicit codes of what women's appearance should be also play out through a moulding of women through styling and apparel - seemingly mandating what a mother should wear, how a young girl's hair should be styled and so on. These beauty moulds are ones that too few women can fit in.

New cliches of representation create hollow depictions of female empowerment, freedoms: There is a tokenism in showing women in spaces beyond the home. Especially the new stereotype of the working woman who is rarely seen at work but is shown as 'returning' home. For example, the 'doctor-mother' or a professional woman are rarely shown in their work settings and most often at home with their family. We end up seeing what are significant aspects of women's self-definitions, represented merely through wardrobe and styling. There is little change in the tasks she is aligned to, or the expectations others have of her. These don't seem to have undergone the make-over the woman has been given stylistically.

understand the depiction of women in advertising. The analysts pored over thousands of ads across categories over a period of time and identified 'stereotypes' of different kinds and developed a narrative on the change that needs to be brought in[9]. Some of the headline thoughts from the study are given in the image.

Consumer Segmentation

One of the most fundamental building blocks of marketing strategy is the consumer segmentation. It enables the business to divide consumers into groups that are similar to each other, so that they can be addressed collectively as a group. The key question that arises is: 'similar to each other' on what aspects? And the answer to that question determines the segmentation strategy. For instance, if there is a 'reason to believe', via consumer research done in the past, that people in different age groups behave differently when it comes to their TV viewing habits, demographic segmentation by age can be meaningful for content creators (and even by the TV manufacturers who could offer different features). Demographic segmentation is a simple and basic one to carry out and often the starting point of the marketing strategy. Other segmentation routes—like the ones based on psychographics such as consumer lifestyle or attitudes towards a category—have also been quite popular in the past.

One of the big criticisms of segmentation is that it looks nice on a PowerPoint presentation but is very difficult to

---

[9] The report is called 'Gender Next: Follow her lead' by the Advertising Standards Council of India and Futurebrands, released in 2021.

use in real life, especially outside of the digital ecosystem. A washing machine maker, for example, can create small and big washing machines depending upon the size of families. However, size-specific advertising or making them available in different shops is not easy because all families tend to have similar media exposure and go to similar shops. So, targeting them differentially is nearly impossible. Similarly, holiday plans designed by a resort for travel enthusiasts vs. lazy travelers may vary significantly, but reaching out to them through different media is a bit of a nightmare. The digital media has, of course, changed a lot of that. We will look at the evolution of segmentation with the digital media later in this chapter.

Partly as a consequence of this criticism and partly with media fragmentation, segmentation has also evolved to make itself more meaningful for new product development, product or service design, communication design, etc. And with the media fragmentation, targeting consumers differentially has also become relatively easier over a period of time. For instance, if Knorr wants to target consumers who are passionate about cooking, using cookery shows and cooking-related articles and web pages can allow the brand to talk to passionate cooks more than others.

The other part that has led to the evolution is the coming together of 'market' and 'consumer' segmentation. Market segmentation traditionally implied dividing the market into different parts that needed different strategies to address them. For instance, urban vs. rural, or institutional vs. retail segments, etc. While the underlying need was to address consumers in these markets differently, several other factors were required to be considered for different market segments. For example, catering to institutional customers requires a different ecosystem than the retail ones; so one doesn't need to think of just the consumer or customer needs but also the way to serve them.

With market and consumer segmentation coming together (with more sophisticated analytical tools and capabilities), organizations don't look at the market and consumer segmentation differently, but in conjunction. This leads to a complete and holistic solution that's lot more actionable than each of them individually. The third segmentation approach outlined in this chapter is a good example of this.

In this section, we look at three different segmentation approaches that are used extensively by consumer-centric organizations. They are by no means exhaustive and there could be multiple different approaches used by different organizations, but these are some good frameworks that can become the backbone of marketing strategies.

Benefit segmentation

This is one of the simplest ones to do and can often be done in-house as well (in the sense, without much primary research but using existing internal and external data sources). In some versions, this is actually not a consumer segmentation but only market or product segmentation done on the basis of benefits offered by different products. Using a database such as NielsenIQ Retail Measurement Services or other similar tools, sizing is then carried out of the resulting segments based on the sales value of those products in the market. Consumer behaviour can then be laid on top of this.

A benefit segmentation done on soap bars in China, Thailand, Vietnam, and Indonesia in 2005 revealed that the benefits consumers expected from bars of soap was quite different from that of body washes. In consumers' minds, the body wash wasn't just a different format that would offer the same benefits as the bar soap; the format actually dictated certain expectations.

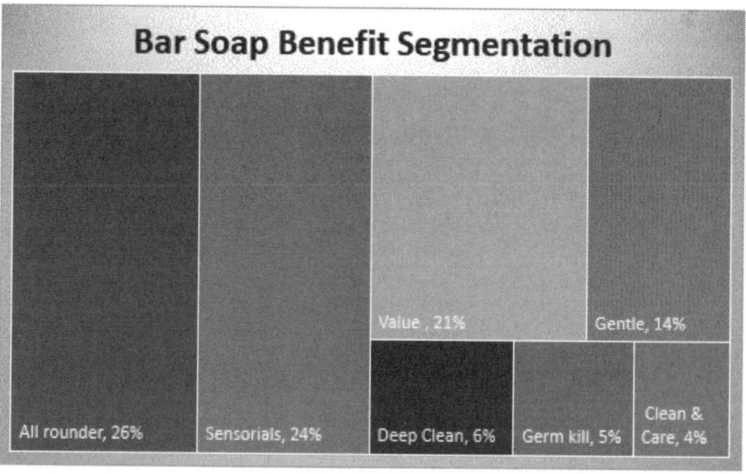

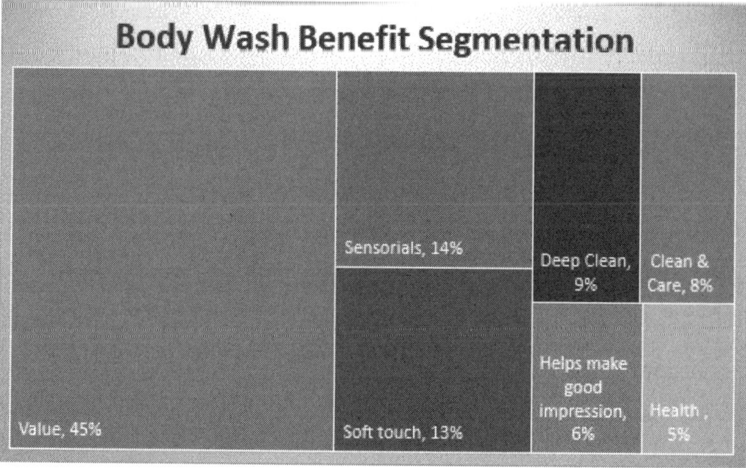

The percentages in these charts and the box sizes, therefore, reflect the size of benefit segment. Strictly speaking, this means that 24% of the share in soap bars is that of the soaps that sell on the sensorial benefits (and 14% in case of body wash), but it is also interpreted as a consumer need. In other words, apart from wanting an 'all-rounder soap' (good in everything), people desire sensorial benefits in soap bars. However, in body washes, they want 'value' more than the sensorial benefit (partly also because body washes tend to be more expensive than soap bars).

Mapping of the brands on these benefits provides insights on the differentiation the brands have in consumers' minds but also the attributes of their equity. Demographic and psychographic profile of people seeking these benefits gave insights into how the benefits could be communicated to them. So, while this is not a consumer segmentation, this way of segmentation makes a lot of sense because same consumers buy different soaps giving different benefits at different points in time. For instance, consumers with flirtatious behaviour, sometimes, would be tempted to buy a small body wash product that smells really nice while sometimes they would be attracted by a good value proposition (e.g., of a larger pack at discounted price). As consumers move between brands for different benefits, it's the benefits that becomes the biggest discriminator of consumers more than anything else, and hence, 'benefit segmentation' can give useful insights for marketers to work on.

In several cases, benefit segmentation is the first segmentation carried out to give a clear 'lay of the land', and hence, it becomes a foundational starting point. Furthermore, segmentation is done subsequently based on the understanding of other dimensions that can discriminate consumer behaviour.

Needstate segmentation

This is the segmentation based on the emotional needs of people that impact consumption. It's about the state of mind that people find themselves in different situations that affect the categories and brands they buy. Consider alcoholic beverages as an example: depending on how people want to feel and who they are with, the consumption changes. When drinking with friends in a pub after work, people prefer beer because the need is to 'hang out' with people and drink something light and fun. The choice of beer brand is also likely to be a brand that everyone likes and is not too heavy or strong. The choice moves, however, to spirits in more intimate situations with one or few friends coming together.

Apart from alcoholic beverages, there are several categories that work on emotional needs quite well, for instance, perfumes (fine fragrances), beverages, cars, food, skin care, etc. This segmentation is a great way of dividing the market into consumers with different needs and understanding how a brand wanting to cater to those needs can position themselves on attributes that matter (for a need) and differentiate from other brands. We look at the example of skin care brands using the tool called Needscope®—the proprietary model of Kantar TNS.

The Needscope® model looks to understand the emotional needs in two dimensions that give an insight on the mindset or state of mind:

1. **How does one relate to the world:** There are times when you want to belong to the world and want to be included with the set of people you are interacting with. Hanging out with friends in a pub post work from the example above is one such instance—you want to be with colleagues and have fun and want to belong to that group. But you maybe in a different mindset at other times when you want to stand out instead: you might be competing with same colleagues at workplace, and you would want to stand out and perform better than others. Hence, there is an 'affiliative' mode and 'assertive' mode of interacting with the world and both have their *own* time and place in a person's life. And that can impact product consumption.

   Let's take clothes as a category to illustrate this further: the clothes that you wear in office with the colleagues and clothes you wear with colleagues at an evening party can be driven by this state of mind (apart from office's policy of dress code). In office, you would want to look professional but distinct from others ('assertive' state of mind), but while hanging out with them outside, you choose clothes that are trendy (and, hence, socially acceptable and worn by a lot of people ('affiliative' state of mind).

   Face make-up can be another category that works similarly on this axis: The make-up that women are likely to wear in office would be something that would make them look professional but not stand out as someone trying to look attractive at workplace. But, in a social out-of-office gathering, the make-up used is the one that makes you stand out from others. This is how the way you relate with the world (and want to relate to) affects your state of mind and product consumption.

2. **How does one express oneself or derive the energy from:** There are two modes of this; outward expression (extroversion) and inward repression (introversion). When you are happy and want to have fun, you could be dancing away your evening (extroverted expression) or you could be spending the evening at a spa chilling out (introverted expression). This expression is not entirely driven by the extrovert or introvert personality type a person might have, because the so-called introverts can also express their emotions to others quite well (verbally and non-verbally), and vice versa. But it is about what your state of mind is at that point of time. At the end of a long, tiring week, sometimes you would want to go out and party but sometimes you would want to sit at home and watch TV—both could be equally good ways for relaxing, but they are different expressions of your energy.

   Typical extrovert expressions are loud, flashy, seductive, jumpy, while the introvert expressions are calm, collected, put together, in control, etc. Make-up, again, proves to be a good example of consumption for this axis: a woman is likely to wear bright red lipstick on a date night when she wants to express the excitement of being on the date, while a subtle-coloured lipstick might be for the comfort of moisturized lips in order to

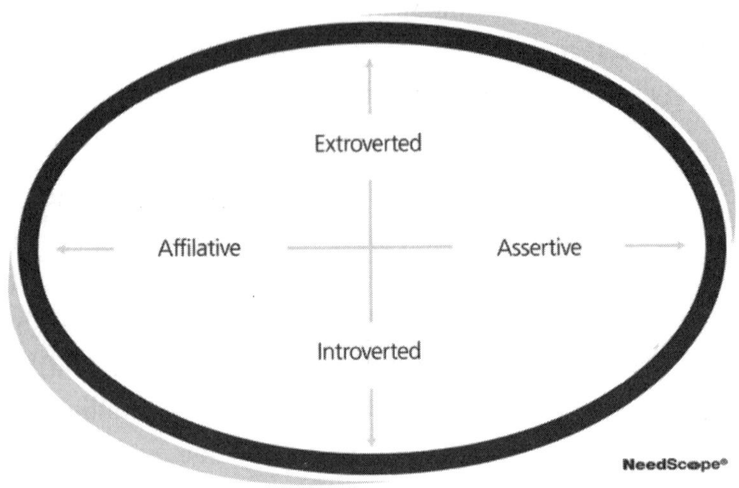

The NeedScope model maps universal human emotions. This provides a framework to map brands and their symbolism.

feel confident and calm (as opposed to seductive) when going to work.

The real magic happens when the two axes are combined—here, distinct territories of human emotions and personalities emerge. Real evocative brands are those that understand and tap into these need spaces quite effectively. Like L'Oréal taps into the assertive dominance space (three o'clock) accompanied with the tagline "because I am worth it" and offers products that can give women (and now men, too) confidence to look their best. Or, Toyota—an affiliative brand at nine o'clock position offering family and pocket-friendly cars.

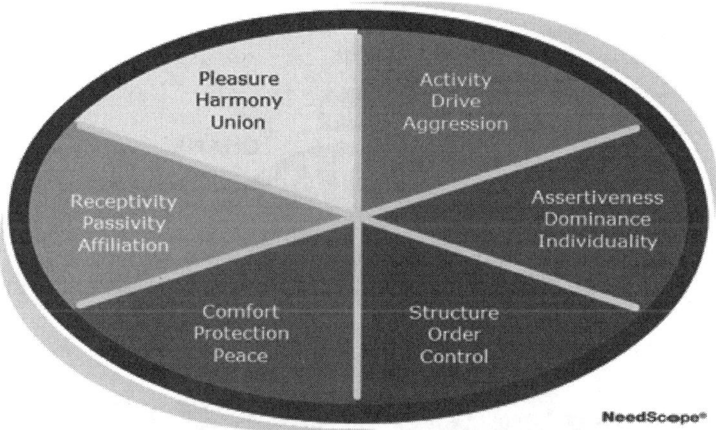

The six emotive spaces

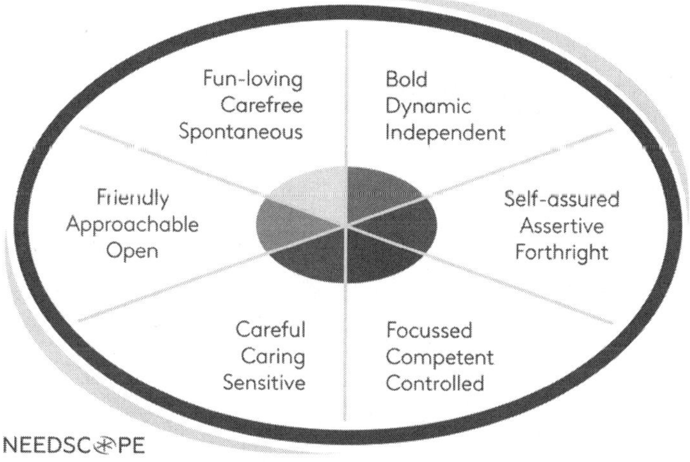

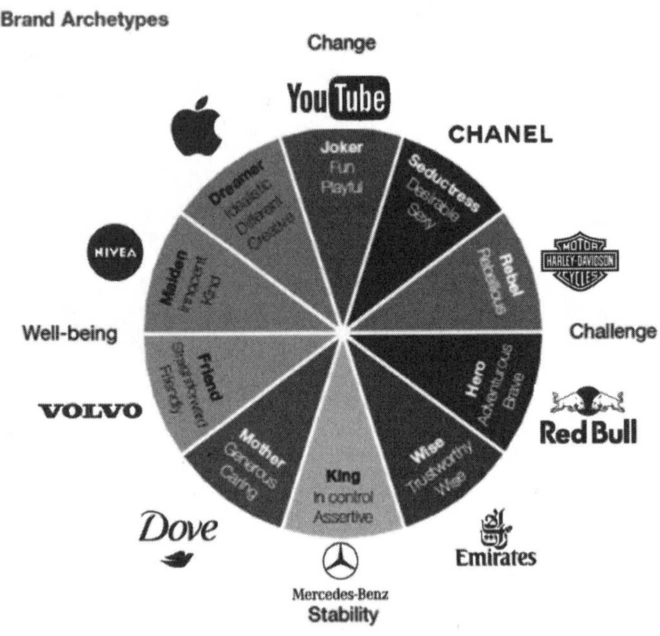
Brand Archetypes
Change
YouTube
CHANEL
Joker
Fun
Playful
Seductress
Desirable
Sexy
Rebel
Rebellious
MOTOR
HARLEY-DAVIDSON
CYCLES
Challenge
Hero
Adventurous
Brave
Red Bull
Wise
Trustworthy
Wise
Emirates
King
In control
Assertive
Mercedes-Benz
Stability
Mother
Generous
Caring
Dove
Friend
Straightforward
Friendly
VOLVO
Well-being
Maiden
Innocent
Kind
NIVEA
Dreamer
Idealistic
Different
Creative

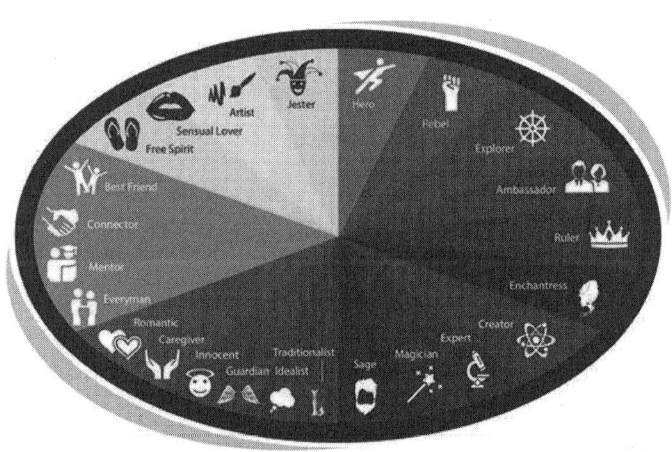
Jester
Artist
Sensual Lover
Free Spirit
Hero
Rebel
Explorer
Ambassador
Ruler
Enchantress
Creator
Expert
Magician
Sage
Traditionalist
Idealist
Guardian
Innocent
Caregiver
Romantic
Everyman
Mentor
Connector
Best Friend

You can see the brands from categories such as cars, beverages, cosmetics, fragrances, etc., using this quite effectively to cater to certain mindset, differentiate their brands, and even develop the brand archetypes. An example of brand archetypes on different positions of the map is shared in the previous image.

Unilever uses Needscope® extensively to define the position of the brands, the attributes that the brands should own, the advertising it should be doing to belong to a position, and indeed, sometimes testing if ad is failing in the intended position.

Consumption segmentation

For some categories, it is quite difficult to find demographic or psychographic variables that can cut the market in segments that are quite different from each other. Think of the categories that are consumed multiple times a day and week like food and beverages—same people within a demographic segment can make different choices on what they eat or drink, where they eat or drink. In other words, demography isn't a variable that determines the choices they make; there is a lot more beyond that like who are they eating or drinking with, what time of the day it is, is it a regular day or a special occasion, etc. In categories like these, it is usually difficult to identify one variable that can divide the consumers in different behavioural groups.

BCG, the consulting company, came up with a framework that they called 'Demand-Centric Growth' (DCG) where they took into consideration the consumer context, attitudinal profile of people, and several other variables that together determined the consumption; they called those moments of consumption as 'demand spaces'. This approach then started getting referred to as 5Ws framework and is used extensively by Kantar Added Value for segmentation. The 5Ws that this framework refers to determine the choices people make:

1. **Who:** Who is the person consuming the category and decision maker of the choice? Demography plays a role here. Let's take the example of food and beverages: is it just for a single person or is it for the whole family? Who are they eating with and what is their affordability and food and beverage preference.

2. **What:** The choice of the food or beverage they choose to consume.

3. **When:** What time of the day or week or year is the choice being made? Everyday dinner or afternoon meals vs. weekend meals vs. special occasions drive different choices.

4. **Where:** Where are they and where do they choose to eat or drink? Choice made in office or college or at a restaurant is different from choices made at home.

5. **How:** How they choose to consume food or beverage is also dependent upon their mood and lifestyle preferences. Are they in a mood to celebrate, are they vegans, are they foodies or food doesn't matter to them as much, etc. This says a lot about psychographics and the way food makes people feel.

If you think about these 5Ws, it becomes apparent that the choices people make aren't dependent upon any one of these, but a combination of all these. Depending upon the category, couple of 'Ws' might matter more than others and that dependence can also vary. Marketers, therefore, need to segment the market looking at all of these and understand what drives demand of the category and what makes people choose some brands over others.

Unilever used this framework quite effectively to segment the market of cooking products globally. The demand spaces created by this framework allowed them to clearly see the choices people make, role of different categories in each of the spaces, what true competition is (e.g., in everyday dinner, people may not choose mayo to go with the sandwich but might use a home-made sauce), and the role that the brand can play. Unilever's brand Knorr (one of its largest global brands) is present in several categories—from cooking aids to bouillons, from sauces to spices to noodles—and, therefore, runs the risk of being a generic brand (means different things to different people and in net sum doesn't mean anything). Managing the brand coherently requires a clear understanding of demands that the brand is catering to and a unique identify that can

Demand spaces are 'moments of consumption' that people with different attitudes to category (typologies) find themselves in. Each space has a different character and hence the consumption patterns are different in each space

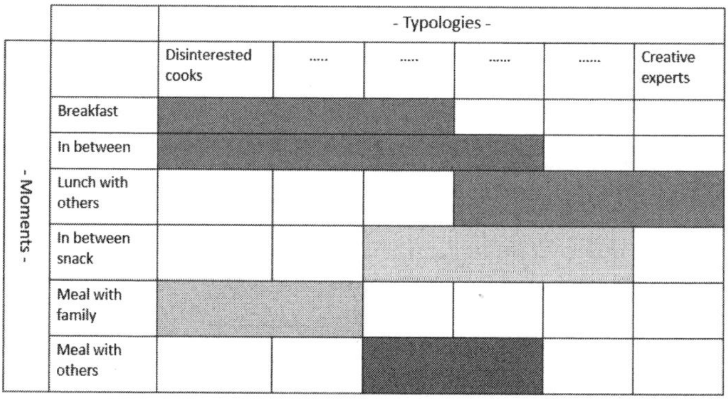

		- Typologies -					
- Moments -		Disinterested cooks	.....	.....	.....	.....	Creative experts
	Breakfast						
	In between						
	Lunch with others						
	In between snack						
	Meal with family						
	Meal with others						

cut across those demand spaces. The demand space framework used looks something like this:

On one axis is the typology—the attitude that consumers have towards food and cooking. The modelling done in the study showed this to be a variable that significantly impacts what people choose to cook and eat. Different typologies were identified through primary research done in several countries around the world which ranged from totally uninvolved cooks to passionate expert cooks to health-conscious cooks.

The other axis is a combination of couple of demographic variables bundled together—what time of the day the choice was made and who they (consumers) were with while making the choice. Breakfast, in between meals (snack time), main meals like lunch or dinner and if they were eating with family or special guests on a regular day or on a special occasion.

The combination of these two dimensions gives rise to different spaces which are distinct from each other on what people eat, the categories they choose, and the brand choices they make. For instance, people find themselves in different demand spaces when it comes to meeting with the family, depending on their attitude to cooking, their expertise in cooking, and what the meeting occasion is:

1. **Family get-togethers:** The focus is on people getting together and enjoying food. The food consumed is something that everyone likes and is prepared or ordered by the organizer.
2. **Approval:** Usually in family get-togethers, the person in-charge of cooking is seeking to get an approval of

sorts from the rest of the family members. Happens on occasions like newly-married woman inviting the in-laws for a meal for the first time—the typical pressure here is to find a way to win the hearts of the extended family through good food. The choice of dishes, how they are typically cooked, and ingredients used matter a lot in such occasions, and brands can come to their rescue and reassure a consumer about the brand heritage and expertise (and can also charge a premium). Seasoning products, particularly for complex traditional dishes, use this approach to help consumers cook a great meal in the approval demand space.

3. **Showtime:** The foodie is trying to show off their skills to their family and friends. It is not the mental pressure of approval, but the need is to get appreciation or seek validation, nevertheless. Hence, the ingredients and brands chosen to prepare the meal has to be of trusted quality and price premium is quite a norm. Food brands in this space talk about premium quality ingredients or process of creating the product that only the most discerning would recognize as a way to assure consumers that their products are most suited for the 'showtime' demand space (and hence commanding a premium).

4. **Creative social meals:** Similar to showtime, but the accent is on being creative with food and, sometimes, people coming together to cook. The mental pressure is much less, and the point is to have fun, but the need

is to think of food that's different and not very easy to find or cook.

This framework allows for sizing of different spaces in different countries or markets, profiling of the ingredients, brands used, and detailed understanding of the reasons behind the choices made in each space. Brands like Knorr can then make informed choices on the spaces they want to operate in, products they want to offer and their pricing, and communication strategy that can clearly signal to consumers what the brand stands for.

Demand spaces is an incredibly rich tool for segmentation but can be quite complex to use, and hence, it needs to be used skillfully. A brand trying to occupy too many spaces can become too fragmented, but equally trying to occupy just one space can become restrictive. Overlaying additional information on these spaces such as the brands playing in each space, consumer journey in each space, and so on, can enrich it further. When they are chosen purposefully, executed accurately, and utilized effectively, demand spaces can still be an incredibly powerful tool to help the businesses access fewer, bigger, and better opportunities for their brands.

Trends

Perhaps the most commonly used phrase in the world of business and marketing, 'trends' is ironically also one of the least understood or the fuzziest of all the concepts. Different people have different ideas of what they are seeking when they look for trends. It's, therefore, important to understand what they are looking for and what do they want to do with them. While this is true for all the questions, this one in particular can send teams into a wild goose chase if the objectives are not clear. To illustrate, here are some perfectly good examples of trends but they all serve different purposes or lead to different kinds of action in a business:

1. Mobile phones have become an integral part of consumers' lives.
2. Fashion is rapidly becoming gender neutral.
3. Make-up for men was one of the largest growing beauty categories in Europe last year.
4. Our environment is under a lot of stress and the damage is said to be already irreversible.
5. Brands like Netflix and Ben & Jerry's are quick to respond to consumers on social media with usually quirky replies (that often tend to go viral).

The problem with the trends above is that they are a mix of trends at different levels. Some are macro trends that are impacting the world (like sustainability), some are about how consumers behave differently, and some are about different categories (emerging or declining, etc.). Therefore, it is important to understand the 'level' at which the trends need to be looked at because those would impact either the overall business outlook or category strategy or tactical activities.

Unilever looks at trends at three different levels and those are monitored and analyzed at different frequencies:

LEVEL	DEFINITION	PURPOSE	FREQUENCY
Macro trends	Broad economic, political, technological, etc., changes that impact the world in the long run.	Long-term business strategy.	Once in three or four years.
People trends	Changes in the way consumers behave—generally as well as specific to certain categories. These are impacted by broad macro trends.	Medium-term innovation and category management strategy.	Once a year.
Category or product trends	Trends seen in the category on the shop shelves—new launches, formats, etc. These are usually a result of consumer trends seen in the market.	Medium to short-term innovation and activation plans.	Continuous or 'always on' throughout the year.

Different organizations—from Google to Kantar, from fragrance houses to food organizations publish trends that they see around them every year. The Unilever trends team assimilates all of those and translates them into the framework above so that everyone in the organization is looking at the same trends in the same way and not getting swayed by multiple trends floating in the market. This allows a focused conversation on the implications of trends and actions to be taken. A look at these trends set by the Unilever team in 2017 were as follows:

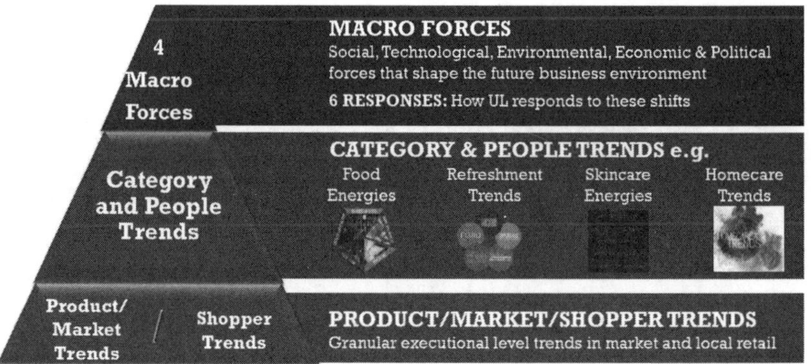

Macro Forces

Multipolar world, environment under stress, digital and tech revolution, and people living differently were identified to be the four key macro forces. These, in turn, were understood in detail to outline implications on how people behaving differently would impact category consumption to identify trends for foods, beverages, skin care, and home care categories. These eventually become the umbrella drivers setting certain trends amongst people and categories.

THE 4 GLOBAL MACRO FORCES ARE UNDERPINNED BY KEY DRIVERS

MULTI-POLAR WORLD

THE ENVIRONMENT UNDER STRESS

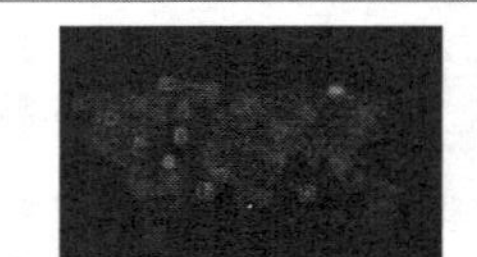

DIGITAL & TECHNOLOGY REVOLUTION

LIVING DIFFERENTLY

KEY DRIVERS

MULTI-POLAR WORLD

- Uncertainty in mature markets
- Crisis of trust in elites
- New business models & competitors
- Slow global growth
- Rise of nationalism, protectionism
- Income & political polarisation within countries

THE ENVIRONMENT UNDER STRESS

- Water stress squeezes us dry
- Our fragile food system
- Spotlight on big business accountability
- Renewable energy transformation
- Dynamic technology breakthroughs

DIGITAL & TECHNOLOGY REVOLUTION

- Digital reshapes home & shopping habits
- Rapidly expanding tech access
- Growth of AI, Robotics, VR & AR
- Data explosion sparks smarter business
- Increasing risks & concerns around connectivity

LIVING DIFFERENTLY

- Changing household roles and structures
- Rapid urbanisation & migration
- A bigger but older population
- Growth of health challenges
- Growing opportunities for women

Category and People Trends

Translating macro forces into category trends is an important step and that requires understanding the impact of these forces on the lives and behaviours of people around the world, and then further translating them into the implications for the category. As an example, looking at how people consume food and how it would impact macro forces described above, following eleven trends were identified by The Whole Foods Market for the year 2022:

1. **Ultra-urban Farming:** Innovation in indoor farming, hydroponics, and aquaponics.
2. **You Do Yuzu:** Tart and sour citrus, tangerine-sized fruit will be added in vinaigrettes, hard seltzers, mayo, and more.
3. **Reducetarianism:** Reducing consumption of meat, dairy, and eggs without cutting them out completely.
4. **Hibiscus is Happening:** Going beyond teas to fruit spreads, yogurts, and beyond.
5. **Buzz-Less Spirits:** Drinks that provide the taste and sophistication of cocktails without the buzz.
6. **Grains that Give Back:** Grains grown through practices that address soil health.
7. **Seize the Sunflower Seed:** Delivering protein and unsaturated fats to crackers, ice creams, and creamy cheeses.
8. **Moringa's Moment:** Matcha's latest alternative.

9. **Functional Fizz:** Sodas with probiotics, prebiotics, botanicals, fruity flavours, and unconventional ingredients.
10. **Turmeric Takes Off:** Packaged foods like cereals, sauerkrauts, and even plant-based ice cream sandwiches.

Mintel, on the other hand, identified five people trends for 2022, which they defined as follows:

1. **In Control:** Brands delivering information and options to make consumers feel like they are in control.
2. **Enjoyment Everywhere:** Consumers are eager to embrace novel experiences, both virtually and in the real, physical world.
3. **Ethics Check:** Consumers want to see measurable progress from brands.
4. **Flexible Spaces:** Public and private spaces must maximize their capabilities to match consumers' flexible lifestyles.
5. **Climate Complexity:** Consumers are looking at brands to help them mitigate their impact on the climate crisis.

Product Trends

The trends at the lowest level (i.e., product or market or shopper trends) are 'always on', and when seen in the light of macro forces and category trends, they become quite self-explanatory. Furthermore, inferring the ones that would stick and the ones that are likely to fade away becomes a lot easier. These lowest level trends are usually about new product launches, ingredients coming in, fragrances in the product categories becoming popular, popular lingo, media consumption, etc. They are obtained from various sources (e.g., Mintel for new launches), including social conversations, search analytics, etc., and are put together in the form of easy-to-use dashboards. One example of the trends on the kind of ice cream that people in Britain are looking for is given below (snapshot of a dashboard). This infographic kind of dashboard below shows the search trends classified into short-term and long-term (using an index) for different types of ice creams in Great Britan, and also summarizes the growing and declining trends. This information is 'always on' and is used by the teams not just for new product development but also for short term promotions and activations.

Mintel—a market intelligence firm gathers information about launches in the market (across the world) and is an excellent source for product trends. They analyze the new launches in every aspect—ingredients, claims, packaging, pricing, etc., and their dashboards can provide not just the intelligence about new launches but also broader consumer and product trends. For instance, the chart below from Mintel shows their point of view on the youth fashion—the size of the market, different categories within it and factors that drive that market. This can be a very useful broad overview for brands operating and wanting to operate in the youth fashion market.

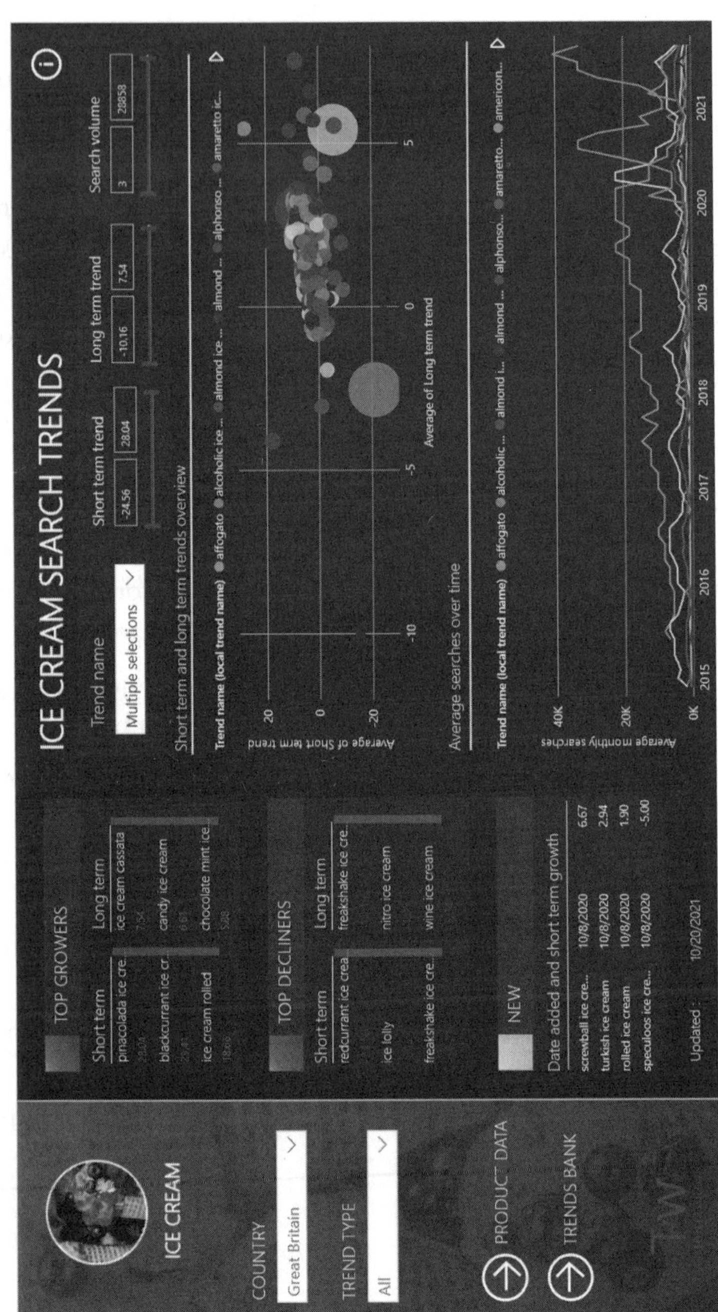
ICE CREAM
COUNTRY
Great Britain
TREND TYPE
All
PRODUCT DATA
TRENDS BANK
TOP GROWERS
Short term
Long term
pinacolada ice cre...
blackcurrant ice cr...
ice cream rolled
ice cream cassata
candy ice cream
chocolate mint ice...
TOP DECLINERS
Short term
Long term
redcurrant ice crea...
ice lolly
freakshake ice cre...
freakshake ice cre...
nitro ice cream
wine ice cream
NEW
Date added and short term growth
screwball ice cre... 10/8/2020 6.67
turkish ice cream 10/8/2020 2.94
rolled ice cream 10/8/2020 1.90
speculoos ice cre... 10/8/2020 -5.00
Updated : 10/20/2021
ICE CREAM SEARCH TRENDS
Trend name
Multiple selections
Short term trend
-24.56
28.04
Long term trend
-10.16
7.54
Search volume
3
28858
Short term and long term trends overview
Trend name (local trend name) affogato alcoholic ice ... almond ice ... almond ... alphonso ... amaretto ic...
Average of Short term trend
Average of Long term trend
Average searches over time
Trend name (local trend name) affogato alcoholic ... almond i... almond ... alphonso... amaretto... americon...
Average monthly searches
40K
20K
0K
2015
2016
2017
2018
2019
2020
2021

YOUTH FASHION

INFOGRAPHIC OVERVIEW

December 2014 - UK

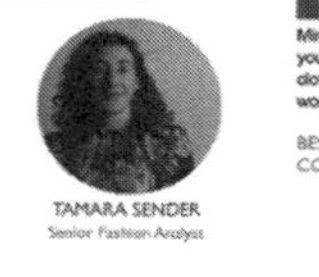

TAMARA SENDER
Senior Fashion Analyst

WHAT WE THINK

"Young people are more inclined to use social media networks such as Instagram, YouTube and Pinterest than other age groups. This is particularly the case when it comes to fashion, with a quarter of 15-24-year-olds using Instagram for engaging with fashion brands and one fifth using YouTube. Instagram in particular has become increasingly popular driven by the trend for selfies and the digital filters that can be applied to the images making them ideal for the world of fashion, allowing everyone to portray themselves as model or fashion icon. The increasing prominence of media networks – with their longer average visit per visitor and greater user acceptance of ads – is a key development for brands and retailers looking to spread a message.

YOUTH FASHION MARKET

Mintel estimates that sales of clothing and footwear by 15-24s rose by only 2.1% in 2014 to £14.7 billion as young people continued to feel the impact of financial pressures and have cut back on their spending on clothes. The youth fashion market has underperformed the total clothing and footwear market. While young women have become more cautious, the youth fashion market has been boosted by rising sales of menswear.

BEST- AND WORST-CASE FORECAST SPENDING ON CLOTHING AND FOOTWEAR BY CONSUMERS AGED 15-24, 2009-19

WHAT MOTIVATES YOUNG PEOPLE TO BUY NEW CLOTHES

Nearly half of young women mainly buy clothes when they are on special offer, showing how this generation have become accustomed to a discount culture and being able to rely on buying clothes when they are on sale rather than at full price. By contrast, men are more willing to pay full price for clothes.

REASONS FOR BUYING NEW CLOTHES, SEPTEMBER 2014

WHAT INFLUENCES HOW YOUNG PEOPLE DRESS

Friends stand out as being the main factor that influences how people dress. At the same time 15-24s are more likely to be influenced by street fashion and what other people are wearing out and about than by popular culture such as magazines, TV, films and celebrities.

FACTORS THAT INFLUENCE HOW PEOPLE DRESS, SEPTEMBER 2014

REASONS FOR USING SOCIAL MEDIA FOR FASHION

Young females are most likely to use social media for style advice or inspiration, with almost four in ten agreeing with this, making it the number one way for females to interact with fashion brands. Both young men and women are equally as likely to use social media sites to take advantage of special offers such as money off when buying clothes.

REASONS FOR USING SOCIAL MEDIA FOR INTERACTING WITH FASHION BRANDS, SEPTEMBER 2014

reports.mintel.com
@mintelnews
helpdesk@mintel.com
EMEA +44 (0)20 76064533
Americas +1 (312) 9320400
APAC +86 (21) 63866609
LAR 0-800-095-9094

Process for Innovation or New Product Development

Having looked at the details of market and consumer context understanding, this section looks at the process of developing new products and innovations. This process is quite similar in several organizations and it goes from generating and testing ideas to checking the feasibility of the full mix, including business forecasting and finally tracking post-launch.

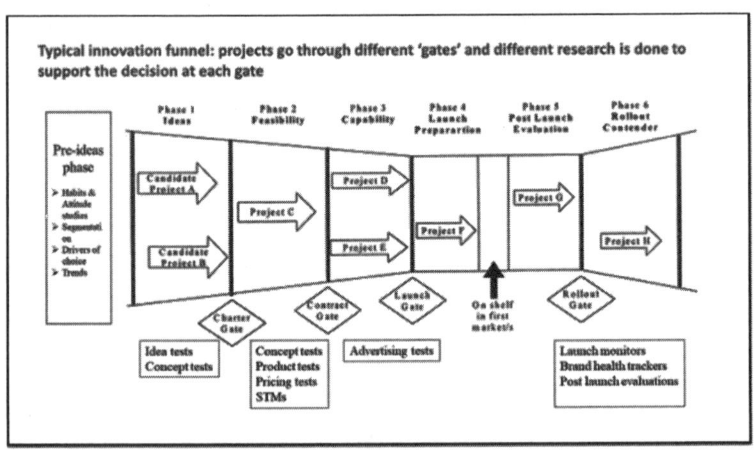

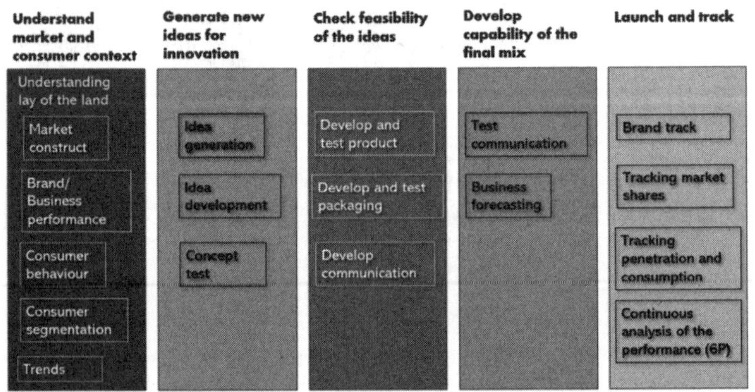

Generating and Testing New Ideas

Anyone in the organization can generate ideas, and everyone should be encouraged to generate them and add to the 'pool' of ideas to be considered. Organizations like Unilever encourage people across functions to generate ideas and submit them to the marketing team working on innovations, who then take it forward for evaluating it (more on evaluation later in this chapter). If the idea gets shortlisted through initial evaluation, then the person submitting the idea is often brought into the conversation to flesh it out further.

But how can people generate ideas? There are a few ways:

1. **Consumer connects:** As described earlier in the book, consumer connects are an excellent way of spending time with people in their context (home or office or kitchen or laundry room, etc.), and understanding the issues they face with different things they need to do. It enables people to link them to the product categories and think of ways of designing better products.
2. **Attending trade events:** Beauty teams at Unilever attend the big fashion shows in New York, Paris, and London to get a sense of latest trends and patterns and sensorials. This inspires them with thoughts and ideas on what new things they could be doing with their products. Unilever CMI has even developed an award-winning, in-house proprietary analytical model—recognized at the global insights and analytics forums—that predicts how fashion, beauty, and food trends travel across the world once they get introduced. It requires

an understanding of from where these trends originate, which ones sustain (while others fade out), how they travel across the world, and so on. The model predicts when a new food ingredient or recipe introduced in New York trade show in 2022 would start showing up in the kitchens of small towns of Brazil, Indonesia, or India—this knowledge enables the food team to prepare an innovation around that new ingredient or recipe and hit the market right on time to stay relevant with the trend.

3. **Working with innovation firms or designers:** Though it may be an expensive route, working with design and innovation firm can bring up new ideas. It is important to have a clear problem definition without which designers can't come up with ideas in this route. There is a famous example of Ideo (a global design firm) redesigning the shopping trolley to make it easier to navigate around the shop and stack goods of different shapes and sizes.

Once ideas are generated, it is prudent to have a quick check to shortlist meritorious ideas in order to take them forward. And the best way to do that is to put them in front of consumers and observe their reactions.

'Idea Clinics' was quite a popular way of filtering good ideas from the bad ones in Unilever for several years. Ideas at this stage are usually one- or two-line descriptions of the thought without branding or pictures or detailed description so that people respond to just the core thought without any bells and whistles. Some examples of ideas for detergents would be:

1. A lather-generating sustainable detergent that doesn't pollute the oceans when drained.
2. Detergent in the form of capsules that come in dissolvable packaging. You only need to throw the capsule along with the pack in the washing machine while washing clothes.
3. A mild detergent that you can use for delicate clothes; it cleans well without spoiling them.
4. A detergent for people with sensitive skin so that clothes washed with it don't irritate your skin.

The typical Idea Clinics involves creating a setting similar to that of a group discussion (around eight to ten respondents from target audience), engaging and initiating them in a conversation about the category to warm them up, and making them think about the category. Then, the ideas are shown to them one by one. They have three 'bins' (physical ones for face-to-face discussions)—'definitely select', 'definitely reject', and 'kind of in the middle' bins. Respondents look at one idea at a time, deliberate on it for couple of minutes, and choose a bin that it goes into. They cycle 25 to 30 ideas in an hour this way, and in the end, they pick up the ideas in the 'kind of in the middle' bin and choose the ones among them to be selected or rejected. These clinics are repeated with same ideas in different cities in a country (or different countries) and with the core and peripheral target audience. Ideas that consistently fall into 'definitely select' bucket are carried forward for further development.

A few things are important here:

1. Warm up begins before the discussion on the idea so that people are in the mindset of thinking about the category. People usually are not thinking about the categories that marketers are working in as a part of their daily lives; so, it is important to bring their minds to start thinking about the category and brands before the ideas are brought forward.

2. Each idea is not presented in a fully-fleshed out form (branded concept or product with full packaging) but just as a thought; this allows true assessment of the core of the idea.

3. Each idea is expressed in a simple manner and debated for couple of minutes. If it doesn't cut ice in that time, it very likely means that either it's too complicated or not strong enough.

4. The ideas ideally don't have to be branded because it's important at this stage to see if the idea is clicking with the consumers; unless the brand is intrinsic to the idea itself (like Apple Car), which usually should not be the case.

This traditional way of idea clinics in Unilever has now given way to Ideaswipe®. Conceptually, it's quite similar to idea clinics, except that it is executed digitally. The underlying premise is that in the world of Tinder, people are familiar with swiping right or left to express their liking. Ideaswipe®—another propriety tool developed by Unilever CMI—presents ideas to the target group on their phones and asks them to swipe right if they like it and left if they don't. (More details on Ideaswipe® are on idea-swipe.com). This allows faster agile assessment of ideas before taking them forward. This tool is now used in over 40 countries around the world and has norms developed in more than 20 countries. Interestingly, the tool is now made available for others to use as well via the research partners Brandscapes Worldwide.

Concept test is the usual next step after ideas have been selected. The concept behind a 'concept' is that it articulates in great detail the key proposition that the product or service would offer. Concept is not advertising but the sum total of information on advertising, packaging, product sampling, etc., that consumers would get across channels. There are times when 'adcepts' are developed as well (which is advertising reflected in a concept, but those are more for testing advertising ideas than product ideas). Hence, it requires substantial amount of work to translate an idea into the branded concept. Great concepts are a profitable intersection of the consumer insights, product facts, and brand truths that is looking to match functional unmet needs, emotional benefits or relevance via the brand's unique point of view.

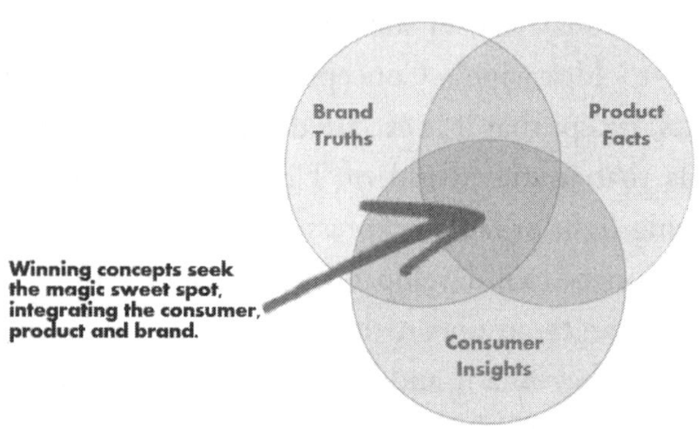

Writing a concept requires gathering of these building blocks and putting them together in a meaningful format which can be put in front of the consumers to get their reactions. Concept is, therefore, primarily a research stimulus—it is something that consumers would never see as a marketing communication vehicle in real life. However, it serves a crucial role of being an anchor for the entire project. Once the concept is finalized and tested well with the consumers, it is used as a reference point for developing the entire mix. R&D teams, packaging teams, fragrance or flavour houses then get briefed for the product development with the concept; it further gets included in the advertising brief, and so on. Concept serves as a compass for reference for every element of the mix to be checked against.

CONCEPT GRID		
CONCEPT NAME		
INSIGHT	**BENEFIT**	**RTB**
• Is it relevant and important to your target market? • Does it accurately underpin and drive the proposition? • Does it contain interesting tension?	• Does it answer the consumer insight directly? • Is it single-minded? • Is it competitive in the market place?	• Do they support the discriminating benefit? • Are they sustainable over the long term?

At Unilever, the teams use concept grid quite often to gather building blocks and create the concept from an idea. A typical grid looks like the above:

This is where having a well-articulated consumer insight plays a huge role. It works as the foundation for the idea to be shaped into a concept that consumers can relate to. It is, therefore, crucial to get the right insight, which often here is about a problem that consumers are facing that the product can solve for them. As discussed in detail in the earlier chapter on insights, the insight has to be sharp, meaningful, real, and expressed pithily. From the insight flows the benefit that the product would offer, which could be functional or a combination of functional and emotional.

Let's take an example of an insight from the world of toothpastes. "Sometimes I feel bad breath from people around me and I wonder if my mouth is smelling equally foul?". This insight is about the anxiety that people feel about their breath freshness and the reassurance they need from their toothpaste of the freshness that would last for several hours. The benefit would then be not just about removing bad breath to make your mouth feel fresh but also about ensuring that the freshness remains for several hours. The RTB (reason to believe) would have to be about ingredients in the toothpaste that can do that, and sometimes, even a claim about number of hours that the toothpaste can provide freshness.

Another example is from the world of fabric conditioners. The grid below shows the different concept ingredients and the resulting concept.

CONCEPT GRID		
CONCEPT NAME	**Comfort One Rinse**	
INSIGHT	**BENEFIT**	**RTB**
• I have to rinse my clothes several times to **be sure there's no harmful residue left.** • I have to rinse my clothes several times **which takes a lot of effort.** • I have to rinse my clothes several times **which wastes a lot of water.** • **Rinsing is a real hassle in laundry**	• Rinse, soften and perfume your clothes, **without leaving any irritating residues**. • Rinse, soften and perfume your clothes in one single step, **making your washing so much easier.** • Rinse, soften and perfume your clothes **in one single step**, **while reducing your water bill.**	• **It cuts the foam** which **prevents detergent residues from sticking onto clothes.** • With a new **foam dissolver**, which **means the foam disappears in less water.**

Comfort One Rinse

To give my family's clothes the best care, I have to rinse several times to remove all the detergent, which wastes a lot of water.

Introducing new Comfort One Rinse Fabric Conditioner.

It contains a breakthrough foam cutting technology: With just ½ a cap it cuts the foam and prevents detergent residues from sticking onto clothes, whilst keeping the great softness and freshness you love from Comfort – all in just one rinse.

New Comfort One Rinse – rinse, soften and perfume your clothes in one single step, while reducing your water bill.

There is a checklist of sorts that can be used to judge how good or bad a concept is before it is released for consumer testing:

1. **Insight:** Is it something that grabs your attention and makes you engage with the rest of the concept? It should be something that's relevant, expresses a need in people's lives, something that can connect emotional and functional benefits offered by the brand.

2. **Benefit:** At the functional level, what does the product offer that's different or better than the competition, including the brand's own existing range already available in the market? Does the usage of the brand make consumers feel that the anxiety or aspiration captured by the insight has been satisfied?

3. **RTB (Reason to Believe):** This is not a reason to *buy* but a reason for consumers to genuinely believe the product would deliver *before* they have bought it. In simple words, how would one consumer describe to another person why they believe this product is effective? While brand credibility plays a huge role, technical mumbo jumbo wouldn't be enough, as it should be simple enough for people to get it.
4. **The 'steel filament test':** Steve Miles, ex-global head of the brand Dove, used to talk about this steel filament test. He argued that there should be a sense of inevitability in how one box (referring to the boxes in the concept grid—insight, benefit, RTB, etc.) flows from the previous one: the benefit should directly respond to the need or tension expressed in the insight; the RTB should clearly be a credible fact that helps us believe the assertion made by the benefit (and not just random interesting fact about the product). In other words, there should be a 'steel filament' of clear, unarguable, inevitable logic around one single thought that runs through the concept from start to finish.

Qualitative research is incredibly useful to sharpen concepts. Furthermore, individual or group discussions with people enable the crafting of each element of the concept. It is then usually tested quantitatively in important markets. Most concept-testing agencies have benchmarks with which to compare the concept results. However, it's often a good practice to compare them with the scores of the brand's concepts tested in the past, particularly successful ones. In case of relaunches, concept of the existing brand mix is tested versus the new concept (though often done monadically). But it is also not unusual to create concepts for competition brands and test them for comparison as well.

When a concept is tested quantitatively, the scores on various parameters are usually compared against the database, rather than looking at the scores in an absolute sense. That's an important step because consumers have a tendency to understate or overstate their responses. For example, it's quite well known that people in Germany tend to understate (in other words, even when they like the concept, they would not say they like it and would buy the product; instead they would prefer to be more cautious and appear neutral in their responses). In India, on the other hand, consumers tend to overstate their responses and would appear a lot more optimistic than they really feel about the concept. And, sometimes, there are differences even within a country. For instance, North Vietnam reacts differently from South Vietnam as the two are culturally quite different. The agency doing the concept test creates a database of responses across concepts it evaluates. The results of a concept test are, therefore, presented against a database in the top, average, bottom quartile. And validations done by agencies usually show that concepts scoring in the top of the database are far more likely to succeed in the marketplace than others. Choosing the right agency partner who has the right database for a country and preferably for the test product category is an important consideration for concept tests.

Survival rates vs. Nielsen BASES' database

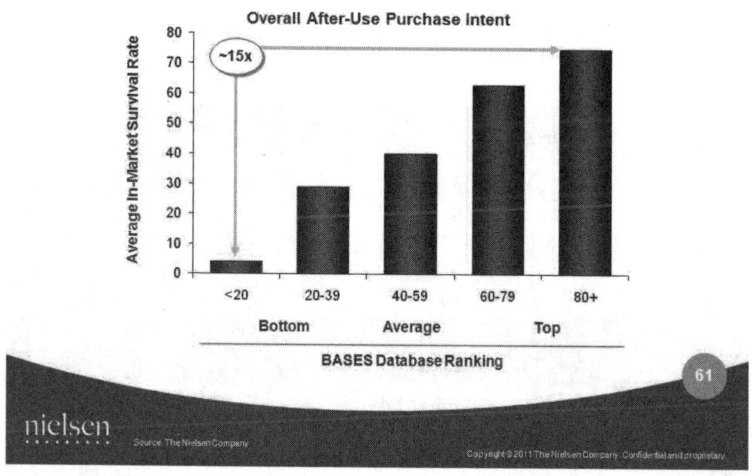

Companies like NielsenIQ BASES conduct the concept test in this classic manner described above. They have an extensive database against which the concept score can be benchmarked. Companies like Ipsos, on the other hand, take a different approach. Instead of developing and constantly updating the database, they prefer to show the test concept in the context of its competition. In order to do that, they show competition concepts and test concepts together and they also create a shelf (physical or virtual, depending on the category and consumer journey), so that consumers can see the test concept in relation to other solutions that exist in the market. This helps consumers position the test concept quite well in their minds. And it also works quite well for fuzzy concepts that are proposing a product or a service that did not exist before. For such a product or service, consumers may not be able to visualize the benefits. When the concept is compared against the competition, consumers can understand the problem it would solve better and can also imagine what it would substitute.

Though NielsenIQ BASES and Ipsos approaches are quite different from each other, both the tests have equally good validations. In other words, the probability of success predicted as against actual success by these systems is almost equally good for both the systems in my experience. And, hence, the choice should be made based on what best suits the concept being tested.

Testing the Feasibility of New Ideas

Once the concept is finalized and tested, the project formally gets kicked off with development investments and cross-functional teams behind it. Different teams would then start working on different elements (R&D on the product, advertising agency on the communication ideas, and so on). As each element is developed, it is tested with consumers to see if it meets the expectations set by the concept. Few key ones are:

Product Development

Once R&D is ready with a few options with different formulations or tech configurations, the testing of these options begins. In an ideal scenario, there is an early-stage testing (which could sometimes be within a lab) to shortlist the final two or three formulations. The final formulations are then put through extensive quantitative product testing (a quantitative survey amongst large number of people who are given the product to use and then asked to rate it on several parameters) to choose the winner. Unilever CMI has developed extensive guidelines on product tests that determine if the tests should be monadic or comparative, branded or unbranded, with or without the concept. Agencies offering product-testing protocols usually have benchmarks and norms for every country or category, but like concept tests, it is always a good practice to keep the scores of product tests done on a brand in the past. These records also provide good benchmarks and guard rails for assessing the success probability of the new products being tested.

A product is usually tested blind (without the brand name and in a neutral pack) in the early stage of development to see if the product is able to deliver the promise articulated in the concept on its own, without the halo of branding. At subsequent stages, especially during volume forecasting, branded tests are recommended.

In consumer packaged goods, products are tested usually in monadic form (only one at a time) because that reflects consumer behaviour; they tend to use only one shampoo or a detergent at time, for example. If the earlier product or the competitor's product needs testing, then those need additional monadic panels. However, there are times when a paired comparison test becomes necessary. In paired comparison tests, consumers test two products one after the other and compare the two on different attributes. This method exaggerates even the smaller differences that might go unnoticed in real life. Hence, it is used when the objective is to see if a small change is noticed and is appreciated. It can also work as good early-stage testing while shortlisting formulations. For instance, the shortlisting of new flavours of soup that are quite distinct from existing ones can be done through paired comparison tests (usually at a central location where product team cooks different soups to serve their respondents, which also ensures that there is no change in the way soups are being made).

Packaging Development

Packaging is an important element of the mix, not only because it helps store and use the product, but also because it is a critical communication channel to signal the key benefits and ways of using the product. A packaging test, therefore, involves not only checking the shelf throw (the ability of the pack to stand out on a shelf against the competition in the retail shops) or noticeability vs competition, but also a detailed pack evaluation to test the functionality. Just like for concepts and products, norms for pack testing play a significant role in judging the results of pack tests.

These pack tests can be very extensive when there is a major change in packaging or a new pack format is being introduced (think of laundry capsules that need to be thrown into the washing machine along with the clothes, as opposed to laundry powder that goes into a specific compartment of the machine).

Pricing

Pricing single-handedly can make or break the business of a product. It's a crucial element to get right and yet, there is no one definitive way of identifying the right price for a product. There are many different ways to ascertain the right price, and the process can be quite daunting. 'Cost plus' is obviously the most basic way. In this method, you have to consider the cost and add the margins you want to make to arrive at the price. However, the marketer needs to understand what price consumers would be willing to pay for the product. As price is also an indicator of quality, pricing a product low might suggest inferior quality, while pricing it very high might signal unaffordability to the majority of the potential consumers. Getting the balance right to arrive at that magical price point is quite an art that needs to be combined with the science of expertise. This is, therefore, one of the most complex and interesting areas in which insights are needed. This is not a book about methodology but about making businesses insightful. So, I will now list some ways in which your gut feeling or intuition about a product's right pricing can be fine-tuned.

1. If the product is being launched in an already existing category, then it makes sense to get the prices of all brands and stock keeping units (SKUs) in the category to work out the relative price index (RPI) of your launch brand. The RPI, then, is simply the ratio of your brand's price to the average price in the category, indexed to 100. This is not a simple average but weighted by the volumes of each brand. If the RPI of your new brand is 125, it simply means that it's 25% more expensive than what a brand sells for, on an average, in the category. The RPI of your brand needs to be in line with the positioning of the brand. For instance, Lifebuoy's mission as a brand is to offer hygiene protection that's affordable to everyone, and hence, the RPI of Lifebuoy soap in most markets is about 80 to 85. On the other hand, Sensodyne toothpaste offers a solution for sensitive teeth and promises quick remedy and complete change through its use. As a consequence, its RPI in most markets tends to be about 200, which means that it's double the average market price.

2. Get a clear understanding on whether it's the absolute price or the relative price that matters to consumers in your category. This differs from category to category and this insight can be gained from the analytics work and from shopper research. Take an example of a category like smart TVs and cooking aids (products that help in cooking). When people buy a TV, they usually have a budget in mind, for instance, TV within $1,000. It's the absolute price that matters and that is the starting point for the purchase decision. Of course, they would look at

different TVs available around $1,000 and then make a choice, but they are likely to stick to the budget they have in mind. TV brands, therefore, need to have offerings in different price points that cater to different budgets.

For cooking aids, on the other hand, people use different cooking aids for different dishes and the price they pay depends on the help that the product provides. Products like seasoning and bouillon (stock) help add flavour to the dishes, but products like meal makers offer a complete solution to make the entire dish (meal makers come with the full set of all ingredients needed to make a dish so that you don't need anything else). So, comparing them on a like-to-like basis required converting them to a standard metric.

Look at the example of cooking products from Germany (prices per pack in €), where we converted the pack prices into money that consumers spent per dish to make them comparable and decide the right pricing for Knorr. Looking at prices in Germany, we realized that for making a specific dish, consumers were spending €1.5 per dish when they were opting for wet meal makers, which gave them a complete dish. However, they were paying €0.03 per dish (for the same dish) while using wet seasoning to make the dish – but they needed to pay for ingredients to make the dish additionally on their own. This gave a good guidance to Knorr on where they were right and where they were off the mark. It must be noted that consumers don't perform these detailed calculations while buying the products. However, they intuitively know that they have to pay more for meal makers as against seasoning. We needed these calculations to get the relative benchmarks and fix the pricing.

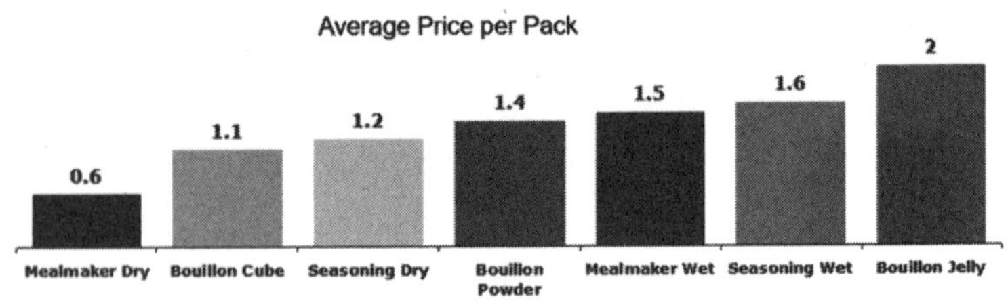

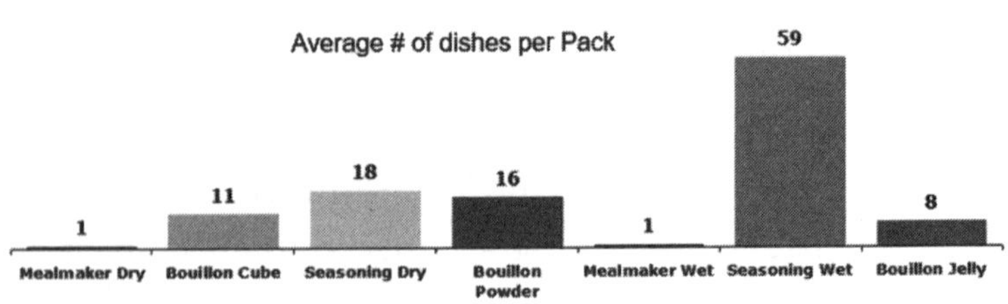

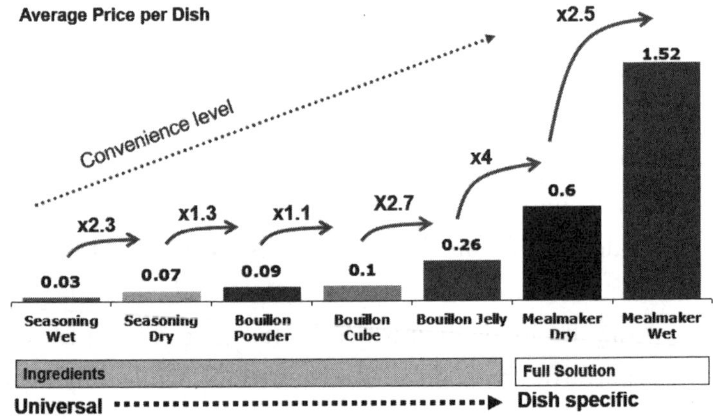

3. Building on how consumers think about the price (absolute vs relative), there is a framework that I developed a few years ago (which is quite intuitive) that I use for classifying categories on the basis of how consumers look at pricing in those categories. In my experience with pricing, there are two dimensions to the way price matters to consumers:

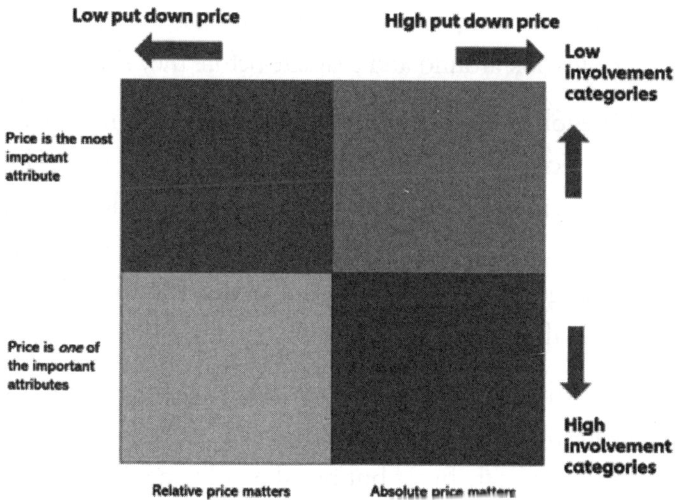

Let's have a look at these axes in some more detail. When the involvement level is combined with the consideration for absolute or relative price, four distinct spaces emerge where people make decisions differently:

1. One axis is about what matters more—the absolute price that people pay or the price relative to other options. Typically, absolute price tends to matter a lot more when the put-down price is high (i.e., money people have to shell out of their pockets while buying).

People think whether it's worth spending money before they walk into the shop. Categories like cars, durables etc., are examples of this.

2. When relative price is more important. Usually, when buying a lot of grocery products, which are also high-frequency, people tend to look at what's on offer and compare different prices before making a choice. Ironically, these are categories where the out-of-pocket prices are quite low (compared to cars, for instance), but people still like to look around and evaluate before they shop.
3. Categories where price is the most important attribute for decision-making. Typically, these tend to be low-involvement categories where the brand differentiation is quite low. People then tend to use price as a means to judge the quality and choose the one that fits their needs the best.
4. High-involvement categories where people think a lot more before deciding. And hence, price is one of the important attributes but not the only one. For instance, the colour of lipstick to be worn at work is a high-involvement choice where apart from price, there are other considerations too.

While these dimensions look like they overlap, they do not in reality. However, their interaction leads to interesting spaces and the choices people make in those spaces are quite different. Marketers need to understand where their category belongs—through analytics, shopper insights, value drivers in the category, etc.,—to be able to use pricing as the effective tool for driving sales.

	Low put down price ←	**High put down price** →	
Price is the most important attribute	You can't make out too much difference between brands and the final choice doesn't matter to you that much. You choose the best deal and display low loyalty. Unlikely to remember price by brand or even total money you spend on it	You are not really bothered about the choice you make, but you know you have to pay a lot. You are unlikely to remember exact price by brand and brand differentiation is low in your mind (but you would remember approximate money you spend on it)	↑ **Low involvement categories**
Price is *one* of the important attributes	You choice is very important to you and you tend to stick to your choice – but there are a lot of options out there and since the financial implications of switching are not high, you compare a lot before you buy	What you choose and how much you spend matters a lot – financial implications and functional/emotional benefits are huge. Recommendations and past experiences matter and you have a good idea of how much you spend and cost of different brands	↓ **High involvement categories**
	Relative price matters	Absolute price matters	

Some examples of categories in each space are:

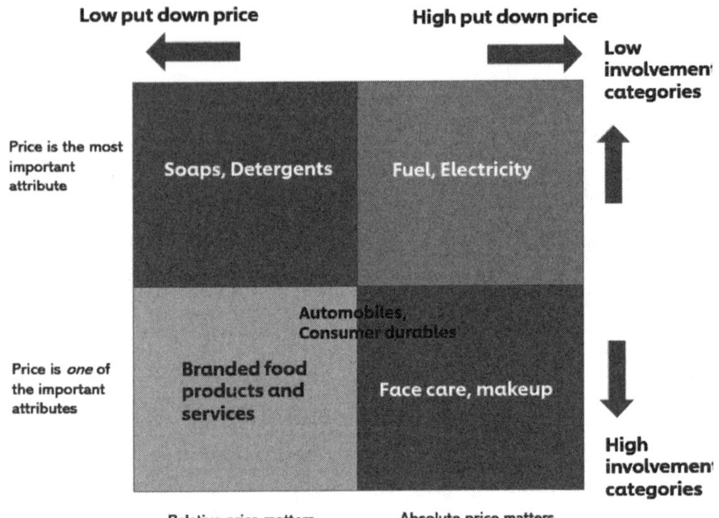

The research methods needed to arrive at the right pricing also differ by the spaces and here is how they fit:

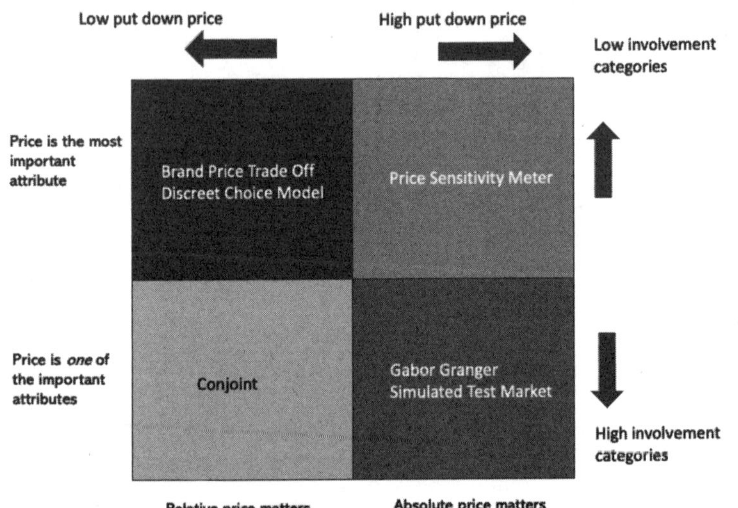

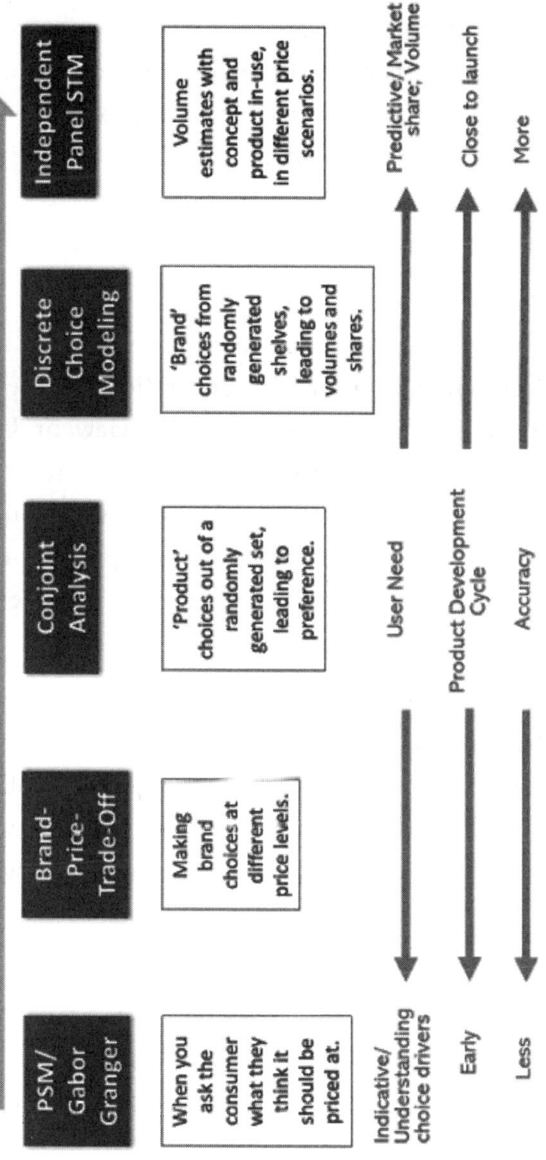
Right ways to apply survey-based research methods
PSM/ Gabor Granger
Brand-Price-Trade-Off
Conjoint Analysis
Discrete Choice Modeling
Independent Panel STM
When you ask the consumer what they think it should be priced at.
Making brand choices at different price levels.
'Product' choices out of a randomly generated set, leading to preference.
'Brand' choices from randomly generated shelves, leading to volumes and shares.
Volume estimates with concept and product in-use, in different price scenarios.
Indicative/ Understanding choice drivers
User Need
Predictive/ Market share; Volume
Early
Product Development Cycle
Close to launch
Less
Accuracy
More

There are different methods of understanding right pricing for the consumer. A lot depends on the involvement levels in the category and absolute put-down price as articulated above, but other important factors are the stage of product development and accuracy expected. Broadly, it works in the following manner in my experience:

Communication

Perhaps the most debated aspect of the new product development, communication often takes several rounds of refinement. From idea generation and testing to script tests to final quantitative test (Preview or Link of Kantar Millward Brown), this process takes several weeks and months. Therefore, starting the process as soon as the concept is finalized is prudent. Previous chapters in this book have discussed the Preview or Link testing in some detail, so they won't be repeated here.

Pre-testing in advertising generates more discussion and debate among marketing, insights, and ad agency teams than perhaps any other marketing work. It is the place where both advertising and research professionals come with passionate beliefs about the work they are doing. Having been through those debates a million times at Unilever, I have learnt a few lessons:

1. Communications testing can be a major point of friction between advertising agencies and insights teams. Inexperienced or naïve advertising teams can see the process as a hindrance to 'creativity' and think of it as too rational an evaluation for ideas that are creative.

But the seasoned professional creative directors usually understand the value that insights can bring in the idea development process, especially at an early stage. It is important to take them along the journey and make the early-stage development a collaborative process with the team.

2. Qualitative testing at an early stage can bring out insightful nuggets on where the communication idea is working and where it is failing in consumers' minds. It is, therefore, really important in early-stage testing and development to split hairs, so to speak, and pull out every little thing that's building the story or distracting from it. For instance, is the protagonist's personality overpowering the brand or story, is the context for the story being set up properly or is the brand jumping in too fast to solve the problem, are there enough branding cues in terms of colours, signs, sounds, symbols that people can make out the brand without the logo even appearing, does the brand have a unique story to tell or is it likely to be misconstrued or misappropriated as competition brand, and so on.

3. One of the biggest criticisms of pre-testing is that it is quite a 'rational' evaluation, where people are asked questions post-exposure to which they respond. In real life, people react to ads subliminally and don't rationalize the understanding of ads in their heads. But the reality is that pre-testing asks respondents questions like how much you enjoyed watching the ad (on a scale), would you like to watch it again and again

(which is an indication of real engagement), words that describe the ads (funny, scary, annoying, etc.) which capture subliminally, and quite effectively, what people feel while watching the ad. And these responses are compared to a benchmark—which is a critical part of the test—to see if the ad is far above or below average; and that comparison overcomes the respondents' tendency to under or overstate their feelings about the ad.

Some agency teams prefer working with qualitative research for the assessment process. While qualitative research can give you detailed insights on the level at which communication is working or failing to deliver, it becomes difficult to predict the success of an ad based on that. An experienced qualitative research expert along with a seasoned advertising creative professional would be able to predict the success of the ad when they work together and do qualitative research. However, that luxury is not available for each and every ad that is developed. And it is important for an organization spending huge amount of dollars on advertising to have a systemic approach for predicting the performance of the ads rather than rely on individual brilliance. Quantitative testing provides just that.

4. There is a notion amongst creative people (and often within marketers) that advertising is a work of art, and therefore, can't be judged by ordinary people (i.e., consumers). Of course, advertising is a work of art and takes the genius of a creative person to be able to come up with a story that can engage people and get a message

to land. However, that 'work of art' is meant to deliver a business result and any prudent businessmen should want to know how good the returns on the investment would be. So, ultimately, the decision to invest in an ad has to be a rational one and pre-testing predicts quite effectively the likely returns on investment behind an ad. It's critical for insights team at this stage to "tackle the ball and not the player" (in the words of Stan Sthanunathan, ex-CMI head of Unilever). In other words, be objective about articulating what the ad is good for and what improvement it needs, without being critical about the creative per se or without necessarily suggesting creative solutions, which is the domain of the creative teams. It's a difficult balance but it is the one that separates the men from the boys in the world of insights.

5. Companies like Kantar Millward Brown do extensive validation of their model, not just to see the relationship between on-air performance and performance in pre-testing, but also to see how the award-winning creatives perform in their tests. They have repeatedly found that several award-winning creative ads actually do quite well in their pre-testing model and those are the ones that stick to fundamental principles of engaging the audience with relevant stories.

6. Brilliant ads that evoke a response in the viewers are almost never a serendipity. They are created through a really good consumer insight, a clear understanding of the brand's strategic needs, and a creative person's ability

to combine these two. If any of these ingredients are missing, then the ad is likely to miss the mark. It helps to get the creative person involved in the insight by bringing it to life for them, getting them to talk to some consumers directly, making them use the products, etc. This is especially true for categories that the creative team may not be the direct users of. This helps them to relate to the consumers' emotions and develop a gut feeling.

7. There is always an ongoing debate between 'functional' ads and 'emotional' ads. Functional ads are the ones that focus on the functional benefits of the brand like germ protection abilities of a soap or a cough syrup that doesn't make you drowsy or a washing machine that takes less time, etc. Emotional ads, on the other hand, create a story from the emotional consequences of either the problem consumers are facing or the positive payoffs of using the brand. Using examples of rational benefits above, the emotional benefits could be children falling sick less often with the germ protection of a soap or being able to be on top of your game professionally despite consuming cough syrup, or having the freedom to do whatever you want with the time freed up from washing clothes. Research done on this by the IPA (Institute of Practitioners in Advertising) in the UK by Binet & Field (Ref: the IPA 'The long and short of it') actually suggests that emotional ads do better than functional ads.

Figure 53 Emotional campaigns are more profitable

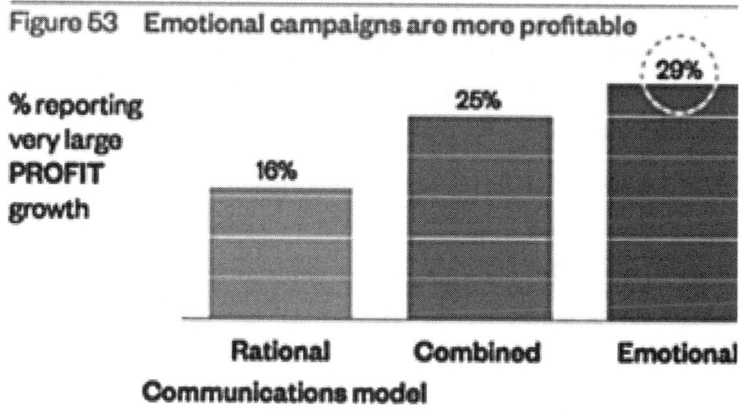

Figure 55 Emotional campaigns are more efficient

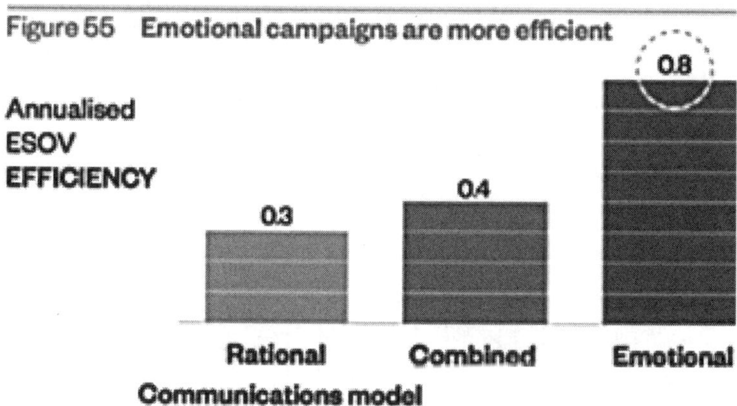

There is no magic formula on what works best for a brand. It's generally a combination of a unique functional benefit combined with the emotional payoff of that benefit (through the right consumer insight), and the unique codes owned by the brand that it might have been using in the past (music, colours, emotions) which can deliver good results. While it is easy to say, it's a tough balance to achieve in reality. Therefore, brands sometimes do emotional ads separately from functional ones, which can be an expensive route but can work well if the spends on the two are balanced well to have overlapping reach and exposure.

8. The ad should ideally have one clear message to land. That should be the key benefit of using the brand but narrated via an engaging story that's relevant to the target audience. It can, at the most, stretch to two messages, particularly if the second message is linked to the first one (e.g., an affordable fridge that can keep your food fresh). But stretching beyond two doesn't work most of the times and there is actually a risk that consumers won't remember any message. As the chart from Kantar Millward Brown shows, the number of

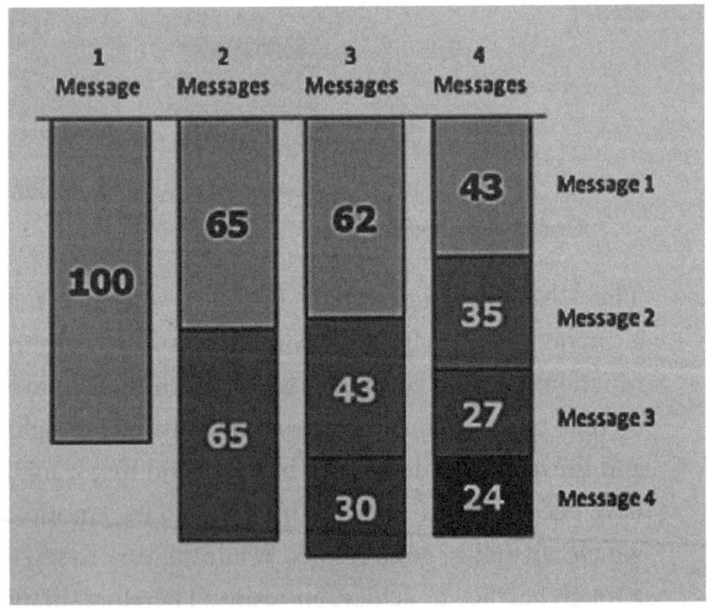

people likely to remember a message goes down as the number of messages increase.

It's unbelievable how many times this lesson is forgotten because there is a temptation to keep adding the messages to an ad. Almost as if there is only one window you get with the consumers and you want to rattle out all the benefits in that one window. Advertising doesn't have to carry the burden of communicating everything about the brand, it should land the key reason for people to choose it (through a relevant and engaging story), but other messages like the price, product superiority, great fragrance or flavours or sensorials, wide range of SKUs etc., should be left to be communicated via packaging, shelf exposure, product experience, PR, etc. Because that way consumers are likely to create a 'sum total' in their minds better which is reflected in the equity of the brand.

9. Advertising pre-testing does not tell you if the ad is on strategy. In other words, it doesn't tell you if you are landing the right message that would help the brand, but it will tell you if the message is landing, if the tonality and style (humorous or clever or serious, etc.) are right fit for the brand, if they are making the ad engaging, if the casting is right for the brand, if consumers are relating to the characters, and so on. The ad pre-testing is not a test of strategy but a test of execution, and a bad result shouldn't be treated as the strategic mistake. There are other ways, usually qualitative, to check if the communication strategy is right and those methods

usually assess if the ad fits the existing brand image (that it wouldn't cause wrong attribution to another brand), and if it further enhances the brand in the intended direction.

Communication development is one of those areas where art truly meets science; where the experience of the creative team has to come together with the expertise of the insights team to create the advertising that excites consumers and drives them to the intended action, i.e., purchase. Communication development is, therefore, one of the most exciting areas for marketers, creative, and insight professionals.

Checking the Final Capability of the Mix

This is the stage when individual elements of the mix (like concept, pack, product, communication idea, etc.) have tested well with the consumers and now the time has come for the organization to develop the capability to produce the final mix. At this stage, several things are set in motion at once: the factory starts piloting the production, the animatics of the advertising are worked out (pre-production), pack graphics are finalized, and so on.

The insights team does the 'full-mix testing' where all the elements come together for the testing. In other words, consumers are shown the concept and given the product in the branded packs to use for a few days; their reactions about the product are then recorded. This is usually a quantitative test, and the scores are used for forecasting the likely sales of the new launch. If the ad is ready (final ad or the animatics), then the team prefers showing the ad instead of concept in this test. However, in my view, it should only be done if the ad communicates *all* the aspects of the new launch. Often different aspects of the launch are communicated through ads that are aired or displayed on different mediums or platforms—TV, print, digital, on pack, in shop, etc. Hence, a single TV ad doesn't communicate the entire 'concept'. In such situations, a concept is a far better stimulus than the ad and should be preferred during the tests.

NielsenIQ BASES is the world's largest provider of launch forecasts using concept product test in the FMCG space. Their claimed accuracy is that in 90% of the cases, the forecast is within +/- 95% of the actual results. This test, therefore, can not only be a useful Go/No-Go test but also an effective diagnostic tool to understand the reasons and ways of increasing the results. Conceptually, the way the forecast is done consists of two inputs:

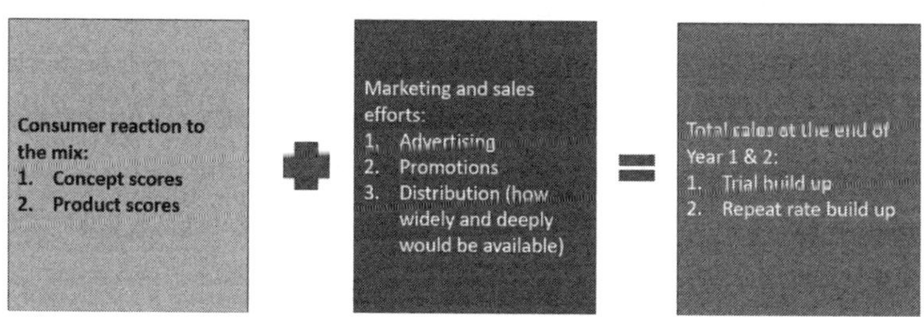

In forecasting the sales of the brand, a few things everyone in marketing and insights teams must be mindful of:

1. The results are not just dependent on how consumers have reacted to the concept and product but are also dependent on how much the brand would be spending

on advertising and how easily would the product be available.

2. It is important to iterate various scenarios of the marketing or sales effort, given certain concept and product scores. These scenarios should be as realistic as possible and compared with the efforts that the brand has done in the past. For instance, it is easy for a naïve brand manager to suggest that the brand would have 60% numeric distribution within six months, but the previous data might show that the brand has never managed to achieve that in the past.
3. More often than not, the forecast fails not because the consumer reactions were exaggerated but because the marketing and sales efforts were not realistically assumed. It's critical to have an independent check on the assumptions made before the forecasting is worked because forecasting each scenario is expensive.

There is a line of thinking that argues that this way of forecasting the business potential is flawed because the foundation lies in its consumers responding to the concept and products monadically. In other words, they are testing just the test idea and not comparing it with the competition, whereas in real life, the new launch would compete with existing products in the market. NielsenIQ BASES argues that the consumer responses are then calibrated with the extensive database they have developed globally, and this calibration of responses when further mixed with marketing or sales efforts, it determines sales. This method has been validated over several categories in various countries across the world for years.

There is a merit in pushing this thought a bit further. If your product is competing with multiple alternatives and people choose by looking at the alternatives, then it is worth doing the concept test in context of the market competition. In most categories people tend to buy just one product at a time, so product testing can be monadic. Ipsos—one of the largest global market research companies—has a model that does the concept test in the competitive context for volume forecasting. Essentially, the method involves consumers reacting to the test concept and a few competition concepts; this generates a relative preference score. The mock packaging of the new launch is placed on the existing category shelf (physical or virtual depending on the situation) and respondents are taken to the shelf to see what choice they make. The methodology is, obviously, far more nuanced than described here (since this is not a methodology book). However, in essence, it is about exposing consumers to choices available in the market and asking them to react to the new idea being fully aware of the options.

Consider categories like soaps or biscuits or savoury snacks where people flirt between brands a lot. It is quite common for people to walk into a shop, look at different options of savoury snacks available, and then decide what they want to buy. In a category like that, if you are launching a new snack, it is imperative to check how attractive it would be against the already available options—not only in terms of concept but also on the shelf. In fact, the competition for a savoury snack may vary from other savoury snacks to fresh snacks to sweets and chocolates. It, therefore, necessitates understanding of the real competition and comparing with those for realistic volume forecast. In such cases, it's prudent to choose a methodology that provides for the relative comparison. Ipsos is one of the agencies that offers this method for forecasting (post their merger with Novaction that developed this method) and perhaps several more today.

A quick comparison of the two methods and their merits:

	SINGLE CONCEPT EXPOSURE METHOD (e.g., BASES)	TEST AND COMPETITIVE CONCEPT EXPOSURE METHOD (e.g., Ipsos, Novaction)
Target Group	Broad-based—representative of the entire market (for all SECs or income and age groups).	Narrow target group that's relevant for the concept.
Concept	Only test concept shown.	Test and competitors' concepts shown.
Shelf exposure	No shelf exposure. Respondents are asked the 'purchase intention' question after showing the concept (along with other questions).	Shelf exposure (physical, virtual, or digital) post concept reactions to check shelf noticeability and likelihood of getting picked up from the shelf.

Likelihood of purchase	Purchase intention question for concept, along with other questions like relevance, value for money, etc., used to calculate purchase probability.	Chip game after concept test to award chips to all concepts shown and product picked on the shelf exposure is used to calculate purchase probability.
Database	Plays a critical role in estimating potential, and all responses are calibrated against the database. Having the right database for country or category is the key.	Doesn't need database for estimating potential, for every study is self-calibrating (since competition products are also shown in the study). However, database is maintained for diagnostic variables.
Category dynamics	The study usually doesn't include category dynamics understanding; it tends to be a pure concept product test.	Study by default includes category dynamics understanding like purchase behaviour, brand preference (via chip game), brand performance, and key category drivers. Those are needed for calibrating the test concept against the competition and estimating potential.

Strengths	1. Simple to get it done. 2. Well-entrenched in several organizations and used as a standard practice. 3. Huge learnings available on what makes a mix successful in the market.	1. Provides a good snapshot of the total category and position of the concept within it. 2. Diagnostics are linked to volumetric estimation. Hence, it's extremely easy to estimate change in volume potential with the change in attribute scores. 3. Works well in 'fuzzy' categories too.
Weaknesses	1. Diagnostics are not linked to volumetrics, so sometimes, it's difficult to see how improvement on attributes would link to volume potential. 2. Category drivers are not included in the study and so need to be done separately to understand concept performance vs. key drivers.	1. Complex to operate—the team needs to create competition concepts (or get ads), shelf, etc., which takes a lot of time, effort, and cost. 2. As a result, it is not so entrenched in organizations as a standard practice.

These companies then provide business forecasting using the concept and product scores. The principles of working it out are quite simple and can also be done in-house—if the insights team has enough expertise and experience in working this out. An example of the business case is given below:

Dove was looking to launch a new hair care range called Dove Moisture Essence Oil in China.

The expected volumes for a launch like this can be worked out with this logic:

Total sales = Total number of households in the country (in this case, China) x Target households (as % of the total) x Trial rate % x Trial units x Repeat rate % x Repeat units x Repeat frequency

TOTAL NUMBER OF HOUSEHOLDS IN THE COUNTRY (in this case, China)	AVAILABLE USUALLY FROM CENSUS DATA
Target households as % of total	Defined based on the target group (e.g., households of certain affluence, women from a certain age group, etc.).

Trial rate %	Estimated from concept test. Purchase intention can be converted into probability of trial using forecasting methods. Alternatively, trial rates available from sources like Kantar World Panel for past similar launches can be used to guesstimate expected trial.
Trial units	Average number of units bought by consumers while buying the new launch for the first time (usually close to one, unless a promotion is being offered).
Repeat rate %	Percentage of households expected to repeat purchase (out of those who tried). It can be estimated from product test scores using forecasting methods. Alternatively, repeat rate available from sources like Kantar World Panel for past similar launches can be used to guesstimate expected repeat.
Repeat units	Average number of units bought repeatedly by consumers while buying the new launch. It can be estimated from product tests or from Kantar World Panel for past launches.
Repeat Frequency (or repeats per repeater)	Number of times consumers are expected to repeat purchase in one year (usually close to one for most FMCG categories).

For this new Dove China launch, this translated into:

Expected Sales = 232.2 million households x 40% target households x 4% expected trial rate x 1.1 expected trial units x 21% expected repeat rate x 1.1 Repeat units x 1.7 Repeat frequency = 5.3 million units.

Applying the price per unit, the sales of 5.3 million units translated to €20.3 million.

The key question then, obviously, is how are the concept and product scores converted into trial and repeat rates? This is where forecasting companies bring in their decades of experience in several markets and categories. But as a user of these forecasts, it is important to know certain guiding principles that drives the forecast and some tricks to check the validity of the forecast. The best validation, of course, is comparing the actual launch performance with the forecast (these forecasting companies do that a lot) but you need some assurance of the accuracy before you decide to launch—that's where these tricks can come in handy.

Let's look at the principles that drive the forecast:

1. That sales is a function of how fast the trial builds up and how much repeat customers the launch is able to attract (which depends on whether the product delivers on the promise) is clear from the forecasting model. But the build-up of trial is a direct function of distribution (also referred to as 'physical availability'):

    a) There is a linear relationship between the two. Higher the distribution, higher is the trial.

b) But the distribution build-up also has an impact on the trial. Slower build-up results in lower trials.

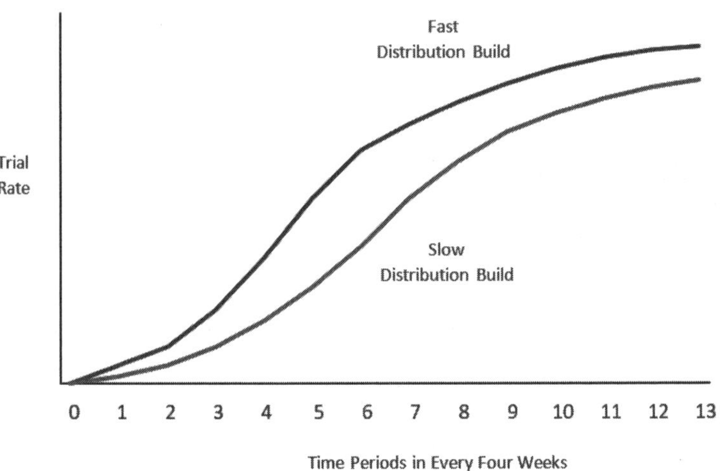

2. The second factor that impacts the trial build-up is awareness (also called as 'mental availability'). Simply speaking, higher the awareness, higher is the trial. The build-up of awareness, however, depends on two things:

   a) Advertising quantity: Higher the reach of advertising (function of money spent and smart planning), higher would be the awareness.

   b) Advertising quality: Better the creative (in line with the brand values, engaging enough to break the clutter, and delivers the message), better is the awareness.

3. Repeat rate, on the other hand, is dependent upon the product performance (if it delivers on the promise made

in the advertising). Of course, physical and mental availability do impact it as well.

These principles are quite the fundamentals of marketing and business and this means that building new business is not rocket science but getting basics right.

Let's look at some common tips and tricks to check whether the forecasting makes sense and is likely to come true:

1. Check how realistic are the distribution levels assumed for the forecast. Often enthusiastic, naïve brand managers set unrealistic estimates of distribution levels (and fast build-up) for forecasting. Even with the average concept or product test scores, the forecast can be quite high if the distribution assumptions are high.

   a) Easiest way is to see the distribution levels that the last new launch of the brand got within a year, or average distribution levels of all new launches of the brand in the past. If it's a new brand, check the distribution levels of competition brands and how much they achieved in the first year of the launch. This provides a good benchmark for realistic estimates.

2. Check how realistic are the assumptions on the advertising and promotion spends. Check the translation of those spends into GRPs and reach:

   a) For example, if your advertising spends will reach 50% of the audience in year one, the awareness levels can't be expected to be more than 25 to 30% assuming fantastic creative performance. In which case, the trial levels would be under 10% assuming that the proposition is quite attractive, and product is easily available.

b) Check the advertising spends for the same brand in the past—how much do they tend to spend and how are the estimates for the new launch compared with that? Some brands spend a lot on new launches, and some don't. Check the pattern of spends in the past to get realistic estimates.

3. Compare the estimated trial and repeat rates from the forecast with the trial and repeat rates that new launches in your category have got in the past. This would give an idea of how realistic the estimates are. This comparison can be done using the Kantar World Panel data—either by comparing expected penetration (combination of trial and repeat rates) with actual launches in the past or by asking trial or repeat rates from KWP team (they are not visible in standard dashboards).

   a) For instance, if your forecasting company is estimating trial rates to be 25% (of the target audience), whereas in the past no new launch in the category has seen over 10% households trying the product in a year of launch, in that case, 25% is likely to be a huge overestimate. That over-estimate could be because of the exaggerated assumption of distribution and advertising spends or because of the concept scores being really high compared to benchmarks—and both these hypotheses can be checked easily.

4. Do a back-of-the-envelope calculation of sales and see how that compares with the forecast. Sounds basic and rudimentary but it's amazing how insightful it can be! Consider this example of Becel in Netherlands:

    a) Becel had a sale of €62 million in Netherlands and that sale can be broken easily to understand the details (using KWP):

        i. Total households in Netherlands = 7.3 million
        ii. Penetration of Becel = 51%
        iii. Yearly frequency of purchase = 7.9 times
        iv. Average number of units bought during purchase = 1.3
        v. Sales = 7.3m X 51% X 7.9 X 1.3 = 39m units = €62 million value

    b) Let's assume Becel is launching a new variant at the same price. Given the money expected to be spent on launch, let's say you can't expect more than 10% people buying it and they would probably buy it twice a year (given that they buy Becel almost eight times a year, two out of those eight times, they could buy the new variant). Sales of the new variant then would be 7.3m X 10% X 2 X 1.3 = 1.9m units = €3m value.

    c) This provides a good back-of-the-envelope estimate of the likely value of the new launch. This kind of calculation is also useful at the beginning of the project to see the financial scale that is feasible.

5. Run different simulations of forecasts with different levels of distribution and spends on advertising and promotions including a realistic one. This exercise is also quite helpful in understanding the sensitivity of the sale to marketing efforts and helps determine the optimum levels needed for success.

Innovation Insights: 3M's Perspective

There are organizations like Apple and 3M that pride themselves for being highly innovative and nurturing a culture of exploring new ideas. How does the insights' function add value to their innovation process? A conversation with Chitkala Nishandar, who created and led the insights function for the APAC region in 3M, provided some interesting perspective on this question. Interestingly, she worked at The Coca-Cola Company for several years prior to 3M, so she is quite well-placed to compare the similarities and differences in the innovation process between the two organizations.

There is a fundamental difference in the way innovation happens at 3M as compared to FMCG organizations like Unilever and The Coca-Cola Company. For instance, an innovation at The Coca-Cola Company maybe a new flavour of soft drink, which maybe a new innovation for the organization but not so much for its consumers, whereas innovations at 3M could be about bringing something new to the world that may not have existed before. Therefore, you can't apply the traditional methods of innovation testing used by FMCGs in situations where you want solutions that people haven't even thought of. Or worse, people don't even know that they have a problem they would like to solve. For instance, before iPod Touch was launched by Apple, no consumer would have said that they need a touch device for music or could have visualized the concept of apps that would run on your device. It is usually someone's vision that drives the innovation; someone with an innovative mind comes along and thinks they can simplify the way people do certain things or use certain products.

This is why Apple talks to highly involved regular users during their product development stage. Because they can tell you the difference that the round edges make as compared to the angular ones, or features that can really be annoying with repeated use, and so on. Otherwise, those nuances get 'averaged out' in large quantitative sample sizes whereas these could be the real nuggets that create innovations for companies like 3M. After a point, the functionalities don't delight you—the delighters are things that consumers often can't even think of. Those have to be fleshed out from these nuances with a lot of expertise.

FMCG organizations typically work on innovations for already established brands, whereas 3M innovations teams work on the fuzzy front end with lots of blue-sky thinking. The insights team, therefore, has to be equipped with different skill sets, which are not about evaluation but a lot more about development. The insights team tend to be highly visual, design-oriented and filled with a lot more 'qualitative' thinkers who are able to visualize a need and explore potential solutions. Companies like The Coca-Cola Company would carry out large-scale quantitative product test using prescribed protocols and study design. But that kind of rigour, sometimes, does not give you a nuanced insight on why the product could have something in it even if it's failing the rigorous product test with consumers. You may know it intuitively, but the quantitative data doesn't come to support.

Hence, the work at 3M tends to be a lot more exploratory. Emphasis is on 'listening' to the voice of the consumer rather than following standardized protocols. A lot of research happens at an early stage of development and the idea is to open the developers' eyes to the customer feedback. Hence, sending out small sample sizes, reaching out to known super users (heavy users of the category or brand) are common practices. This is something FMCG companies would not do that often. It requires a lot of caution because of the inherent bias in the design, but when followed carefully, the process is really high on cross-pollination and development of innovative ideas. As a result, establishing the insights' function and embedding it in businesses like 3M is a different kind of challenge compared to FMCG companies. "It is best not to talk about yourself as an 'insights' or a 'market research' person, but talk about yourself as a problem solver," says Chitkala.

Roll up your sleeves and spend time with the businesses, understanding the issues and the problems they face; run workshops with people to explain what we know from consumers, build it to see what it could mean to the business; and provide ideas and potential solutions. Getting into the trenches and getting your hands dirty is the only way to do it and it is highly gratifying as well.

Have some quick wins and scale them—this may seem like a simple mantra, but it may not be as easy to apply because of the complexities that exist in running businesses. The greatest joy, however, of being in insights is to see the team collectively arrive at that 'aha' moment when the team is not stuck at the data or problem level, but they are finally able to see light at the end of the tunnel. It is crucial for teams in the end to create an action plan with clear accountabilities. Insights teams also often take the responsibility of tracking the action plan which gives them a real sense of impact that their insights have made, and they can see their clear contribution to the business.

This way of working and embedding insights into business results in three things for the function:

1. The role of insights in the minds of stakeholders changes. From the perception that they don't really need 'market research' for innovative cultures like theirs to seeing them as a part of the very fabric of innovations.
2. Insights team starts feeling accountable for the business results. The whole team sees the action points coming out of their work and they track those actions and hold businesses accountable for carrying them through.
3. It builds salience for the function. Everyone in the organization thinks they know insights but most of them don't really understand what the insight function does. This kind of work brings opportunities to talk about real consumer stories and build regular communication like newsletters that create further demand for the function.

Implications for Marketing and Insights Professionals

While the process described in the (rather long) chapter is a process that good B2C companies follow, every company has to identify a process that works for them. And the category context would also necessitate suitable modifications. For instance, pharmaceutical companies making OTC drugs would have some additional considerations. The marketing and insights teams looking to boost their new product development (NPD) should:

- Identify and articulate the need of NPD in their organization based on their context, which would dictate how often the new products should be developed and launched, including relaunches of existing products.
- Define and codify the NPD process for the organization which would enable them to create a system or repeatable model.
- Adapt a system that works in the organization and category context. The system described above is suitable for a CPG or FMCG organization but the same can be adapted for other industries with suitable modifications (just like 3M has done it for themselves). There are research and analytics organizations that specialize in different industries and offer expertise in creating such processes.

- Establish a system to constantly keep an eye on the evolving competitive landscape. This is usually a combination of subscription to syndicated reports (e.g., Mintel gives a report of all new launches in different categories, including pack shots, claims made, pricing, etc.), listening to consumers on what they are using, watching consumers shop, scanning the virtual and physical shelves (and other consumer touch points), and reviewing advertising of your competition with the help of ad agencies.
- Establish a process for continuous idea generation and recycling in the categories of interest.
- Identify ways of quantifying the business opportunities for the shortlisted ideas—this chapter discussed BASES and Ipsos methods, but there would be others specializing in specific industries.

Epilogue

It has taken me a couple of years to write the book, and in a way, it condenses my life's learnings in one place. While it is not possible to put down everything I know, I have attempted to touch on various aspects of insights, challenges, and complexities of working on them. Most of the examples are derived from my experiences at Unilever, though I plan to add experiences from other companies in subsequent editions. The book articulates the definition of insight and uses the understanding of what makes a person insightful to create a framework for what would make an organization insightful. I took the BCG model of evolution of 'market research team' in an organization and used my Unilever experience to illustrate how Unilever's insights team has evolved—which was an interesting experience for me as well to reflect on and see how good the model is. I hope that other organizations can plot themselves on the continuum and discover ways to grow further.

The book delves deeply into various methods of gaining insights across different areas. This is not a methodology book, so I have avoided going into technical details, but that wasn't possible everywhere. My idea has been to broadly explain how these methods work and add my experience and learnings on how to make them work better. Reflecting on my experiences on each of these methods and fleshing out learnings was quite enriching for me as well and I hope that readers, too, would gain something substantial out of this. All the Unilever examples and charts have been collected from various Unilever documents some of which are already in the public domain. The Hindustan Unilever Limited team has reviewed and given a formal approval to use them in the book, for which I am forever grateful.

While this book is intended for insights, analytics, and research professionals, it would also be useful for marketers who want to leverage insights for their business and enhance consumer centricity within their organizations. My intention is not to propagate hiring of large insight teams, but to promote consumer or customer centricity and use some of these practices to make the entire organization insightful—insights are not just the responsibility of insight managers, but of everyone in the organization.

I hope you readers enjoy reading this book as much as I enjoyed writing it.

Acknowledgments

I began writing this book in 2020, amidst the COVID-19 pandemic. It took me two years to complete the manuscript, followed by another year of editing and securing approvals. The endeavor demanded considerable time, as it involved extracting case studies, collating data, interviewing various individuals, and weaving all of these elements into the broader narrative of the book. This monumental task would not have been possible without the immense and invaluable contribution of numerous people around me. I have tried to acknowledge them all; my sincere apologies if I inadvertently missed anyone.

First and foremost, I extend my gratitude to Unilever as an organization and Hindustan Unilever Limited (HUL) for providing such a highly stimulating environment that always pushes the boundaries, encourages innovation, and promotes high-level thinking. The leaders there recognize the need to balance nurturing individual sparks with the larger organizational growth, a rarity in today's corporate world.

I must start by thanking Mr. Sanjiv Mehta, who was the CEO at HUL when the idea of this book was conceived. He was highly encouraging of the idea and believed that a book like this was truly needed in the industry. He has been kind enough to write a foreword for this book and providing his perspective on how insights help an organization.

Nitesh Priyadarshi, who was the head of CMI for the South Asia region of Unilever (HUL) when I finished writing the book and is now Global Head of Insights at Danone, read through the book for official approvals, gave me valuable suggestions and also participated in an interview on the future of insights.

Many thanks to Prasad Pradhan, the then head of corporate communications at HUL, and Suranjana Nandi—both went through the book in detail and provided their valuable suggestions. Swagata Sharma played an active role in the middle of all this exchange. Stan Sthanunathan, with whom I have had several discussions about many of these topics when he was global head of insights, also wrote a foreword for this book.

In my two decades at Unilever, living and working in different parts of the world, I had the opportunity to work on all the key brands of Unilever—Lux, Pond's, Vaseline, Dove, Glow & Lovely, Knorr, Hellman's, Surf, Axe, Pepsodent, Closeup... the list is long and glorious. Marketers working on different brands have helped me shape my thinking and have provided their invaluable insights along the way: Oliver Lloyd, Anuj Rustagi, Purnima Lamba, Late David Steele, Late Richard Clegg (Ogilvy), Samir Singh, Kartik Chandrasekhar, Rajev Shukla, Fernando Acosta, Catherine Sleight, Jonathan Affleck.... Our partners from advertising agencies Lowe, Ogilvy, JWT have helped me immensely in understanding the role of advertising (and challenging me on its testing). My colleagues and bosses in the CMI function who gave shape to my career and my way of looking at insights: Richard Davies, Stan Sthanunathan, B. V. Pradeep (who recruited me in Unilever after a three-hour long interview), Robert Kitching, Chet Henderson, Oslando Desouza, Alex Owens, Anila Vinayak, Namita Mediratta, and so many others. Our research agency partners—Kantar, NielsenIQ, Ipsos, Brandscapes Worldwide, Quantum, Wy Consulting, Firefish—worked hand-in-hand with me across the years, producing tonnes of great work together. I couldn't have asked for better partners.

I was fortunate enough to interview some truly remarkable people while writing the book and incorporate their perspectives. Rebecca Wynberg, a close friend and professional partner on my journey in Unilever, helped me on several occasions, letting me bounce off some thoughts and give them direction. Madhav Srinivas from Quantum and Sam Gomez (now Founding partner of 8th Day) gave me their perspectives on the evolution of qualitative research, which was a fascinating conversation in itself. Chitkala Nishandar took me through how 3M thinks about insights and the systemic thinking she has had to put in place. Preethi Reddy provided her thoughts on the future of insights.

My journey in the world of insights began at a research agency ORG-MARG in India, where I gained invaluable lessons during my initial few years. This fantastic organization later became part of NielsenIQ. I'm grateful to Praveen Tripathi and Ravi Moorthy from ORG-MARG, who interviewed and hired me, and continued to guide me in various ways throughout my career. Ashok Das provided essential insights on research methods and interpretation. Nehal Medh, who was my boss back then patiently nurtured the naïve researcher in me and later became a dear friend, read through the first draft of this book and provided feedback. Amit Adarkar, with whom I worked closely on some truly cutting-edge projects, those learnings will always stay with me. Sakina Pittalwala opened my eyes to the world of Qual research. Additionally, I'm grateful to all my colleagues and friends at ORG-MARG who inspired me to appreciate the value research could bring to the business.

I initially thought that I just had to write down the book and that would be the end of the journey, totally unaware of the long road that lay ahead with the publishing team. The team at Jaico has been incredibly patient, letting me navigate the ropes of the publishing world. Thanks also to Rishi Piparaiya who introduced me to Jaico and Venkatesh Babu for guiding me through the art of writing proposals for publishers.

Writer's block is a real challenge—you need to be in the right frame of mind to write well. Though this book appears as the diary of a researcher, it did require significant inspiration to capture my thoughts on various subjects. Doing so amidst the chaos of COVID-19 pandemic demanded even greater mental energy and control to focus and pen down my ideas. This would not have been possible without the unwavering support of my wife, Savy (Savithri Swaminathan), who patiently supported me not just in completing this book but also in nurturing and advancing my career (sometimes at the expense of her own), without which, I would not have gained the experience that I did. Thanks to my lovely daughters, Ira and Nisa, for being my strong anchors and, of course, for providing constant joy and laughter at home.

About the Author

Manish Makhijani has spent 28 years in the fields of insights, analytics, and marketing, with 19 of those years at Unilever, working across various parts of the world and in diverse business sectors. He thrives on 'bringing music into mathematics to uncover previously untold stories', combining his insatiable intellectual curiosity with a passion for unlocking potential. Recognized globally as a thought leader in the insights space, Manish has won prestigious international awards, including the Ginny Valentine Award in New York in 2013 and the global Insight250 in 2023.

Now an independent consultant, Manish helps different businesses become more consumer-centric, trains marketing teams on the art and science of insights, and teaches at a couple of management institutes. He lives in Mumbai with his wife and two daughters. This is his first book.

JAICO PUBLISHING HOUSE

Elevate Your Life. Transform Your World.

ESTABLISHED IN 1946, Jaico Publishing House is home to world-transforming authors such as Sri Sri Paramahansa Yogananda, Osho, the Dalai Lama, Sri Sri Ravi Shankar, Sadhguru, Robin Sharma, Deepak Chopra, Jack Canfield, Eknath Easwaran, Devdutt Pattanaik, Khushwant Singh, John Maxwell, Brian Tracy, and Stephen Hawking.

Our late founder Mr. Jaman Shah first established Jaico as a book distribution company. Sensing that independence was around the corner, he aptly named his company Jaico ('Jai' means victory in Hindi). In order to service the significant demand for affordable books in a developing nation, Mr. Shah initiated Jaico's own publications. Jaico was India's first publisher of paperback books in the English language.

While self-help, religion and philosophy, mind/body/spirit, and business titles form the cornerstone of our non-fiction list, we publish an exciting range of travel, current affairs, biography, and popular science books as well. Our renewed focus on popular fiction is evident in our new titles by a host of fresh young talent from India and abroad. Jaico's recently established translations division translates selected English content into nine regional languages.

Jaico distributes its own titles. With its headquarters in Mumbai, Jaico has branches in Ahmedabad, Bangalore, Chennai, Delhi, Hyderabad, and Kolkata.

SINCE 1946